CW00942768

Holy Anarchy

Holy Anarchy

*Dismantling Domination, Embodying
Community, Loving Strangeness*

Graham Adams

scm press

© Graham Adams 2022

Published in 2022 by SCM Press
Editorial office
3rd Floor, Invicta House,
108–114 Golden Lane,
London EC1Y OTG, UK

www.scmpress.co.uk

SCM Press is an imprint of Hymns Ancient & Modern Ltd
(a registered charity)

Hymns Ancient & Modern® is a registered trademark of
Hymns Ancient & Modern Ltd
13A Hellesdon Park Road, Norwich,
Norfolk NR6 5DR, UK

Permission is granted by the author and publisher for the hymns and Appendix
material to be used in non-commercial group performance and accompanying
printed hymn and service sheets. Due acknowledgement must be made
to this book as the source publication.

For all other material, all rights reserved. No part may not be reproduced,
stored in a retrieval system, or transmitted,
in any form or by any means, electronic, mechanical,
photocopying or otherwise, without the prior permission of
the publisher, SCM Press.

The Author has asserted his right under the Copyright, Designs and
Patents Act 1988 to be identified as the Author of this Work

Scripture quotations are from the New Revised Standard Version Bible:
Anglicized Edition, copyright © 1989, 1995 National Council of the
Churches of Christ in the United States of America. Used by permission.
All rights reserved worldwide.

British Library Cataloguing in Publication data

A catalogue record for this book is available
from the British Library

978-0-334-06190-8

Typeset by Regent Typesetting
Printed and bound by
CPI Group (UK) Ltd

Contents

To Sheryl and Bethan for their love and inspiration,
tolerating the anarchy which happens around me
and encouraging me to believe in what can be.

Foreword

I remember the day like it was yesterday. I was driving my younger brother to London as he was going to study at the London Metropolitan University for a degree in Caribbean Studies. All had gone very smoothly driving down the M1 motorway until we got to the outskirts of London. Then, suddenly, in London we got into a furious argument. I remember shouting at my brother: 'What is wrong with you? Can't you see where we should be going?' We had set off at the crack of dawn in order to beat the worst of the traffic, travelling from Bradford in West Yorkshire all the way down to the 'great smoke' that was London. Neither of us knew the way to the university but, armed with a detailed road map that my brother was reading and two keen pairs of eyes, we felt we could not go wrong. But, sadly, go wrong we did, and in spectacular style! When you find yourself going down a one-way street in the wrong direction, with a cacophony of blaring horns and flashing headlights serenading your path, you know that you are lost and big time!

My brother and I had the map in front of us and the street signs ahead, and yet we still got lost. The central problem we had was that the real, three-dimensional, concrete landscape of London did not look anything like the flat, uncomplicated world of the road map. All this was before the days of Sat Navs that talk you through the complications of road navigation.

On the map it all looked very simple. There were no cars to interrupt or impede one's progress or blow their horns at these slow, dim-witted youths from 'the provinces'. Suffice it to say that on such occasions, friendships and filial bonds are stretched to the limit, as trying to match theory to practice becomes a painful and sometimes nerve-wracking experience. This was October 1988.

I have retold this story because reading *Holy Anarchy* reminded me of the incredulous moment my brother and I surveyed the flat road map unable to figure out how to match it to the three-dimensional world in front of us.

Holy Anarchy is a brilliant text that seeks to help us interpret the world differently. Christianity has traditionally used resources such as the Bible, allied with the continuum of Christian tradition, to assist us in navigating our way on the spiritual journey towards the alternative reality that is God's reign. But much like the physical journey my brother and I undertook over 30 years ago, trying to navigate one's way to the desired destination is not as straightforward as one imagines. Graham Adams' book provides a compelling set of metaphors, theories, ideas and reflections that seek to help readers navigate the treacherous terrain towards the destination that we believe God has fashioned for the whole of creation.

Holy Anarchy wrestles with the multifarious nature of empire and how its nefarious tentacles have shaped our collective imaginations in what we see as reality. Using the metaphor of a journey, *Holy Anarchy* invites us to rethink what we see and what direction of travel we should take.

Many of us who have grown up in church will know the temptations of assuming there is a natural clear-cut journey of A–Z. Such unambiguous map readings rarely turn out to be as 'obvious' as one imagines. And the more complicated the terrain becomes – due to constant changes in physical features such as metaphorical road works and detours – the greater the difficulty in navigation.

Holy Anarchy is a gift that seeks to help us untangle the diversions, roadblocks and poor signage that has often prevented many of us from seeing the correct direction we should be taking. The book offers no easy answers or false panaceas. Rather, via critical analysis, robust theological reflections and poetry-hymnody, Adams has fashioned a text that offers alternative ways of seeing and different ways of possible navigation. Given the continued complexities with which we are living, *Holy Anarchy* is a refreshingly honest and insightful vision for a journey that is compelling, joyous and inclusive, one in which all persons are supported and loved and no one is considered inconsequential or irrelevant to the community of fellow travellers.

Holy Anarchy demonstrates that there are no perfect metaphors for understanding the truth of God's ways in the world, and will, I am sure, become an indispensable resource for fellow travellers as we journey ahead in the years to come! Thank you, Graham, for writing this important book!

Anthony G. Reddie,
Director of the Oxford Centre for Religion and Culture,
Regent's Park College, University of Oxford

Acknowledgements

I am hugely grateful to all those whose support has enabled me to give shape to this book. Firstly, over nearly 20 years, the insights, inspiration and encouragement of Andrew Shanks have been instrumental. This has been further enriched through teaching – so I am also thankful to the theological students who allowed me to imagine possibilities with them, asked probing questions and urged me to develop my angle on things. I hope they don't regret it!

I am indebted to the Council for World Mission for enabling me to participate in several theological consultations concerning 'Empire'. This deepened my appreciation of my dissenting Christian heritage, sharpening my readiness to be critical of the tradition to which I belong and enlivening the hope of anti-domination.

Of course, my teaching colleagues at Northern College (United Reformed and Congregational) and the wider Luther King Centre partnership, in Manchester have been integral to this process. At the risk of overlooking some, I must nevertheless name Noel Irwin, Glen Marshall, Rosalind Selby, Graham Sparkes and Kim Wasey for ongoing conversations and support. Thanks, too, go to Jason Boyd and Mike Walsh for valuable encouragement. And over many years, the wisdom of Andrew Pratt and Janet Wootton has been crucial in helping me to develop my hymn-writing.

As the material for the book was developing, particular people kindly read drafts of it – Clare Nutbrown-Hughes, Noel again, and my friends Janet Lees and Bob Warwicker, who also meandered with me in what we called spiritual (mis)direction.

Many thanks, too, to David Shervington, Linda Crosby and all at SCM for responding so helpfully to my questions or anxieties and walking alongside me.

Huge thanks to Anthony Reddie for his generous Foreword, which really captures what I was aiming to do, without my ever knowing for sure whether I was actually achieving it!

Using the hymns and Appendix material

Permission is granted for the hymns and Appendix material to be used in non-commercial group performance and accompanying printed hymn or service sheets. Due acknowledgement must be made to this book as the source publication.

PART I

Introductions

Jesus told us about 'the kingdom of God'. It seemed to be his central concern. He invited us to compare it with things and images in our world. It is a realm that does not play by the rules of business-as-usual. It defies expectations of what a kingdom ought to be. It is coming. It is here. It is within us. But at the same time it is elusive, seemingly out of reach even as some would claim it too tightly. So what is it?

Inspired by the work of British theologian Andrew Shanks, who renames the kingdom 'Holy Anarchy', I explore this image and its implications for our understanding of the world as it is and as it may become. In doing so, I offer a particular framework for how we may think of the challenges we face, the nature of divine action in the world, and the calling of the church in a context of diversity. It is an alternative horizon that beckons us to discern the structures in which we are embedded, to build communities of solidarity, and receive from those whose differences have much to teach us. It is a vision that seeks to take as seriously as possible the awkwardness, pain and potential of our realities, so we may attend empathetically to one another's stories, while exposing and subverting the very systems that hold us enthralled. It is not a blueprint for an ultimate resolution of all the tensions in our world, but rather offers the possibility of more honest engagement with the messy, ambiguous and interconnected nature of our lives, faith and actions.

Part 1 introduces the vision of Holy Anarchy in more detail and opens up various concepts and themes associated with it. In Chapter 1, I explore what this alternative expression is attempting to say, rooting this in my understanding of theology and my own context. In Chapter 2, the focus is on why there are such contrasting visions of Christian faith, engaging with different kinds of truth and their implications for Christian identity. These insights are applied to racism and the ecological crisis.

Parts 2 to 4 then address the particular challenges posed by Holy Anarchy's exposure of life as we know it. In Part 2, I attend to the very structures of domination that attempt to suppress and contain the movement of Holy Anarchy and the way in which God makes possible the subversion of such structures. So Chapter 3 identifies those structures in terms of Empire or Dominion, and Chapter 4 explores how Holy Anarchy evokes our discernment and decolonization of them, focusing especially on the question of divine agency, the significance of smallness, and the implications for mission.

In Part 3 the focus is on the calling of the church to be an alternative community, witnessing to and embodying Holy Anarchy, however imperfectly. In Chapter 5, I consider how themes in Jesus' ministry offer us insights into the church's vocation in terms of solidarity among the impurities of life, responsiveness to those with other stories to tell, lamenting the cries of pain, and an ever deeper openness to God's world, drawing on the resources of our faith to help sustain these commitments. Chapter 6 develops further what it means to be an awkward body of honest hypocrites, both religious and spiritual, prayerful and playful as adventurous children, mediating between diversities and agitating where systems hold people in their place. I offer a new approach to the marks of the church.

Part 4 recognizes that it is not only the church that addresses the systems of domination; there are wider partners to engage with. So how should we make some sense of and engage with such diversity? In Chapter 7, I explore the way in which faith opens us up to ever deeper neighbourliness with others, recognizing how Holy Anarchy cuts across other loyalties, but also urges us to be open to what is genuinely strange to us. We do not know the whole story. Chapter 8 is focused on worship and how, when we worship the God of Holy Anarchy, we are being opened to an alternative horizon, like witnesses at an empty tomb, even as we continue to live in the world as we know it.

The Conclusion brings some of the key strands together, outlining what this vision means for the gospel as a whole, exploring 'Anonymous Anarchy' in terms of the many small contributions to it that are not seen in such terms, and recognizing the challenge we face to witness to this alternative horizon.

In the Appendix, I offer samples of worship material to evoke your own creative responses.

I

Holy Anarchy is Close at Hand

With what can we compare the kingdom of God,
or what parable will we use for it?
(Mark 4.30)

Holy Anarchy!

It is the alternative horizon declared by Jesus. It is the realm or reality that he conveyed in stories and which his actions demonstrated. It is the world in which God's will is done. It's where things are as they should be. But it's not blatant. It's not quite here, and yet it is, in part – almost imperceptible; under our noses; even within us. It's partially hidden, but still present; close at hand and on its way. Arundhati Roy expresses it as a personification of the coming reality:

> Another world is not only possible; she is on her way.
> On a quiet day, I can hear her breathing.[1]

If only we would learn to discern this presence. Or *un*learn our ways of burying it. It is the 'thing' we should seek most. It is a party, a feast, a day of jubilee: abundant life for all. But to enter it, we need to be like little children. Take a leap. Ask 'why?' in the face of injustice, or 'why not?' in the face of inertia. Imagine things differently. It is the kingdom of God. Yet it is a notion that has been used in starkly different ways to justify conflicting visions of truth and hope. Was it the World Order defended by the Christian crusaders, or is it present at a foodbank run by people from different religious traditions working in collaboration? Is it represented by 'traditional values' of religion or by alternative possibilities? By a society in which everyone knows their place or the vision of a table where there is space for everyone to feast? Is it limited to those who explicitly confess faith in Christ, or is it uncontainable, a condition that defies capture, whether by words or by human will?

What is this elusive treasure at the heart of Jesus' vocation? What is it, exactly, that he invites us to glimpse and head towards? With what can

3

we compare it? There are many ways of reconceiving it, to help us understand in our own time and place what Jesus might have meant. Some call it the kin-dom of God, the reign of God, or the commonwealth of God, all of which are valuable. John Caputo calls it 'sacred anarchy', which is not dissimilar to Andrew Shanks's term: 'Holy Anarchy'. I will say more about various options in due course, but I begin here by affirming that Holy Anarchy draws me in and beckons me out, and that this book is an attempt to unpack it, to identify it in today's world and to encourage the possibility of it, as a horizon that is close at hand.

But before I say more about the words, first a question of punctuation, as we begin to dig into the meaning of this alternative horizon, Holy Anarchy! I admit that I feel some affection for the exclamation mark, but I was in two minds: should I use it after Holy Anarchy? (Or is the question mark more appropriate?) If I do use the exclamation mark, this would reflect the surprising, disruptive quality of this alternative reality, in some sense bursting on to the scene. God's kingdom! Holy Anarchy! It's here! However, it is not always like that. Even if its nature is strikingly different from the dominant conditions in our world, its emergence is not always energetic. It's not always even noticed. In fact, it often isn't. Which is part of the reason why it's different from the dominant state of things – it just doesn't present itself as the next shiny thing for our consumption. After all, it is not exactly attractive. Not as such. Not in the way we often think of 'attractive'. And it presents itself almost sideways, as a new horizon in our peripheral vision; perhaps a little fiery but still only fleeting; yes, illuminating the true nature of things, but somehow shrouded in shadow. Sometimes it appears slowly, surreptitiously, under the radar. So it doesn't always need an exclamation mark. It almost needs brackets instead, since it is glimpsed *in the gaps*, between other things, not where our central focus is. In any case, the phrase in itself – as a re-expression of 'the kingdom of God' – is not the sort that is normally finished with an exclamation mark, like an imperative or command, or an expression of surprise. It's the name of a thing. Not a command. Nor a verb. And yet. A living thing or, rather, a state of affairs that is loaded with transformative power – even though it can be small, like a seed, or like yeast, or signified by a child. A state of affairs loaded with transformative power. Fizzing with possibility. And to glimpse it, however briefly, is to begin to see this, and to sense that even in its quiet form, maybe it deserves an exclamation mark: Holy Anarchy!

But I also recognize that the use of an exclamation mark can be risky. It can seem flippant. It can turn something weighty into something rather less serious. It can trivialize an idea. And this could certainly be the case with regards to Holy Anarchy! Some people will hear an echo of a comic-book reference. Surely that wouldn't be helpful, would it? In the 1960s there was a TV series, *Batman*, in which his assistant, Robin, uses a wide range of bizarre exclamations beginning 'Holy' – including 'Holy Taxation!', 'Holy Semantics!', 'Holy Cosmos!', 'Holy Ghost Writer!', 'Holy Interruptions!' These all need the exclamation mark. So why not 'Holy Anarchy!'? The echo of the comic-book humour, aided by the punctuation, could seem to trivialize something of ultimate significance, connecting the grandeur of the kingdom of God with something far less weighty and pulling 'Holy' away from its sacred origins. But actually this echo is useful. It helps to make a point pertinent to my argument, even if it is risky as well. The thing is this: the echo caused by the exclamation mark is only there if you know and hear the reference to *Batman*. If you know the reference, you hear the echo. If you don't know the reference, it passes you by. This illuminates an important tension or, in fact, a double tension.

On the one hand, there is a tension between those who are 'insiders' to an in-joke, who know the reference and hear the echo of it, and those who are 'outsiders' to the joke and miss the point. Obviously Christian faith can be like this, with its in-jokes and boundaries, and those of us who are insiders don't always notice how things are heard by 'outsiders'. We don't even always notice when our terminology *creates* outsiders! Concern over this is certainly not the only motivation for changing the language from 'the kingdom of God' to 'Holy Anarchy', but it is part of the picture – because language can be deeply problematic. It reinforces walls and power dynamics. It makes 'us' feel 'at home', so presumably others can feel 'homeless'. And even if it is intended to be good news, *including* for outsiders, it goes stale, ceasing to reflect what it originally intended to say, if not reversing those intentions. So we need to keep asking: are there better ways of articulating something as radical as God's alternative horizon? The exclamation mark (in Holy Anarchy!) reminds me that, if our language relies on people 'hearing particular echoes', then we must wonder where that leaves those who don't get the joke. We may have intended to laugh with them, even to weep with them, as God's kingdom beckons us, but actually it can feel as though we are laughing *at* them.

On the other hand, there is another tension, between 'getting' some-thing and not getting it. This is different from the first tension, because – if we are being honest – we insiders are not always very good at 'getting' what being inside this story is all about. We lose sight of the heart of it. We spend energy on less crucial things, even sometimes on the wrong things at the expense of what is lifegiving. As a result, I may delude myself about the identity of this tradition. Furthermore, there may be in-jokes where I am exactly the sort of person who will not 'get it', because I am busy preoccupied with distortions of what matters. My seemingly relevant experience has not included the particular concerns that are more instructive. Others, outside of my own experience, are better placed to get the joke or recognize the truth, even though they do not fit with my assumptions about 'my' tradition. Yet others, walking a very different path and using very different language, may be more 'in tune' with the echoes of truth than I am expected to be. So I must listen and learn, while being mindful of how my own in-jokes, my presuppositions and language leave others wondering what is going on.

Opening up

Of course, I'm writing this book because I believe I have something to say about 'what it's all about', my organizing principle being Holy Anarchy. But it is vital that I make clear as early as possible that at the heart of this is the recognition that insiders like me are not always the best people to see it – we need perspectives outside of ourselves. And not just because we sometimes lose track of it and need others to help us get back on track. It is something more fundamental than that.

The very nature of this story, this Christian tradition, this particular religious identity, is to *be opened up* to reality in all its awkwardness and ambiguity. It is not best understood as something self-contained at all, but is intrinsically concerned with 'neighbour-love'[2] as the basis of divine and human solidarity. This implies a readiness to *learn* from and with neighbours of all kinds – those who also belong to 'our' tradition but whose experiences are starkly different, those outside of it with distinct insights into reality, or for whom the struggle simply to survive is more pressing than 'learning about reality' as such. This is not about this tradition desiring to be the ultimate absorber of everyone's experiences, like an Artificial Intelligence growing in knowledge and power. Rather, at the heart of Christian faith, as it witnesses to and pursues Holy Anarchy, is the recognition that the whole story is always more. We are not the sole witnesses to Holy Anarchy. Nor the sole pursuers of it. But we may have a particular role, a distinct calling or vocation, as we play our part in faithfully pointing to it (and receiving the wisdom of others as they point to it too), embodying it (however imperfectly) and furthering it (in solidarity with any who are hurt by whatever and whoever resists it, including us). I aim to explore these vocations more fully through this book and to pose questions for us, wherever people are trying to live them together.

All I am seeking to do at this stage is acknowledge that, when it comes to 'getting it', the Christian story highlights that those who conceive of themselves as – or act as if they were – insiders are not always the first people to 'get it'. So there must be room for 'anarchic' conversation, as different perspectives unsettle prevailing assumptions – whether it is those who have a long history of trying to get our attention but are wearied by our unwillingness to listen. Or those who wouldn't even think that their experiences represent important lessons for the church. We should anticipate disruption, because God often comes to us *in strangers*. I will return to this more directly in the final part of the book, but I need to be clear from the beginning about the desire to work with a tension between two anxieties: on the one hand, an understandable concern that this project should root itself in the particularities of Christian faith, rather than claiming to be 'what *everyone* thinks already', as though to colonize territory outside of ourselves. On the other hand, a legitimate worry is that it should not close itself off, but must regard the creative power of chaotic strangeness to disrupt and colour it. And Holy Anarchy *anticipates* and *demands* such sensitivity. It is a consciously Christian perspective on God's new realm but such that the place of Christians is not taken for granted; rather, we are alerted to the contributions of others.[3] There may be echoes of others' stories in our own story, or echoes of ours in still others' stories, but regrettably we keep missing them by drowning them out with our own conversations. This is why we need Holy Anarchy's destabilizing impulse – not only to unsettle our language, and our 'insider assumptions', but to help us be receptive to other stories in God's awkwardly varied world.

In other words, the possibility of 'getting it' can cut across other loyalties. It will not always be insiders who 'get it'; rather, people who are insiders to a range of traditions may sometimes 'get it' better than any single group, and those outside every formal tradition will have vital insights to challenge them all. According to insider notions of what understanding looks like, people who might have had no reason to 'understand' can actually be the ones who get it much more incisively. And anyway, who decides that 'understanding' is so important? And whose 'understanding' counts most? Usually those with the power to decide that it does. What we see, though, inspired by the exclamation mark and the question of who 'gets' what it's all about, is that clusters of issues are being gathered.

So, in Part 2, we will focus on the structures of power exposed and addressed by Holy Anarchy, and the potential response as agents of this alternative horizon; in Part 3, we will focus on insider-assumptions about the many-layered nature of Christian tradition, and what it means to embody community that signifies the world we're aiming for; and, finally in Part 4, we consider the question of receptivity to strangers, and how we might celebrate this challenge and demonstrate it.

A motif that will recur is the presence, or indeed the absence, of child-likeness – especially if little children are meant to be benchmarks of entry into this new realm, with their power, assumptions and receptivity differing from that of adults. So, for example, I may debate with myself about the significance of an exclamation mark – which in itself is symptomatic of much church and academic conversation. Meanwhile, a little one (whether a child or someone short of power), who specifically *needs* Holy Anarchy to disrupt things, *may be precisely the person who 'gets it'*. In which case, ironically, the exclamation mark serves a crucial purpose: it helps to remind me, at least, that Holy Anarchy confronts prevailing structures, it stops me in my tracks when I take my own position and assumptions for granted, and it alerts me to experiences, wisdom and questions beyond my preoccupations.

Holy Anarchy – *Holy Anarchy!* – signifies this sort of energy, as God shakes the structures and boundaries that keep things a certain way and makes possible new solidarities among people. It confronts us with the dangers of taking words or ideas for granted, not least 'the kingdom of God' itself, a term so easily spoken and repeated, but that can become a cliché, as though we all know what we mean. But who are 'we'? Are we a block of people who speak with one voice? Are we really all the same? Or are we merely using the same words but meaning very different things? And who decides the 'proper' meaning? And if the term becomes an in-joke, for people 'like me', or supposedly people 'like us', then we should ask who is really laughing? Does the joke fall flat, or does it only echo for some? And despite our best efforts to laugh with others, as well as to weep with them in solidarity, are we effectively laughing at them, anxious too that they are laughing at us? Whose side are we on? And whose future are we pursuing?

Despite these challenges with 'insider language', I am not at all saying we should avoid it, because it is part of the story of a community; part of our richness and complexity – and, indeed, it is intrinsic to our arguments as we wrestle with our own sense of identity and purpose. The words are symbols of underlying questions and catalysts for ongoing self-examination – or they should be. But it is by being attentive to the words, and by seeing what happens when we change them, that we return to important questions – not only about our own identity, but how such questions cut across other identities. For instance, is it possible that other people are asking related questions? How do their questions pose vital challenges for us? Holy Anarchy, with or without the exclamation mark, prompts these quests – for better self-awareness, deeper connection with others and meaningful solidarity.

I imagine it seems that most of this energy is associated with the 'anarchy', rather than the 'holy'. I will elaborate further on 'anarchy' in due course, but a word about 'holy'. I noted above that the echo of *Batman* may seem to trivialize it. Robin's exclamations appear to pull 'holy' away from its sacred origins, by associating it with a wide range of things, mundane and bizarre. Doesn't this undermine its significance? There is a counter-argument. While 'holy' means 'set apart', this certainly need not mean 'physically separate'; in fact, especially in Holy Anarchy, it is not about being physically separate but very much embedded in the mess and struggles of life.

As we have seen, there is a danger when an 'insider mentality' assumes that the boundaries are proper and permanent, taking them for granted – and so it is with holiness. It cannot be contained by the way that a certain group thinks or behaves. It cannot even be contained by serious-ness, or by sincerity. Because it turns up in unlikely places, among unlikely people, teaching unlikely lessons. That's what Jesus' ministry demonstrates. Partying with 'sinners'. Turning up at the 'wrong' people's houses. Touching people regarded as impure. Receiving the faith of those who were publicly rejected. This is *Holy* Anarchy. Or, as Jesus declared, 'Wisdom is vindicated by her deeds' (Matt. 11.19). In the mix, in the mess, in the impurity. Holy Anarchy – not 'holy' only when groups of Christians meet to affirm special ideas that Christians believe. Not 'holy' only when all things are found to be in good order. But 'holy' in the midst of the chaos of life. 'Holy' when the ways of the world, in all their dis-tortedness and self-deceit, are illuminated and held in hope. 'Holy' when the brokenness of things is acknowledged and not ignored. 'Holy' when the inequalities that get in the way of human flourishing are put front and centre of our gaze. 'Holy' when the inadequacies of Christian community are not denied but laid before us, humbly. 'Holy' when the need to learn from the wisdom of others is tapping on the glass through which we see only dimly.

This is why, if I end up turning 'Holy Anarchy!' into an in-joke, some-thing that only 'people like me' can hear and understand, the irony is that I do not understand it at all! It passes me by. I tame it to suit my own interests, but miss the point entirely. The secrets of the kingdom, which Jesus shared with his close friends, were painfully hard for the church to bear – and they still are hard for us to bear – because they are anarchic secrets. They destabilize our assumptions about God and about the world. They shatter the glass that we are inclined to hide behind. They break us open, too. But when I say 'us', I don't mean 'we' in terms of one neat block of people being affected in exactly the same way. No, the secrets of the kingdom, or Holy Anarchy, are destabilizing especially for those who enjoy most 'insider-power'. The rich and mighty are humbled. The poor and forgotten are raised up. There is indeed a particular 'identity' at play, but who gets to determine its nature is a crucial question.

So it is that 'Holy Anarchy!', with or without the exclamation mark, confronts 'us' with realities and dynamics we would prefer to ignore. Whether it is some people being opened up to the pain and potential of others, or it is others being set free from forces inhibiting their flourishing, or a messy mix of both – the existing distortions of the world affect us in messy ways. The in-joke begins to laugh at our delusions. The despair is heard and held. An alternative is glimpsed on the horizon: what is it saying to us? Is it tears or laughter that I hear? This new reality may sometimes be quiet, surreptitious, gentle, but it still packs a punch of surprise, subverting business-as-usual. An exclamation mark makes perfect sense!

Holy Anarchy is an attempt to express the truth of God's kingdom as it reckons with these questions and tensions. The exclamation mark does not simply remind us of the risk that only people 'on the inside' will grasp the echo of the story that they already know. As I said above, the exclamation mark also represents the surprise, cutting through the assumption about who the insiders are. A rupture that comes in the midst of a world where mighty forces are at work: forces of domination, whether in terms of economic power, racial and gender injustice, and the exploitation of the Earth. The systems within which we live and move and have our being encourage us to view these forces in terms of our own freedom, the freedom to choose, the freedom to be ourselves. But the reality is that, despite all of the apparent freedoms, still a tiny minority enjoy a disproportionate amount of power and wealth. There Is No Alternative, we are told, to the prevailing socio-economic models. Meanwhile, millions are hungry, uprooted from homes or security, desperate for meaningful hope rather than fantasy. In response, those of us with far greater privileges can feel guilty, and we can be paralysed by that guilt, consumed by a sense of powerlessness in the face of overbearing systems. Or we are in denial, trying to hold these realities at bay.

And it is in the midst of such a world, a world of borders and boundaries, stark inequalities, apparently unchanging truths, that Holy Anarchy comes with its exclamation mark: an abrupt puncture of this-is-how-things-are, breathing new life where the ambiguities make alternatives possible, where the tensions, the paralysis and the power can be turned on themselves, and inviting all of it, all of the mess, to take a step towards this ancient-but-new horizon.

The thing is, Holy Anarchy is not simply the end-point, what happens when everything is put right. It is also the route-map, the means by which the end takes shape. So it illuminates the current order of things, rather than denying it, while rubbing this current order against its alternative horizon. It is the way as well as the goal; both companion and trailblazer. And it is a shaking experience: especially for those who need to be shaken by the possibility of change.

But it does not always need the exclamation mark, because it often comes quietly, under the radar of everyday life, sprouting in the cracks of normalcy. Skimming across a border wall, as free as a bird. Slowly splitting the concrete in our minds and public spaces, until statues begin to fall: statues in honour of Establishment-interests. It comes at night, like a thief, stealing from vaults of privilege. It comes as a whisper, a seed, a cry of solidarity, an evocation, a catalyst. Holy Anarchy. Under the noses of those resistant to its call. Seeping into the wells from which hope is drawn, but making its home in the places of despair, not glossing over such realities, but enabling deep lament to find voice. Living with the ambiguities of human meaning and purpose, in which the vision of a beautiful alternative takes root – *not* one where all ambiguity and tension is neatly resolved, as we shall explore, but where such things are lived with constructively, justly, empathetically. After all, no-one who gives voice to it is perfect. We are all entangled in its denial, its negation. And this moral complexity matters – it is part of the picture, the chaos. But the seed can still grow through the thorns. Though the cross is truly power-ful, it does not have the last word. The tomb is empty.

Holy Anarchy is at hand. It is close by. But it is almost imperceptible. Like a hidden pearl. Like yeast that has been mixed into the dough of everyday life. Like a small seed. Buried, but ripe with potential. It is close by. But to enter into it, or to participate in it, we may find ourselves stooping to be like children. Seeing things differently. From a new per-spective. Through the eyes of those who are little. Even the least of these. This may not be entirely comfortable, but for many it will be gloriously good news. Holy Anarchy! Dare we trust ourselves to it? Dare we believe it is here, beckoning us? Dare we nurture it and scatter its seed further afield, and find that others have done the same? Dare we?

It depends

Whether anyone dares to embrace Holy Anarchy will depend, of course, on a number of things. There will be various conditions, or impediments, that obstruct our desires to embrace it and our efforts to pursue it. As I indicated, these will be addressed in Parts 2 to 4. Whether this alternative horizon resonates with others will also depend a little on the authenticity of what I offer, in terms of why it concerns me – which I will address in the following two sections. But of course it will depend too on the particular content of it, which I have begun to outline; but how does the change in language, from 'the kingdom of God' to 'Holy Anarchy', reflect this content?

It is worth noting that we do not know for sure how exactly the words we use relate to the thing in itself, specifically 'the kingdom of God'. This is an issue that will be developed further in Chapter 2 in terms of the different kinds of truth, but here I explore briefly the question: what do we think we mean when we name this alternative realm 'the kingdom of God'?

We could be using the term as an analogy, because our words cannot quite grasp the thing in itself, so we make a creative comparison, saying 'it's a bit like this'. This surely is partly what we are doing, because it is commonplace to say, 'it is a kingdom but like no other' – so we are acknowledging there is a problem with the term since it only takes us so far, but nevertheless it serves a useful purpose by giving us recognizable reference points: other kingdoms. But the 'otherness' of it remains an issue. So perhaps it is more like a metaphor, which is where a term plays creatively with a tension: on the one hand reflecting how it 'is' like the reality and, on the other, how it 'is not'.[4] This way of understanding the term also has difficulties, as we shall see, but at least it gives us a way of holding things in tension. For example, when people say 'God is my Rock', this can only make sense as metaphor, because it *is* the case but also *is not*. God is not *literally* rock – unmoving, cold, susceptible to erosion – so a literal understanding of it cannot make sense. But as metaphor, it brings 'God' and 'rock' into creative interplay, so reflects how the notion of rock-ness does express some truths about God, such as God's foundational or steadfast qualities. There may be similarities in the understanding of 'God's kingdom', which is partly like what we know of as kingdoms but partly not. So too with 'Holy Anarchy', which we will explore in due course.

The problem with 'kingdom' language is the *extent* of the 'is not' in relation to God's realm, because there are many problems associated with 'king' and 'kingdom'. There is the exclusive gendered language, the authoritarian (and often violent) nature of power exercised by kings, their location 'above' their subjects, the explicit or implicit subjugation of people, and the ways in which any kingdom's boundaries tend to be defined and enforced. Of course, people argue 'this kingdom is uniquely different', but this places a considerable strain on the imaginative connection being made: it requires us to associate God's realm with something *unlike* all other examples of such realms. This is even more problematic since the New Testament Greek word *basileia*, which is translated as 'kingdom', is also the word for 'empire'. So we are being asked to imagine an alternative *unlike* all other instances in the world – an empire but like no other empire. In which case, why call it an empire? Or a kingdom? It is precisely this *difference*, or we may even call it an 'untruth', that makes it good news – the gospel of God's *alternative* empire/kingdom, which is so different that it is unrecognizable.

The use of the term *basileia* expects us to place so much emphasis on the *unlikeness* of God's alternative that we must consciously and constantly remind ourselves that it is not like any other kingdom. The 'is' becomes seriously misleading, unless we are proactively alert to its unlikeness. Because of this demand on us, we are quite likely to opt for an easier path: resigning ourselves to the sense in which God's kingdom is partly recognizable as other kingdoms. The 'is not' finds itself losing ground, as we succumb to the view that God's empire is actually another realm of top-down and gendered power, a realm with a ruler and subjects, a realm with distinct boundaries between insiders and outsiders. Even if we tell ourselves that it is different, the weighty historical resonances of the term can undermine our best intentions. We may *want* to view it as different, but the metaphor struggles to hold the history of kingdoms and empires at bay. It is because of this challenge that we find ourselves seeking alternative terms, better language, to reflect what is arguably intended.

The alternative notion, 'kin-dom', offered particularly by feminist theologians,[5] makes the point that it is right to scrutinize these terms again and again, because if we take it for granted too easily we risk collapsing 'the kingdom of God' into any other understanding of 'kingdom'. Kindom, by contrast, calls into question the model of 'king' – its maleness and its authoritarian power – and affirms that in this alternative realm we are 'kin' to one another. After all, a kin-dom is where God's will is done and, as Jesus said, any who do God's will are his family (Mark 3.35). However, when read as a metaphor, kin-dom also involves an 'is' and an 'is not' in interplay. It 'is' the case in its aspiration to affirm what the alternative realm is like, not one of authoritarian and male-centred power, but of mutuality and familial bonds between us all. Yet it also 'is not' the case, since 'kin' may not resolve the issues entirely. The problem is that, while the language of 'kin' seeks to overcome the difficulties with kingship, its appropriateness may also depend on people's experiences of 'kinship'. Not only can kings be damaging, but many people also suffer at the hands of kin. No term may be entirely innocent, as I shall explore in Chapter 5, but a realm in which we are kin to one another may not be good news for all.

Interestingly, Elisabeth Schüssler Fiorenza opts for the Greek word itself, *basileia*,[6] deliberately making English-speakers pause to consider what is intended, rather than using the problematic kingdom/empire while retaining the term's political reference. In contrast, Gerd Theissen's term *'sym-basileia'* – *'sym'* meaning 'with' – reflects the different dynamic within *this* empire/kingdom: divine and human agency collaborating 'with' each other. None of these alternatives resolves all the problems; no analogy or metaphor ever could, but they are helpful contributions to the conversation as we continue to find parables in our own time and place.

Another option is Roger Haydon Mitchell and Julie Tomlin Arram's constructive notion of 'kenarchy'.[7] 'Ken' is from the Greek term *kenosis*, meaning 'emptying', as in Philippians chapter 2, in which Christ is described as 'emptying himself'. However, Mitchell defines 'archy' simply as 'a way of ordering or relating in social space',[8] whereas, as I elaborate below, my understanding is that it is more specific than that: 'archy' indicates 'rule over'. So, for Mitchell, 'kenarchy' is a vision of a society shaped by self-emptying, what he also calls 'the politics of love', since one's self-emptying is directed towards the wellbeing of 'the other'. I affirm much in this, and certainly the ethics that flow from this vision resonate with me.[9] There are, though, two ways in which I would contrast it with the approach I take. First, since the term does not engage directly with the 'ruling over' dimension of 'archy', it implies that self-emptying can coexist with 'ruling over', or at least that *kenosis* is a way of reconfiguring how we should conceive of 'rule-over'. But I am not sure that the apparent tension between 'emptying' and 'rule-over' can be maintained. It is more of a contradiction, because to rule is not to empty oneself and to empty oneself is not to rule. The creative interplay of the term is under considerable strain.

Second, I also have a difficulty with *kenosis* itself, because it suggests that God *had* the power to rule over, but chose to give it up. Rather, as I shall argue further, the nature of divine power is, and always has been, awesome by virtue of its childlike weakness. To the extent that this is wild, or manifest in unpredictably significant outcomes, this is in accordance with 'chaos': small events can indeed generate huge consequences (I develop this theme in Chapter 4). Nevertheless, I acknowledge some synergy between 'kenarchy', with its respective interplay of 'is' and 'is not', and Holy Anarchy.

Alternatively, Caputo speaks of 'sacred anarchy',[10] to which I will return, because there is a good deal in common with Shanks's term which I use. For them, 'anarchy' is understood in the literal sense of 'an-archy', where *arche* is concerned with 'ruling over' and *an* represents the negation or reversal of this – not merely a tension with 'rule-over', but its subversion and reversal. 'An-archy', therefore, is a realm of no-domination,[11] or even anti-domination, the active subversion of rule-over. (Below, I address the way in which rule-over and domination are related.) Whether 'sacred' or 'holy', the point is that true 'anarchy' is godly; it is a condition, state of affairs or reality in which God's will is done; things are as they should be.

But of course, as many people would argue, *surely God's kingdom is precisely the realm in which God 'rules over' all things?* That is what it means for God's will to be done. God is sovereign. God is in control. But this is exactly the problem that I am hoping to address – with allies like Caputo and Shanks – because the language of sovereignty, control and ruling over is all inappropriate, as I aim to show. In terms of our discussion of metaphor, the notion of 'ruling over' again stretches the imaginative connections to breaking point, because it invites us to associate this alternative vision with whatever we *do* know to be 'ruling over' (wherever other people exercise such authority) while at the same time affirming that God's exercise of 'ruling over' is unlike all others. The traditional argument is essentially saying that the alternative kingdom is still a kingdom, because there is still a king, God, who rules over all things within this realm, and because God rules in this realm, God's will is done, which is what happens when someone rules – even if God's rule is different from any other rulers. By contrast, my commitment is that God's will is done *precisely* by virtue of God's *not* 'ruling over'. Rather, God's will is done wherever the work of anti-domination bears fruit, and life in its fullness can flourish. It is neither 'rule' as such (command and control) nor 'over' (as though above), but something quite different. More akin to 'solidarity' (as opposed to 'rule') 'in the midst' (rather than 'over').

Of course, it could be argued that when I conflate 'ruling over' with 'domination', as though they are one and the same, I specifically miss the point – which is that God's 'rule' is different *precisely because it is not domination*. But I am not convinced that there is enough of a distinction between 'ruling over' and 'domination'. I understand that they are not intrinsically the same, because a good leader or a good employer may be said to exercise an element of 'ruling over', without resorting to 'domination'; and to the extent that we speak of God's ways as 'higher' than ours, this could seem to point to such 'ruling over': in the sense that God *holds to account* and *enables* rather than *disempowers*, God's higher ways could be ruling over ours. But, for me, problems remain. First, to rule involves having sanctions to draw on, the possibility that if someone defies my rule, I may sanction them in some way. I do not believe that the nature or power of God consists in sanctions;[12] rather, the reality of things may be revealed to us, but there is no door to close on us, even temporarily. For God remains intrinsically inseparable from the whole cosmos, neither averting the divine gaze from situations of brokenness nor heightening the brokenness through withdrawal, but embodying solidarity 'in the midst' through love in the cause of justice, justice in the cause of love. (We will return to this tension in Chapter 2 and the nature of divine agency in Chapter 4.)

Second, it seems to me that when God's 'rule-over' is defended – not least to make the very point that God's rule is innately never dominating – it is defended in the cause of God's capacity to *make things happen*, to *ensure* that God's will is done, with or without the agency of others. That is, a 'command and control' model. This represents a real difficulty, not only because Jesus contrasted the kingdom with all other models, stressing that God *serves*, as distinct from 'ruling' (e.g. Mark 10.35–45), but for a whole manner of reasons: first, if God 'rules over' to ensure God's will is done, how should we account for all the ways in which God's will is *not* done, and the suffering that results? (Of course, 'sin' is usually the answer, but it can feel rather abstract in the face of the similarly abstract insistence on divine power – as though one abstract notion is inhibited by the presence of another abstract notion. In fact, it can even sound rather glib, like an act of theological convenience to get God out of a hole: but does it even get God out of the hole? After all, if God rules over everything, why not negate the power of sin *and suffering*?[13]) Second, is this really how God exercises God's power – 'over' us, 'making' us do things, 'ensuring' outcomes; or is the reality rather more ambiguous, if not 'weak' (to which we shall return in Part 2)?[14] Third, if God's desired outcomes are constituted by a realm of dignity, community, liberty, justice and peace, then God's means ought to reflect those ends, so divine agency should be enabling of our agency, not least of those who are 'least', exercised through dialogue rather than monologue, and building solidarity. 'Rule-over' is intrinsically not like this.

In fact, Holy Anarchy may be a better way of reflecting this anti-kingdom,[15] though it too has an element of the metaphorical interplay. On the one hand, it 'is' the case that God is present and active through the very dynamics of anti-domination – wherever the seemingly powerless are engaged in the renewal of possibilities, wherever those who take their status for granted are subverted by alternative movements. The hungry are fed. The outsiders are welcomed. The little take their place at the table. But there remains a degree of 'is not' in the sense that the term 'anarchy' (like 'kingdom') has its own baggage, and this vision is not exactly like the anarchy that people tend to visualize. Though we will come to questions of chaos and disruptiveness further, which are important, it is vital that *Holy* Anarchy is not understood as being precisely synonymous with any specific human vision of anarchy, whether understood negatively or indeed positively as in one form or another of anarchism.

Even so, Holy Anarchy can indeed be 'hosted' by movements, institutions and programmes which capture it inadequately, whether religious or political as such.[16] Other writers, such as Dave Andrews in *Christi-Anarchy* and Van Steenwyk in his description of Jesus as *That Holy Anarchist*, have also used the language of 'anarchy' to reflect the subversive politics of Jesus.[17] After all, the centrality of the ethic of 'the first shall be last and the last shall be first' points to an anarchic vision: not one in which rulers should simply be replaced with new rulers, but one in which the social dynamics are repeatedly reconfigured. As Shanks states, 'He was crucified as an *anarchist*.'[18] Nonetheless, the metaphorical dimension of 'Holy Anarchy', with its interplay between 'is' and 'is not', remains important: *this* Anarchy 'is not' *exactly* the same as the anarchies of the world, though I certainly regard it as having far more in common with them than any 'kingdoms' do.[19] The imaginative stretch is not at all as great; the truth outweighs the untruth.

However, I am not attempting to outline a political programme as such, though I engage with the anti-imperial horizon of Holy Anarchy in due course. Here, my point is that the shift in language, from 'kingdom of God' to 'Holy Anarchy', is authentic to Jesus' original vision, because the an-archic quality of his message and ministry consistently demonstrated what Elisabeth Schüssler Fiorenza also described as 'an anti-imperialist egalitarian movement that seeks change for all those living on the bottom of the kyriarchal pyramid of domination'.[20] In other words, its defining feature was its commitment to 'anti-domination', a movement where no-one ruled over anyone else. A world where the dignity of each is recognized and celebrated. Whether it is an analogy or a metaphor, or indeed something else again, the notion of God's alternative realm as 'Holy Anarchy' is appropriately disruptive; in fact, its disruptiveness is a mark of its authenticity. Not that disruption per se is always a sign of the presence of Holy Anarchy, because – as we shall explore further in Chapter 2 – all sorts of movements claim to be 'anti-Establishment' but not all of them are. In fact, Establishments sometimes promote the idea that they are not in control, to distract from their privilege and accuse others of being the elite. Meanwhile, of course, even sincerely revolutionary movements can contradict their own ideals.

As I will identify again and again, Holy Anarchy can cut across a whole range of other loyalties, erupting even in a self-deceiving Establishment as well as among those struggling for freedom and dignity. The main issue, therefore, is not how we label ourselves but whether domination is subverted, enabling life to flourish. Since these words can obviously mean many different things, I will unpack the vision in more detail.

> ### Holy Anarchy so far ...
>
> An alternative horizon, not yet here, but closer at hand than we imagine; a realm in which there is no domination, no 'rule-over', neither by humans nor by God; rather, a realm marked by solidarity in the midst of everything, solidarity as the basis of the flourishing of life.

Context, Shanks and shakenness

So where am I coming from? And why am I drawn to this vision? It is important to root these issues and concerns in my own story, to help explain why they matter.

I teach in a theological college where our approach is 'contextual theology'. This means we try to take as seriously as possible the ways in which theology emerges out of and engages with particular real-life contexts. Often, this approach is also committed to particular kinds of change, in the light of specific challenges experienced in a context. So, for instance, liberation theologies are 'contextual', because they emerge out of situations of oppression – often poverty, but any context where particular groups suffer as a result of a relative lack of power or freedom, and the theology concerned helps the issues to be brought into focus, and potential paths for change to open up. Feminist theologies are also contextual, responding to the experience of women in the face of patri-archy, male-centred systems of power ('patri-archy': in which men are the ones to 'rule over'). There are also Black theologies, Asian theologies, African theologies, disability theologies, queer theologies, postcolonial theologies, and many more: each arising from a context, giving shape to the Christian story in such a way that an injustice is illuminated and the possibility of transformation is nurtured and pursued.

However, contextual theology is also an approach which asserts that theology has always been done contextually, even where this is not conscious. After all, the giants of Christian faith (however we decide who they are) are traditionally understood as though their insights speak into the situation of every person and every place. The supposition is that they may have lived at a particular moment, but their wisdom is universal. Now, there may be elements of truth in this, but it also has its dangers. So, for instance, when White middle-class western men (like me) were the main teachers of Christian faith, they did not stop to think how their 'Whiteness', their economic power, their global positioning or their gender had informed their theology; rather, they sought to tell the whole world that their truth was the truth for everyone. They did not notice that their ideas were 'contextual', emerging from particular situations, where particular questions were on the table and other questions were not. They came up with particular theological frameworks which they insisted were 'universal' for all time and space. But these frameworks grew out of specific cultural contexts, mapping the whole of God's story from a particular angle, with particular goals in mind. They may have been good, faithful people, but still their power has been disproportionate: so not only society, and the global network of power, has been defined largely in terms of White middle-class western men, but theology has been infused with these biases too, and has reinforced them as processes of imperialism, colonialism and the exploitation of the Earth have gone hand in hand with Christian mission. We consider this further in Chapter 2.

Consequently, not all contextual theologies are therefore liberating.[21] Some emerge from the contexts of those with privilege and are promoted as though they are good for everyone. In fact, people all around the world live with the legacy of particular 'contextual' theologies – theologies emerging in the hands and mouths of White western men, which have clearly not been liberating for many. As a discipline, however, contextual theology at its best should be and can be deeply self-conscious, alerting us to the ways in which ideas and lived experiences interact with one another, and drawing our attention to how any single context – especially one with disproportionate power – needs to be interrogated by voices from other contexts. It is never straightforward to be able to say exactly where a theology begins: some say it must begin with life-experience, and yet it takes particular concepts and commitments to enable us to draw out the significance of the experience; others say it begins with scripture, and yet we always bring life-experience to bear on our interpretation of scripture. It is widely acknowledged that when we do theology – and it is indeed something we 'do' rather than merely 'receive' – we draw from scripture, the wider traditions of the church, our own human reasoning and our life-experience; each contributes to the whole, though different people give more weight to one or other of those sources. Still others, including the late Archbishop Desmond Tutu, have added the importance of imagination, since scripture, tradition, reason and experience can sometimes only get us so far; what is needed is an imaginative leap, especially in contexts of oppression where it is hard to conceive of the world differently – so it is legitimate to *imagine* where our *reasoning*, or what we believe to be 'revelation', leaves us with gaps.

Essentially, we cannot say for sure where we begin – with ideas, which we use to interpret experience, or with experience, which is the basis for reflecting critically on preconceived ideas. But what matters is the conversation, a rich and dynamic conversation, between theory and practice, ideas and experience, particular contexts and multiple contexts, voices around the table and those who would either like a place at the table or who set up alternative tables right under the noses of the powerful. It is important to acknowledge, too, that when we talk about drawing on these various sources to inform and shape our theology, this thing called theology does not exist in a vacuum, because ideologies, politics, psychologies, economics and more are woven into the very stuff of scripture, tradition, reason, experience and imagination. There is no 'theology only' space, just as there is also no 'theology free' space, because God is present in those interacting voices and disciplines. The conversation of contextual theology is therefore especially alert to its messiness, with its ambiguities and loose ends, its capacity to overlook all sorts of factors which may be at play, and its differences in power among those participating.

As a result, I am interested in three particular dynamics in theology – the challenge to hold a Christian identity generously, since words and traditions are interpreted diversely and cannot capture it all anyway; the challenge to reckon with the limits of what we hold and the insights that come to us from others; and the challenge to acknowledge and transform the power structures that frame our sense of what is possible. In each case, as I will show through Parts 2, 3 and 4, Holy Anarchy sharpens our awareness of these dynamics and enables creative engagement with them. The awareness of these three dynamics is greatly informed by the theology of Andrew Shanks, which has influenced me for nearly 20 years – and conversations with him personally have been part of that journey. At the heart of his work is 'the solidarity of the shaken', a concept he borrows from the Czech thinker and activist Jan Patočka, who spoke of people being 'shaken' out of the lies, half-truths and propaganda of Soviet rule.[22] Shanks reflects theologically on the image as his other way of understanding the kingdom of God: a reality as 'catholic' as possible by virtue of all sorts of people, from as many backgrounds as possible, expressing 'solidarity' with one another; but he states that such expansive solidarity is only possible because a spirit of shakenness prevails, opening the people up empathetically to ever more of reality in all its awkwardness, pain and potential.[23]

It is not about setting out to 'shake' people, because such imposition would be a denial of solidarity; but through the struggles of life, there exists the possibility that we are being shaken open – though equally there exists the entirely understandable possibility that we may withdraw for some security. The point is not to judge how people respond, since God is in solidarity especially with those judged by the world; rather, the point is that God is inviting us to become more alert to reality – sometimes this will be utterly gradual; at other times it will involve a revolution in thinking and practice. Shanks explains:

> The solidarity of the shaken, being in principle the most difficult of all forms of solidarity to organize, can only thrive in the context of other forms of solidarity, playing host to it.[24]

That is to say, it will not exist in its purity, but rather will always be mixed in with the dough of life, whether in flawed religion, political or protest movements, civil agencies or communities. The solidarity of the shaken will cut across all such boundaries, with some individuals or groups being attentive to some forms of shakenness while others attend to different forms, each with the potential to learn from one another. Shakenness, then, is a never-ending process because even where we feel shaken out of one half-truth, others remain, and we always run the risk of lapsing into indifference, a false sense of innocence, or manipulativeness.

As Shanks puts it, there are three particular 'dishonesties' that condition us against shakenness.[25] The first consists in the editing or whitewashing of our own story, or identity, to feel better about the world; we may call it the 'identity' distortion. The second consists in our disregard for the truth-potential of others – the 'difference' denial. The third consists in the silencing, scapegoating and sacrificing of those who undermine vested interests – the 'solidarity' suppression. These are at the basis of the discussions in Parts 2, 3 and 4; Part 2 is concerned with the power structures and the question of solidarity; Part 3 considers the dynamics of Christian community in response to such forces and its particular, awkward identity; and Part 4 addresses issues of difference and strangeness. Together, the quest to address these interweaving dynamics represents an 'inter-contextual' theology, an approach that brings different kinds of contextual theology into dialogue in order to challenge and enrich each dimension.

But if these are the ideas, what have been the experiences that have shaped my engagement with and attachment to them?

Here I stand

I was raised in a Christian church, specifically Highbury Congregational Church, in Cheltenham. Congregationalism is a British dissenting tradition, with a history extending right back to the seventeenth century when the monarchy and Church of England were trying to achieve greater conformity in the churches. Dissenters represented greater freedom and variety, in response to the liberating movement of the Spirit, and they suffered in various ways as a result. Though Congregationalism is significantly smaller, and its modern history is arguably less political, than it was in the nineteenth century, nevertheless this echo of dissent and nonconformity lives in me. I do not want to idealize the tradition, because I have come to understand its shortcomings more sharply, while also appreciating how radical contributions to Holy Anarchy have emerged from hierarchical churches: such as liberation theologies, much feminist theology and queer theologies, and more. Nevertheless, Congregationalism represents a vision of 'the small' – since even a small church (the autonomous 'congregation') is free to govern its affairs, as inspired by the Spirit and through seeking the mind of Christ as revealed in the midst of the covenanted church meeting, unimpeded by powers-that-be, in theory. At the same time, it offers a vision to transcend each locality, speaking up for freedom of conscience and social reform on the national and international stage, not simply in its own interest, but in solidarity with others who are 'little'. Or it offers the potential for such a vision, in accordance with its radical heritage.

My church in Cheltenham was also a wider family for me, and I became very much aware that these wise 'aunts' and 'uncles' were deeply committed to the world beyond the welfare of the church. It was not merely that the building was used by many different organizations but that church members were themselves involved with various bodies and agencies, such as the Samaritans. In terms of its understanding of the Christian faith, this showed me that it was lived through practical commitments, but it was also a church where people were free to discuss, think, explore, doubt, disagree. The Junior Church was subdivided into several age-groups, the oldest of which was called the Anvil Group, because it was where we were free to 'hammer out ideas', the questions of faith and life, as though on an anvil. All of this mattered. In hindsight, it was a witness to the possibility of the solidarity of the shaken.

The church belonged to the Congregational Federation, the largest voluntary association of Congregational churches. The Federation itself belonged to a global mission partnership called the Council for World Mission (CWM) – the successor to what had been partly the London

Missionary Society (LMS), an ecumenical missionary society established in 1795. Its history is complex, having engaged in mission mostly in the countries of the British Empire, along with the other British missionary societies, so its contribution to proclaiming the Christian gospel often went hand in hand with commerce and the colonial presumptions of 'civilization'. In recent years, since becoming CWM, it has been critically revisiting that history and its legacy to identify, for example, where former slaveowners had contributed to its funds and what reparation now might look like. In fact, the evolution from LMS to CWM began in the middle of the twentieth century, as more and more countries became independent, the global ecumenical movement also wrestled with new ways of doing things, and 'daughter' churches sought their own autonomy. Ultimately, rather than being a donor agency, sending missionaries in one direction, from North to South, CWM is a partnership of churches in mission: not an agency that 'does mission to' or even 'through' 'foreign' churches, but an equal partnership of churches in many countries, from the Church of Bangladesh to the trans-national United Congregational Church of Southern Africa (across five countries), from the churches of Taiwan to Tuvalu, Guyana to Hong Kong, Malawi to Myanmar. As each church is autonomous, and thus works out what mission means for them, they contribute to and draw from the collective insights, resources and programmes of the global partnership.

It would be possible for me to idealize this organization, to paint a picture of it that whitewashes its failures, because it has been an organization that has had a huge impact on me, but I have also encountered several ways in which it is far from perfect, in part connected with its imperial history. Thankfully, however, it is committed to examining itself, asking hard questions and learning – and it seeks to encourage its member churches to examine their location in insidious systems of Empire.

When I was 16, I participated in a youth workcamp in Penrhys, an estate in South Wales, with other young people from the CWM member churches. It was invigorating to be with representatives of the global church. We celebrated and wept together, misunderstood and understood one another, used the same words (in English) but meant different things by them, and built community. Subsequent experiences have included several conferences, in the UK, South Africa, Botswana, Brazil, Thailand and Korea. These included one with representatives from the World Council of Churches as we sought to understand and critique features of the global economy and envisage alternative models (leading to the São Paulo Statement 2012[26]), and a series of events with diverse participants as part of CWM's Discernment and Radical Engagement (DARE) programme, leading to publications such as *Scripture and Resistance*.[27] So it is CWM that has helped me to explore the nature of Empire, a name for the matrix of power structures that need to be addressed, and which is one of the areas of focus in my teaching at Luther King Centre.

Previously, though, I had studied law, which I enjoyed, but I began to feel called to Christian ministry. In one of the courses, legal philosophy, I could see how law was resourcing me for something else: it helped me to understand how texts are interpreted from different perspectives and to divergent ends; it enabled me to examine the authority of a text and what lay behind it. Increasingly, I realized more clearly how laws serve some interests more than others. The playing field is never exactly level when it comes to the creation of law, access to law, navigating through the system or legal judgment. During my law degree, various strands of politicization were fused more firmly; and my enquiring faith also found expression in hymn-writing – which has continued, so various lyrics punctuate the narrative of this book.

After graduating in law, I undertook a year of voluntary work; I was placed as a pastoral assistant in an Anglican church in an urban estate, while further discerning my sense of call. Then, once accepted by the Congregational Federation, it was time for formal theological education to prepare me for ministry – I studied at Northern College (United Reformed and Congregational), part of the partnership for theological education at Luther King House (now Centre), in Manchester. A unique place. I was the only Congregationalist, but my United Reformed peers ensured I was at home; and contextual theology, with church placements throughout the degree, helped to embed this sense of the interaction between faith and life, faith and politics, faith and justice. I loved it. And when my time there was drawing to a close, I knew it was right to find a way to keep doing theology alongside my new ministry. So, in 2002, I had a busy year: I married Sheryl, was ordained and inducted to serve as minister of Lees Street Congregational Church in Manchester, and I began a PhD at the University of Leeds.

The church is in an inner-city area, where social deprivation was multiple and complex, and during my ten years there it also became increasingly diverse. The area had experienced a series of clearances, where houses were subject to compulsory purchase and people were re-housed elsewhere, so there was a sense of wariness about what might happen next; therefore much of my focus was on trying to help the church to rebuild confidence to engage with its community. There were small victories, in terms of a collaboration between churches to clean the church garden; a creative art project, telling the church's story in a series of mosaics on the outside wall; people going forward to train for ministry; hosting placements of ministers-in-training; and particular services where the church's newfound diversity was well demonstrated. Children were integral to the celebrations. We practised Messy Church, at many levels. But there were struggles and losses. People. Money. Stability interacting with transience. Fragility. Exhaustion. But hope remained, and it still does, through many traumas. It was a church working at being 'catholic' – that is, for all-comers, in the midst of struggle. It showed signs of shakenness and signs of weariness. We wept and laughed. We shared disappointments and we dared to dream.

At the same time I was researching Christology: how different theologians understand Jesus, and in particular how this relates to different understandings of religious diversity. What emerged, ultimately in my thesis and the book based on it, *Christ and the Other*, was not only about Jesus and other religions, but a more comprehensive argument about how Jesus was the person he was *always through interaction with others* – those within his own tradition, those in other traditions, and those under the radar of respectable society. In other words, I came to see how Jesus is not only the initiator of events, but was also responsive to others, and how he himself was affected, and even changed, through encounter: by insiders, by outsiders, and by 'undersiders' – those at the bottom of the heap. It was also a commendation to churches – to be alert to how the church's identity must be in flux, how it has wisdom to receive from those outside, and how it is both caught up in transforming systems of domination and has a part to play in them.

But despite my training in contextual theology, I did not explicitly connect this research with my ministry. I had found it helpful to keep the two worlds in separate boxes. Since then, though, I have recognized the interaction between them: in ministry and through involvement with the global church, I have experienced the truth of people shaking me open. This included people in my own community, people in other traditions (a Council of Christians and Jews study tour to Israel and Palestine had fed my interest in religious diversity) and those struggling at the margins – not that I am claiming of course to be as alert to any of these realities as fully as I could be. The fact that I had not exactly seen the truth of my research in my own ministry indicates that these things do not reveal themselves easily, or consistently. And still I am being surprised by shakenness, even as I continue to be blissfully unaware of threads that others recognize. This is why resources such as *Young, Woke and Christian*[28] are so important, drawing attention to aspects of the matrix that might go overlooked. For instance, I am slowly realizing that a number of my privileges mean there is relatively little cost to me in navigating the expectations of religious and educational institutions, since I can 'fit in' with the norms and 'play the game' more easily. Even where I want to be subversive, there is enough room for this, and enough forgiveness. Whereas for others, both fitting in and acting subversively is more costly.

This leads me to the ways in which my family story is a part of the inter-weaving picture. As I indicated, I was raised in a churchgoing family. My father was a retail salesman, a gentle man, caring, witty, self-deprecating, and a lay preacher. He died as a result of dementia in 2016. My mother was a physiotherapist, accomplished at many things, highly organized and creative – but multiple sclerosis (diagnosed when I was eight) would increasingly affect her mobility, so she had to give up paid work, though continued to be a volunteer with Girlguiding and at church, in various capacities. She died in 2015. These threads represent further catalysts of shakenness. Grief itself, with two such significant losses just a year apart, and followed a year later by my father-in-law's death, was such a shaking experience. Shanks's interpretation of the Beatitudes had identified that the blessings are for those who are shaken in a range of ways, including those who mourn: blessed are those who are shaken; blessed are those who mourn. I felt it. It was a disorienting sense of living at right angles to reality or, rather, coming to see the truth of reality's fragility at last, and wondering why other people seemed to be getting on with normal life, as though indifferent to the trauma of loss. Of course, many of them may also have experienced loss, each alert to what they knew, or perhaps having to put it in a mental box. But at one and the same time, I felt as though I was drifting in a world that belonged to other people, while also feeling as though *this was reality*. I had previously ministered 'to' people who were grieving, but it was quite different experiencing it first-hand. A shaking experience.

So, too, the experience of disability that had preceded grief – or 'dis/ ability' as I refer to it elsewhere, because of the ambiguities around some-one being measured by their 'dis-' while also having so much 'ability'. It was a huge part of our world as a family: learning to see how the social architecture around us was not prepared for wheelchairs, how people in wheelchairs can be viewed and ignored, and making connections between such a concern for justice and things of faith and church life. My mother would not have regarded herself as political but, even so, she became an advocate for all sorts of 'disability matters'. Meanwhile, as a child experi-encing various kinds of 'unfairness', I was spurred to be attentive to such questions, however inconsistently. It was a means of shakenness, helping to generate empathy, but also a sharpened sense of injustice in face of prejudice, behaviours and structures.

Regarding structures, socio-economic class is obviously a significant feature of them. The fact that I find it hard to describe, in personal terms, is no doubt because I am middle class, so it is part of my context to take for granted certain privileges and securities. And of course, perceptions from within a class can be quite confusing. On the one hand, I was conscious that our family income was below the UK average, because of my parents' circumstances, which obviously informed the choices we made. On the other hand, I could see that we did not have to struggle. While some at my grammar school and in the town of Cheltenham seemed far wealthier, I was gradually waking up: in knowing what the average UK income was, and how many earned more than this, it was dawning on me, in my naivety, how very many more must earn less than it. 'Middle class' is also a matter of inherited assets, access and assumptions that insulate me from many aspects of reality. Specific experiences, however, were gradually alerting me to the contrasts in people's economic security. The workcamp in Penrhys had briefly immersed me in a very different world, sparking much greater interest in social justice. Studying law at university, and conversations among friends and peers, increasingly politicized me. Subsequently, through the placement as pastoral assistant in a housing estate, my theological education, whether in an inner-city Roman Catholic parish or throughout our contextual learning, and my own ministry, I came to understand my own story (its securities, education, norms) more starkly in contrast to urban poverty. Experiences of the global church with CWM also heightened awareness of inequalities.

In addition, while most of my childhood was starkly 'White', family and church lives have become more 'racialized' – that is, conscious of the social constructions of 'race', its prejudices and power differentials. Even within my 'Whiteness', however, I was alert to the complexities of identity because my father was English, my mother Welsh, and this dual identity was important to me. I cannot describe myself as 'English', whereas I do see myself as 'British', *because* it incorporates my English and Welsh heritages. I recognize, however, that such 'incorporation' is precisely what annoys Welsh and Scottish friends, who do not view themselves as British. Nevertheless, it is frustrating to be categorized as English simply on the basis that I have always lived in 'England'. This gives me partial insight into the injustices concerning those of a Global Majority Heritage – both those born in the UK but who continue to feel 'othered', and those who have migrated here. The dynamics of nationhood, race and community are complex, but Whiteness has its grip on such discussions, because 'Britain' is yet to reckon with its imperial history and legacy. These insights developed further because my wife Sheryl is dual heritage, her mother being originally from Singapore, so our daughter is rightly alert to her heritage tapestry. But I have also seen people's assumptions at work when engaging with East Asian heritage. Furthermore, as my church and Luther King Centre became spaces of deeper encounter between people of different racial and national backgrounds, I woke up to some of my own unacknowledged prejudices, as well as those of others and, despite alertness to issues of Empire, I realized that anti-racism had not been so explicitly part of my vision – but it is becoming more integral.

I teach in the area of mission studies, and for me anti-racism is part of the mission of God into which we are called. Environmental justice has also come to be more central as well, despite all the many ways that I am conscious of my complicity with systems that continue to exploit the Earth. This is the thing about shakenness: its particular challenge is alerting us to the ways in which we remain unshaken, or at least stuck in habits of unneighbourliness. I recognize that this book, though it seeks to discuss and promote a comprehensive horizon of Holy Anarchy, will not cover every aspect of this vision evenly or justly. I seek to engage with shakenness in the midst of sexual and gender diversity, differing abilities, neuro-diversity, religious diversity, as well as concern for economic, racial and ecological wholeness, but will not do justice to every dimension.

The thing is, I am being shaken, but it is very much a work in progress. It is uncomfortable, challenging, disruptive. Anarchic. But it's also good news. Holy. There are things that I see, things I do not see. There are moments of movement forwards, moments of withdrawal and retreat. Sometimes I become conscious of my complicity with injustice; sometimes I realize the guilt paralyses me, then I remember what a luxury it is to be morally paralysed while others must get on with the pain and try to survive. As an educator, I feel the sense of 'escape' that Jennings talks about,[29] while also feeling that education sometimes brings me up against more dimensions all at once, the complexity of the matrix in which we live and move, with the 'intersecting' dynamics of injustice, and too little time (or will) to respond to it all. It is a quest to be self-aware, in and through relationship with others, alert to the distortions and delusions, but not only self-aware.

While contextual theology as a discipline, and discipleship in the way of Holy Anarchy as a commitment, both confront me individually with the challenge of understanding how I am personally located in these dynamics, they also open me up beyond the individualism of the western self. The deceit of individualism urges me to be the self-sufficient man on his own pedestal, as western consumer culture expects. But attentiveness to this temptation, and to the reality of my connectedness with the rich diversity of people and to the web of life that is Earth, helps me not to sink into self-loathing on the one hand or self-justification on the other. Because although I own that this articulation of Holy Anarchy is mine,

I am acutely aware that it is profoundly dependent on, and enriched, troubled and far better demonstrated by, many others as well. In fact, I would be foolish to try to control this; it slips through my hands, waits to surprise me in unexpected places, and beckons me to new dimensions of faith, discipleship and justice. I'm not always brave enough to follow, but the alternative horizon continues to captivate me.

A hymn

Imagine a temple of trees and a voice*
inviting the people to make a bold choice:
to grow in God-likeness, our eyes opened wide,
to face all the tensions – within and outside.

Imagine a desert where Jesus would choose
the ways that God-likeness will shape the good news:
enticed towards grandeur, to revel in fame,
or walk with the exiled, those cast out in shame.

Instead of the glamour – of bread made from stone,
fantastical leaps from the temple's high throne,
or harnessing empires to serve him through fear –
he sits with the hungry to show God is here.

Invited to grow in God-likeness through loss –
from garden to desert, from temple to cross –
this freedom affords us no way to stay pure,
but God's love is steadfast, though no simple cure.

Graham Adams (2020)
Suggested tune: *Stowey* – or create another one
*The 'temple of trees' is an allusion to the Garden in Genesis 2, since much scholarship argues that the Jerusalem temple included a garden, so the story is an allegory of the people's exile from Jerusalem as a result of their defiance of God. But it is striking that the serpent in Genesis 2 (an icon of healing, ironically) is simply inviting the people to be more 'God-like' – and isn't that how we are called to be? The early church theologian Irenaeus proposed that, though we are made in God's image, we need to grow into God's likeness; that is the tension we live with. And then in Jesus' temptations, he shows us what growing in God-likeness means: rejecting models of glamour and power in favour of solidarity with those in the wilderness – arguably, solidarity with those exiled by any religious or political establishment. It is an anarchic vision, with no luxury of staying pure.

> ## Questions to ponder
>
> 1 How does this initial picture of Holy Anarchy compare with your understanding of the kingdom of God? What are the differences and any similarities?
> 2 In what ways do you think churches are living with theologies derived from particular contexts, which may not speak for or to everyone?
> 3 Do you have any experiences pointing to the anarchic spirit of God, shaking and disrupting the assumptions and systems of your world or our shared world?

Further reading

John D. Caputo, *The Weakness of God: A Theology of the Event* (Bloomington, IN: Indiana University Press, 2006).

Roger Haydon Mitchell and Julie Tomlin Arram (eds), *Discovering Kenarchy: Contemporary Resources for the Politics of Love* (Eugene, OR: Wipf and Stock, 2014).

Cynthia D. Moe-Lobeda, *Resisting Structural Evil: Love as Ecological-Economic Vocation* (Minneapolis, MN: Fortress Press, 2013).

Joerg Rieger and Kwok Pui-lan, *Occupy Religion: Theology of the Multitude* (Washington DC: Rowman & Littlefield, 2010).

Elisabeth Schüssler Fiorenza, *Jesus and the Politics of Interpretation* (New York: Continuum, 2000).

Andrew Shanks, *God and Modernity: A New and Better Way to Do Theology* (London and New York: Routledge, 2000), especially chapters 1 to 3.

Andrew Shanks, *Faith in Honesty: The Essential Nature of Theology* (Farnham: Ashgate, 2005).

Andrew Shanks, *Hegel and Religious Faith: Divided Brain, Atoning Spirit* (London and New York: Bloomsbury T&T Clark, 2011).

Notes

1 Arundhati Roy, speaking at the World Social Forum, Porto Alegre, Brazil, 27 January 2003.

2 Cynthia D. Moe-Lobeda, *Resisting Structural Evil: Love as Ecological--Economic Vocation*, Minneapolis, MN: Fortress Press, 2013, p. 15.

3 As we shall see, especially in Chapter 7, many before me have made this argu-

ment, including Stanley Samartha, Aloysius Pieris, Kosuke Koyama, Chung Hyun Kyung and Grace Ji-Sun Kim.

4 See Paul Ricoeur, *The Rule of Metaphor: Multi-disciplinary Studies of the Creation of Meaning in Language*, London: Routledge and Kegan Paul, 1978, pp. 247–8.

5 First coined by Ada María Isasi-Díaz.

6 Elisabeth Schüssler Fiorenza, *Jesus and the Politics of Interpretation*, New York: Continuum, 2000, p. 28.

7 Roger Haydon Mitchell and Julie Tomlin Arram (eds), *Discovering Kenarchy: Contemporary Resources for the Politics of Love*, Eugene, OR: Wipf and Stock, 2014.

8 Mitchell, 'Introduction', in Mitchell and Tomlin Arram (eds), *Discovering Kenarchy*, p. 3.

9 For example, the blog https://kenarchy.org/ (accessed 6 January 2022) identifies ethics such as: instating women, prioritizing children, welcoming strangers, reintegrating humanity and the environment, and more.

10 John D. Caputo, *The Weakness of God: A Theology of the Event*, Bloomington, IN: Indiana University Press, 2006, p. 14.

11 Andrew Shanks, *Hegel versus 'Inter-Faith Dialogue': A General Theory of True Xenophilia*, New York: Cambridge University Press, 2015, p. 162. In *Faith in Honesty: The Essential Nature of Theology*, Farnham: Ashgate, 2005, p. 146, Shanks explains that *archein* is 'to rule'. In *The Weakness of God*, p. 101, Caputo speaks of sacred anarchy as 'the unruliness of the rule of God, a kind of divine madness that runs roughshod over the settled ways and rules of the world'.

12 Andrew Shanks, *Hegel and Religious Faith: Divided Brain, Atoning Spirit*, London and New York: Bloomsbury T&T Clark, 2011, p. 82. Shanks speaks of those models 'where "God" is understood ... as the celestial *Enforcer*' (his emphasis). Caputo describes the 'unconditional' call of the kingdom as 'a promise without the power to enforce its promise ... an appeal whose realization is exposed to the hazards of chance' (*The Weakness of God*, p. 105). In Chapter 4 I return to 'chance' in the context of 'chaos'.

13 At this point, we could engage with huge arguments about sin, the death of Jesus, human freedom and the final resolution of all things. However, I am not getting into those debates here. My point is simply that whenever God's 'rule over' is part of the argument, various problems follow, which are not easily resolved. Of course, the negation of divine 'rule-over' leads to different challenges, but I aim to address those constructively with reference to experience and faith. Whether I succeed is for others to determine.

14 See Jacques Ellul, trans. Geoffrey W. Bromiley, *Anarchy and Christianity*, Eugene, OR: Wipf and Stock, 1991, p. 33; he disputes concepts of God as Master, Lord, King – that is, concepts of dominating power.

15 Joerg Rieger and Kwok Pui-lan, *Occupy Religion: Theology of the Multitude*, Washington DC: Rowman & Littlefield, 2010, p. 74: 'this kingdom is better understood as an anti-kingdom'.

16 Shanks, *Hegel and Religious Faith*, p. 85: he speaks of 'the solidarity of the shaken', which I explain shortly.

17 Dave Andrews, *Christi-Anarchy: Discovering a Radical Spirituality of Compassion*, Oxford: Lion Publishing, 1999; Mark Van Steenwyk, *That Holy Anarchist: Reflections on Christianity and Anarchism*, Minneapolis, MI: Missio Dei, 2012.

18 Shanks, *Xenophilia*, p. 153 (his emphasis).

19 See Ellul, *Anarchy and Christianity*, p. 13: he notes different kinds of anarchisms. He goes on to acknowledge that anarchists believe true anarchy is possible, whereas Ellul believes the struggle for it 'is essential' but 'the realizing of such a society is impossible'. This speaks to its comparison with God's kingdom.

20 Schüssler Fiorenza, *Jesus and the Politics of Interpretation*, p. 113. Note: 'kyriarchal' pertains to 'kyri-archy', where there is any kind of 'lordly' (*kyrios*) 'rule-over'.

21 A point made by Anthony Reddie.

22 Andrew Shanks, *God and Modernity: A New and Better Way to Do Theology*, London and New York: Routledge, 2000, p. 5, citing Jan Patoçka, *Heretical Essays on the Philosophy of History*, Chicago and La Salle, IL: Open Court Publishing, 1996).

23 Shanks, *God and Modernity*, p. 5; *Hegel and Religious Faith*, pp. 74, 84–5; *Xenophilia*, p. 25.

24 Shanks, *Hegel and Religious Faith*, p. 85.

25 See Andrew Shanks, *Faith in Honesty: The Essential Nature of Theology*, Farnham: Ashgate, 2005, p. 11. He calls them: 'dishonesty-as-disowning', 'dishonesty-as-banality' and 'dishonesty-as-manipulation'. Here, I re-express them as 'the identity distortion', 'difference denial' and 'solidarity suppression', respectively.

26 https://www.oikoumene.org/resources/documents/sao-paulo-statement-international-financial-transformation-for-the-economy-of-life (accessed 22 December 2021).

27 Jione Havea (ed.), *Scripture and Resistance*, Washington DC: Rowman & Littlefield, 2019.

28 Victoria Turner (ed.), *Young, Woke and Christian: Words from a Missing Generation*, London: SCM Press, 2022.

29 Willie James Jennings, *After Whiteness: An Education in Belonging*, Grand Rapids, MI: Eerdmans, 2020, p. 3.

2

Handling Truth and the Other God

When a strong man, fully armed, guards his castle, his property is safe. But when one stronger than he attacks him and overpowers him, he takes away his armour in which he trusted and divides his plunder.
(Luke 11.21–22)

No one can serve two masters … You cannot serve God and mammon.
(Matthew 6.24)

In the beginning, shakenness

On 6 January 2021, there was an insurrection in Washington DC, also described as a riot and an attempted coup. The Capitol building was stormed; police, civil servants and politicians were abused, threatened, attacked; five people were killed, and in its wake a further four police officers took their own lives.[1] The background to this is obviously multi-faceted, but at the heart of it was Donald Trump's promotion of the idea that the November 2020 election was 'stolen' from him by Joe Biden and the Democrats. Up the road from the Capitol, on the day when Congress was confirming the election result, Trump gave an hour-long speech repeating these unfounded allegations, urging his supporters to 'never give up', asserting 'We're going to the Capitol' and exhorting the crowd, 'If you don't fight … you're not going to have a country anymore.'[2] After his speech, the crowd marched to the Capitol, at 1.30 p.m.

Among his supporters, people carried Confederate flags (symbolically siding with slavery) and others with slogans such as 'God, Guns and Trump', 'Jesus is my Savior. Trump is my President', and 'Jesus is King'.[3] As police officers would later testify, Black colleagues were subjected to racist abuse and intimidation, while the rioters tried to coax a White officer to join them.[4] The building was overrun, Congress was evacuated, the site of lawmaking was controlled by the insurrectionists. At 2.38 p.m. Trump tweeted 'Stay peaceful!' and, at 3.13 p.m., 'No violence! Remember – WE are the Party of Law & Order'. Crowds gathered in other state capitals, with violence breaking out in Los Angeles and in Salem. At 4.05

p.m. Biden called on Trump to 'demand an end to this siege' and, at 4.17 p.m., Trump tweeted a video repeating the claim that the election was 'fraudulent' and telling his supporters that he loves them but that they should 'go home'.[5]

Facebook and Twitter removed some of Trump's messages and closed down his accounts – first temporarily, and then Twitter permanently suspended him. It is undeniable that he played a hugely significant part in the events of that day, having already been the presidential figurehead of various movements among the Christian Right, Christian nationalists, and conspiracy theorists such as QAnon. The coup included people wearing Camp Auschwitz shirts, bearing nooses and gallows – as well as crosses – and beating a police officer to death. As Annette John-Hall argued, in an opinion piece on 16 January 2021, 'the insurrection was never about the election. It was about white supremacy.'[6] It was not simply about who won, but whose votes should matter, with the electoral counts most questioned being in cities with large Black populations. The echo of previous times when Black voices and votes were suppressed was striking. The Christian nationalists among Trump's supporters saw in him someone who advanced the cause of White Supremacy. After all, he had previously declared there were 'very fine people on both sides' of the protests in Charlottesville in 2017, not distinguishing between them at all: on the one hand, neo-Nazis, anti-Semites and White Supremacists and, on the other, anti-racists.[7] In response, Republican Senator John McCain tweeted, 'There is no moral equivalency'.[8]

Why do I begin a chapter about truth and the other God with an account of this insurrection, its backdrop and significance? The lie at the heart of the riot is important, and I will come to the question of truth in the following section. But I want to explore the nature of Christian identity and three further features of this story are especially pertinent: first, many of the rioters were explicitly and vocally Christians. Second, that when some people, including Christians, claim to be anti-Establishment, they may consciously or unconsciously defend other age-old Establishments or systems of entrenched injustice, such as White Supremacy. And third, it took such a traumatic and violent event to alert many people to the dangerous connections between Trump and anti-democratic movements. This is also relevant to our understanding of Christian identity, since we do not always see the connections between religious and political commitments.

It did not go unnoticed, of course, that 6 January is also the Feast of Epiphany for many Christians – a feast marking Christ's revelation or 'manifestation' to the Magi, representatives of the wider world.[9] But although the rioting represented a truth utterly different from the barrier-breaking message of Christ's manifestation, the events of 6 January 2021 were nevertheless 'revelatory' in other ways. They alerted people to the reality that many had previously refused to see. They brought into focus the distortions of 'Christian' nationalism and the violence of White Supremacy. They helped to 'shake' people to the truth of reality: though we do not like it, Christian faith has some disturbing manifestations. In fact, it has different gods. On the one hand, the 'God' honoured by the solidarity of the like-minded, a tribal deity in the service of vested interests. And alternatively, the 'other God': celebrated by the solidarity of the shaken, an unfinished solidarity.

It is important to say, though, that the former 'God' is not only found among the insurrectionists of 6 January 2021, but is honoured far more widely than that. It is found beyond the USA, but also elsewhere within it. For example, among the critics of the insurrection there was also arguably recourse to this false God, even if for better intentions. When Biden straightforwardly called it 'fundamentally un-American',[10] he implicitly distanced an abstract 'America' from anti-democratic practices that serve White Supremacy. This implication betrays a fundamental editing of US history or identity. It is easy to exhort 'the majesty of American democracy', to affirm that 'America's so much better than what we've seen today', as Biden did on 6 January 2021, but this is profoundly selective. The history of the USA includes anti-democratic behaviour, sanctioned by the state, within and beyond its shores; institutionalized White Supremacy; and Constitutional endorsement of violence. Attempts to whitewash this history, on the basis of a supposedly 'true America', are a further reflection of the insidious power of an idol: the 'God of the good guys', believed by one Establishment or another to vindicate 'our side', avoiding any real self-examination. It is the God of the like-minded, whether honoured through a delusional insurrection against the state or through uncritical defence of the nation.

The same delusion can be found throughout the world, where God is claimed to be 'for us' in particular ways, without asking hard questions of 'us'. It is not that God is always, only, 'universal', because God can certainly be partisan,[11] in the interests of those suffering under systems of domination – as we shall explore further. God can and does 'take sides' in struggles for justice, because there was no moral equivalency in the Charlottesville demonstrations: God is anti-racist, not White Supremacist. But the problem is when 'God' is co-opted by the will-to-domination, by groups with a vested interest in the status quo, by those of us who are disinclined to ask hard questions about the social structures that, even if only in some respects, serve us well. This is when God is assumed to be on 'our side' against an impure 'them': those who do not 'fit' with cultural norms or who destabilize the False Order which benefits the powerful. This is present in certain strands of all religious traditions, and in supposedly secular cultures where the gods or idols of politics and economics hold sway.

In Chapter 3, I will consider more explicitly the issue of this 'false Lord God' projected by versions of Christian faith that arise from the lust for power – that is to say, what is the difference between God and 'God'? Here, I simply begin to highlight the struggle between contested visions – of faith, truth and God. Christians in churches that reject, in particular, such 'Christian nationalism' might simply want to distance themselves from it, or do as I did above: put 'Christian' in inverted commas when assessing this faith-infused nationalism. Inverted commas, however, do not resolve the problem: Christian faith has many divergent manifestations, some of them so divergent from its central message of love and justice that it can be agonizing to regard them as Christian.

But there are too many ways in which mainstream churches have behaved appallingly through history for us to say, 'They weren't really Christian'. The sins of the Crusades, the Inquisitions, slavery, colonialism, racism, sexism, homophobia, the exploitation of labour and the Earth – these were, and are, committed by people self-identifying as Christian. People who did (and do) good things in some ways can do bad things in others. Bad things sometimes flow unintentionally from good things, and good sometimes flows inadvertently from bad; and, of course, not everyone even agrees about what is good and bad. Even where there is an apparent consensus, people still find themselves doing what they didn't mean to do. And not just 'them', but 'us' too. Me. In response, we may be tempted to believe that simply by cutting off the bad fruit of such sins, we will purify the church, but this is to make three errors: first, it becomes harder and harder to be a true Christian, with fewer and fewer people living up to its standards; second, it feeds the lie that innocence and purity are possible, even as we are entangled in tentacles we cannot see; and third, we fail to ask why it is that these fruit keep growing, even from such good roots.

Crucially, our task is to engage with the ambiguity of Christian identity: it never has been and it never will be perfect; not even Holy Anarchy in all its fullness is a realm where all ambiguity is resolved. Rather, we are called to live more honestly and constructively with the mess, while holding out the possibility of meaningful transformation. We can be encouraged by the fact that transformation has occurred many times in history and will keep occurring, even if new challenges emerge and we realize there are issues we have not yet identified. To help us engage with this state of possibility, which generates the depths of inhumanity and great heights of moral achievement, we should attend to a struggle between two kinds of truth – a struggle throughout our reality, under-pinning the tensions within Christian identity, and which takes us to the risk at the heart of the divine life.

Two kinds of truth

I need to distinguish between two kinds of truth, as Shanks does. He calls them 'truth-as-correctness' and 'truth-as-openness',[12] but I am call-ing them 'truth-in-hand' and 'truth-in-process'. They are two different ways of conceiving of truth. Or we could think of them as two different ways of articulating and presenting what is fundamentally important to us, of ultimate value.[13] The problem is that, including in debates about Christian identity, there is a general inclination to give more weight to one kind of truth rather than another, or even to reject the other 'truth' – and what I am proposing is that we need to give more weight *to the other kind* instead. Not denying the connection between the two kinds, since they relate dynamically with each other, but learning to prioritize the other. This effectively points us to *the other God*. So I will explore these two kinds of truth, relate them more directly to the gospel and Christian identity/ies, then look at some particular issues about who decides the story, before seeing them related to the specific examples of racism and the ecological crisis.

There are, of course, many ways of categorizing truth. The approach I take starts with an image: imagine a piece of paper with 'truth' written on it. It may be the word 'truth' itself, or indeed something that you understand to be true. It captures the essence of a matter. Now imagine two different ways of holding it. In the first image, the fingers are closed in, the piece of paper is secure within the clasp; it is held, it is 'in hand', grasped, safe. This is what we mostly tend to mean when we conceive of 'truth'. Something that we can pinpoint. Something held to be 'correct'. Something that we can articulate, because it has boundaries, or limits – '*this* is truth, because *that* isn't', *that* being outside of the clenched fist; untruth. The boundaries of the fist help to create the clarity. The truth.

Of course, you may hold a piece of paper with your truth, I may hold one with mine, and we may argue over the differences, but at least we know what our truth is. Hopefully there would be something in common between yours and mine, to help us have the argument, but if there isn't, or if we come across something that is 'non-negotiable' between us ('this is where I stand'), then we have to decide how to proceed: do we live and let live with our different truths, or do we battle over them until one of us prevails? It will depend how serious we think the difference is: for example, it may be affected by whether we are both Christian or we belong to different traditions; whether we are from the same nation or different nations; from the same or different racialized groups; and so on. In other words, how we view the truth (which is 'in hand') will depend on things that are apparently external to it, like race, politics, nationality, gender, sexuality, age, abilities, history and dreams. But actually, even those things may have informed our very notion of the truth that we hold. It may not be in such a vacuum. In fact, our grasp of it will almost certainly have been conditioned by other commitments.

So, the 'truth' does not only consist in what we hold, but exists in the manner of our holding: whether we hold it lovingly, as something to treasure and pass on, or defensively, even aggressively; why it is that we hold it, to what end, and in whose interests. In other words, 'truth' is not simply contained on the paper, but is part of a wider web of meaning. Even so, from a 'truth-in-hand' perspective, essentially we tell ourselves that the truth written on the piece of paper is the very truth of something. All of those other complications are peripheral. What matters is what is written: the statement that we regard as fact – whether that is a law of physics or a religious creed, a political conviction, or a textbook answer to an exam question. Truth is what we capture correctly in our words, hold affirmingly, and use as the unambiguous basis of our actions. In a sense, it is also about having a certain quantity of truth – the right amount of it, secured in hand; an economy of truth, a bank balance of truth; it's what we've got, while others may lack it.

Truth-in-hand. Grasped. Contained. Sufficient.

For 'truth-in-process', however, the piece of paper rests on my palm, which remains open. To the person whose hand is closed, this may appear somewhat reckless or as though I am indifferent to the significance of what I hold. After all, it is susceptible to a breeze which may blow it away, or someone else may grab it and destroy it. Do I not care about preserving the truth? Am I not bothered whether its integrity is maintained? How would I even react if it got mixed up with someone else's truth? But from the perspective of truth-in-process, those questions miss the point, though they are certainly understandable. Truth-in-process is about being conscious that truth is not contained on the piece of paper. It is not the sum of supposedly unambiguous facts, or even the statement of authentic emotion ('this is what I feel to be true'). It is more like an event, or a happening. A state of becoming. It is attentive to the web of meaning in which the open palm is only a part of the whole. It is not an 'economy' of truth, which others may lack, but an 'ecology' of truth, a living network of movements and responses, from which we receive and to which we give. Truth is what *happens* when the palm remains open. The potential for, and anticipation of, *connection, conversation, collaboration*. An open-endedness that defies the boundaries of any fist.

In this image, the truth on the piece of paper may stay exactly where it is, or it may move; it may be challenged or enriched by another slip of paper, or it may fly away, riding a wave of wind. Of course, this may sound far too fuzzy, vague and ambiguous, especially for those who give more weight to the truth-in-hand they hold tightly. It may sound carefree, lazy, indifferent. But the reality is that this ecology of truth is far more demanding; it exists in a state of perpetual risk, open to multiple possibilities, while remaining unanxious about that, because the 'event' of this truth is conscious that any account of truth is fleeting. There is always another angle on reality. Always further to dig beneath the surface. Always more connections to be made. Always an 'otherness' to unsettle the presumptions of what I am inclined to hold tight.

Though a good deal of effort is needed to safeguard truth-in-hand, as energy is spent keeping it secure, holding it tight, it is arguable that this effort serves the cause of *editing reality* rather than *attending to it*. To be committed to truth-in-hand is to ask oneself, 'What must I do to prevent "otherness" encroaching on the purity of my truth?' It is a desire to keep the truth pure, but – whether wittingly or unwittingly – it actually maintains the *impurity* of its edited truth. Whereas commitment to truth-in-process involves putting energy into alertness, the potential for new learning, readiness for greater empathy towards otherness, so creating the possibility of deeper solidarity with others, whether their hands are open or closed.

Truth-in-process. Truth as event, conversation, an ecology of potential, attentiveness, the making possible of greater empathy.

It is crucial to understand that truth-in-hand is not being demonized here, because we always need some degree of it to articulate ideas about the world, and to build common cause with others. In fact, when I articulate the priority that is to be given to truth-in-process, I am using the strategies of truth-in-hand to express this – specific language selected and deployed to convey a particular idea. Truth-in-process therefore relies on truth-in-hand; it is a necessary part of the overall picture. Both kinds of truth are an intrinsic part of our psychology, woven into our evolutionary heritage.[14]

On the one hand, truth-in-hand is about making assessments of our environment, processing it, sharing accounts of things with one another, forming manageable bonds between people who share space and common interests, safeguarding appropriate boundaries whether they are mental or emotional, or something more physical derived from how political communities have mapped territory and defended it. Truth-in-hand is the basis of our communication, policy-making, economics – and, in many ways, our religion too as we decide what is valuable and worth preserving. Truth-in-hand draws lines between things and defends them.

But truth-in-process is a necessary corrective to all of this; an artistic response to what we are often inclined to 'reduce', an awareness that reality can't be packaged, held within boundaries, or preserved simply as it is received; there is always more; our encounter with or grasp of things is always partial, provisional, imperfect; and as adventurous creatures, we keep suspecting this, probing the limits of our own preconceptions and wondering, 'What am I not seeing?'[15] Truth-in-process draws lines to connect things, not to separate them, while knowing no line says it all. Both kinds of truth are valuable and to be preserved, but different cultures, in different moments, fail to appreciate the need for partnership between them[16] – but not an equal partnership; rather, something more dynamic.

In short, truth-in-process is the higher kind of truth, because it resists the editing of reality. Ironically, it runs the risk of being fundamentally misunderstood, as though it is 'Truth' with a capital T, throwing its weight around by colonizing and absorbing all other truths according to its predetermined agenda. But it is, in fact, the very negation of this: it cannot throw its weight around, because it is better understood as an open palm, patiently receptive to the multiplicity of experiences, stories, pain and potential, any preconceived frameworks being empathetically shaken open by such new encounters and, on that basis, offering up the possibility of deeper solidarity among all-comers.

It is truth-in-hand, by contrast, that is more closely aligned with the throwing of weight around, with clenched fists imposing truth on others and misinterpreting what others say in order to fit it with what they already claim. It is truth-in-hand that is linked with the lust for power, the will to domination, whereas truth-in-process, the higher kind of truth, risks being subjected to such things and to misinterpretation, effectively in solidarity with any who are also subjected to domination. And yet it is also truth that cannot be pinned down, as though captured or contained, because it is the very defiance of premature closure. Nevertheless, because it is so hard to grasp, so uncontainable, our meaningful efforts to represent it will mean it is 'hosted' by our more limited truth-claiming and communities; we will witness to it, allude to it, reflect it, as we aspire to its solidarity-building capacity, conscious that we continue to be shaken open by its impulse, even as we recognize that our words and actions do not fully resemble its generosity-of-spirit – but we dare to dream.

Truth-in-hand – the claim to possess a truth, as though by articulating it we grasp the very truth of something. It is a necessary feature of communicating and connecting with others, even if its sensible limitations deny wider realities, complexities and ambiguities. Although we may use energy in preserving its 'purity', we are actually preserving an edited grasp of reality, cut off from the fullness of itself, which arguably makes it 'impure'.

Truth-in-process – attentiveness to the 'uncontainability' of truth; the appreciation that what we hold cannot be the whole story. Though it seems to involve passivity (merely being open), it actually invites us to use our energy in the cause of attentiveness to other experiences, stories and insights, so commitment to it deepens empathy and builds the solidarity of all-comers.

Two kinds of truth and the gospel

How do we see these two kinds of truth playing out in relation to Christian identity? Following Shanks,[17] I argue that the gospel essentially witnesses to the truth of divine love in terms of truth-in-process. I recognize that the notion of 'truth-*in-process*' may not be intuitive – it can feel unsettling to conceive of its ambiguity, but that is part of the point, and I will elaborate on this 'process' further in Chapters 4 and 5 especially. Here, though, the image of the open palm is a good place to start, as the central motif of Christian faith: the openness of divine love towards all of reality, including open to it in all its other-than-God-ness.

This is grace: love that is receptive even to us as we defy it; love that is expansive, exercising hospitality even to those who are inhospitable; love that is scandalously embracing even of those who would try to tame it by demonstrating much more limited versions of it. Love that is neighbourly even towards enemies. Love for sinners and all of creation.

That is the point, the very truth of the gospel: its empathetic openness to all of creation, since nothing can cut us off from the breadth and depth of divine love. Nothing. Such is the extent and scale of divine love. This is grace: relating lovingly to all-comers, without precondition; the very epitome of empathetic truth-in-process. But one way or another, our inclination is to convert this higher truth into something more manageable. Something tamer. Something less scandalous. We convert the 'uncontainability' of divine love into truth-in-hand. An edited reality. An edited truth. An edited love.

Of course, even the assertion of the truth-in-process of divine love involves an element of truth-in-hand. To articulate its scope, I must use words carefully, precisely, purposefully, as though my words can capture the very reality of it. It would be misleading to use words less precisely, though it would also be misleading to suppose that my words can be precise enough, because such uncontainable truth is hard not only to conceive but also to express. But the thing is, the words in themselves *are not the truth of it*. After all, I may say the words but completely defy them by the manner in which I defend them or my attempts to demonstrate them. This is inevitable.

The very truth of divine grace is that it cannot be fully encapsulated, neither by words, attitudes nor actions. Yet it is real – even if imperfectly glimpsed and enacted. It is the basis for the alternative horizon, Holy Anarchy, which is similarly real but imperfectly glimpsed and enacted. The truth of it is the highest kind of truth, the greatest of open palms, alert to reality in all its ambiguity and awkwardness, attending empathetically to it, revealing it for all that it is, while offering up the possibility of its transformation – a transformation that comes about on the basis of its patient, conscious receptivity to all of life, evoking in us and in others a yearning to be receptive, empathetic, neighbourly, and so build an ever greater solidarity.

It is not a truth that 'rules over' us, but is in the midst with us, in solidarity with us, open to us, waiting, revealing, evoking. Such a truth is a risky truth, one that dares to be susceptible to misunderstanding, misuse, misapplication. One that finds itself converted to a kind of truth that is more recognizable to us: a truth that is encapsulated, as though held in a fist, and that can use that conceit to wield power, to build walls, to foster solidarities of the like-minded.

In fact, we do not merely tame it to suit our interests. Or, rather, it is not merely tamed by those with vested interests, as though to convert its truth-in-process to something less risky and more powerful, a gospel of truth-in-hand, in which its community of faith puts more energy into preserving the so-called sanctity of what it holds than it puts into attentiveness to what it does not – more energy into maintaining the edit than reckoning with its ignorance. This is the relatively wilful act of those who know what they are doing, diverting our gaze from scandalous grace to something more limited. However, as a result, something more insidious occurs: a general confusion, in which we do not see the difference between the two kinds of truth. We may use the words of grace, but we do not see how easily we betray them, because we think that the particular truth-in-hand of our commitments *is the very truth of things*. A delusion. The community of faith fails to be properly alert to the shortcomings in what it thinks, says and does. It lacks the rightful humility that is incumbent on any who profess to witness to the very truth of things.

It is, of course, dangerous to generalize about these things, because in many respects all sorts of Christians and churches are adept at reckoning with their ignorance. Many churches are not as arrogant or complacent as they have frequently been perceived to be. But what I am trying to tease away at is the subtle ways in which we tame the scandal of truth-in-process, in particular the empathetic openness of divine love. I suggest this can happen in a number of ways, each of which tells us about the complexity of Christian identity, the sheer difficulty of trying to capture what 'the gospel' is exactly, which is a helpful lesson in itself: because we are not all the same, and it is intrinsic to the gospel to recognize difference, to attend to it for all its glorious awkwardness, and so make possible the most catholic of solidarities, with room for all-comers, not least those who would reframe any settled assumptions. That is the vision, occasionally manifest in small ways, but more widely elusive.

What, though, are the means by which we tame this expansive gospel, confusing it with more limited forms? To explore these, I consider issues in Christian identity concerned with *belief*, *grace* and *justice*, and their interactions. To begin with, there is a 'belief-focused' Christianity. I will explain shortly why I particularly use the word 'belief' here, rather than 'faith' – but my judgement is that this approach runs several risks. Essentially, the issue is that even when people say their emphasis is God's grace, or the power of faith, sometimes their central concern is 'proper belief': believing both that particular things are true, and that people must believe those things. In this way, the truth-in-process of the gospel is very much reconstructed as a matter of truth-in-hand: believing in such things as the Trinity, the incarnation, the atonement, the resurrection, and so on. It is belief in these things that becomes the marker of true Christian identity, faithfulness to the gospel and the basis of salvation. Of course, it is not belief in anything, but in specific things, because these particular truth-claims testify to *the very means* by which God's grace is revealed and enacted. So it is not just about believing for its own sake, but believing that God's prior agency has been embodied in certain events – and we must believe in the truthfulness and effectiveness of those events.

This approach is how many conceive of orthodox faith. After all, it gives priority to God's initiative, the Christ-centred nature of God's engagement with and salvation of us, and the emphasis not on our action in response but on our faithful acceptance of God's acts. But there are various issues with this approach, all concerned with its confusion between the different kinds of truth.

First, it has to be recognized that, even within the parameters of a supposed orthodoxy, there is a variety of beliefs: both in the sense that different people hold to different lists of what are required beliefs (some include far more instances of truth-in-hand than others) and in the sense that people interpret the same truths differently. So, if we try to say that Christian identity consists in believing certain truths-in-hand, the debates will understandably and legitimately continue – because diversity is inevitable. It is inevitable *because* the higher truth is truth-in-process, divine receptivity to the multifacetedness of reality, creating space for multiple responses, each of which may be encapsulated imperfectly in a truth-in-hand. Each economy of truth is cut off from the broader ecology of truth; each has a particular 'take', arising out of a distinctive context, truly valuable but not the whole.

Second, a belief-focused faith may be qualified with reference to sincerity: for what matters is not so much the precise accuracy of one's beliefs – after all, beliefs cannot fully capture the mystery of divine love – but one's sincerity in believing them. Sincerity is, after all, very attractive. We are encouraged to admire it. However, social and political movements like those upholding Donald Trump tend to appreciate authenticity – which is related to sincerity, but not quite the same. The leader who says it as it is. The one who does not edit themselves but dares to say the truths that others won't say, who connects with people by being audaciously 'real'. What you see is what you get. Authenticity. Different from other leaders, because apparently there's no pretence. He means it. So, authenticity and sincerity become confused – even though he probably doesn't believe all of it and sometimes knows he is lying. Authenticity and sincerity are not the same, but can be mistaken for each other, and even sincerity is not always good in itself. Being authentic, or sincere, does not necessarily make our commitments true. Sincerity is no guarantee of the gospel. In fact, churches have often sincerely defended positions that were untrue and unjust. They have upheld racist and sexist policies, justified war, excused poverty and inequality, all on the basis of sincere convictions. This does not mean the antidote is insincerity, but sincerity should not be celebrated for its own sake. Instead, we can dare to examine our sincerely held beliefs, to see what they justify. That would be gospel.

The third issue helps to bridge the second and fourth. It is the way conservative Christian theologies often say they are sincerely all about grace, while actually constructing and defending systems of belief that look more like legalism. To benefit from grace, you must believe this. To enjoy salvation, which overcomes the deadening power of Law, you must accept these rules. To rest in the unconditional grace of God, first accept these conditions. In a sense, this approach is insufficiently conservative, because it purports to have faith in grace but then gives up on it, converting it into something different: not grace, but obedience to certain forms of Christian tradition. Not the priority of God's acts, but the primacy of church authority. For Shanks, there are signs of this whenever Christians condemn other traditions as mere 'religion', as though Christianity is instead pure 'faith'.[18] What this betrays is the delusion that 'we' are entirely different, while our self-regard confirms that we are enthralled by a certain truth-in-hand: what we 'hold'. The fact that our key cornerstone is a building-block called grace, to which we give boundaries. Instead, though, it is not Christian tradition or biblical authority that heals and saves; it is the higher truth of divine love, uncontained by any such tradition, though we are called to witness to it, even through our fragile words and deeds.

The fourth issue is the way in which 'faith' and 'belief' are confused, such that even where people profess to celebrate the saving power of faith, they only know how to determine or measure it with reference to correct beliefs. But faith is not belief. If belief is about accepting the truthfulness of particular ideas (at least where truthfulness is defined as truth-in-hand), faith is the relational act of trusting in an experience or reality, arguably the truth-in-process that goes beyond words or ideas. We consider faith much more fully in Chapter 7, but here the issue is simply that to have faith in God's grace is not about being tested with reference to the supposed correctness of one's beliefs. In fact, I can have faith in grace in different ways.

I can have faith in grace as embodied in particular events, trusting that those are the definitive events in which God's grace is revealed and enacted, without necessarily having a clear sense of what exactly I am believing. So I may not be measurably sure about one or other interpretation of the Trinity, or of atonement theology, but I may nevertheless trust that God's grace comes to us in Christ. Perhaps only a mustard seed of faith, but it is plenty. On the other hand, I may trust that God's grace is itself uncontained by the particular events of Jesus' life, death and resurrection, that it may be represented and demonstrated by other people in other historical situations, while still being the same grace – and I may be quite sure what I believe about this, while trusting faithfully that my particular beliefs are not the whole story. The 'building-block' of grace does not have borders, but builds bridges beyond the limits of what I can ever hold. Or, differently still, I may not have the intellectual means, or the specific experience, to help me respond to and accept particular claims of God's unique activity in Christ, but what I do have is faith that witnesses to the higher reality of grace by way of my own flawed efforts to be gracious. That is to say, I may or may not have heard a good account of the gospel, or I may or may not know what it *means* at a cerebral level, but somehow, truly *somehow*, I witness to grace in my action, in my life-style. My faith may be weak, or it may be implicit, or it may not even be what I label as faith, but what matters most of all is that my attitudes or actions are evoked to be gracious. I may not know how.

In this way, we have begun to see how belief-focused forms of Christian identity interact with grace-focused forms. Of course, grace is significant, or it is meant to be, in all forms, but it is when faith is explicitly distinguished from belief that this becomes more evident. Then we can celebrate the possibility of trusting – or having faith – without necessarily pinning the experience down in particular beliefs. This reflects the higher status of truth-in-process which need not be converted into truth-in-hand.

But there is also an issue. A focus on 'faith', however understood or measured, is still to give a certain sort of priority to the human response: the issue of whether someone happens to manage to respond to the prior event of God's initiative. That is to say, *if* they believe x or y, or *if* they demonstrate faithfulness to the Christian way of life, or *if* their attitudes and actions reflect God's grace, it is by such things that we know they are responding to the prior initiative of divine love. On the one hand, this is a good thing, because it affirms human agency, recognizing how, even imperfectly, we play a part in the divine/human drama. And especially for those who are not used to being given a significant part in the drama of life, this is immensely affirming, dignifying, liberating. We will come, in Chapter 5, to the ways in which Jesus made room for people to reshape his own story and insights, showing that he did indeed celebrate the agency of those who were otherwise wasted by society. This matters. Agency matters. Sometimes Christian theology has distinguished between justification and sanctification to help explain the relationship: God acts to justify us, to put us in the right, and in response God continues to work in us through our sanctification, our becoming holy in the light of what God has already done for us. Our faithful response matters.

On the other hand, this distinction itself witnesses to a difficulty, because faith is often more closely associated with justification; that is, it is not simply that God acts, followed by the question of whether we have faith, but that God's action and our faith are entwined: for we are justified by faith in grace. And what follows is the process of our becoming more holy – in theory. This understanding leaves open the possibility that particular interests will assume control of what constitutes justifying faith. In other words, the problem with making room for human agency is that some people then claim the right to determine the adequacy of others' agency. Does their faith match up? Are they properly faithful? While it is good to affirm that people bring something to the process, the temptation is to expect what they bring to conform to a certain truth-in-hand – a conforming that is likely to be determined by those with power, and power determined by class, 'race', sexuality, gender, ability. In the face of such expectations, many people will not be 'justified'. Even where the church purports to celebrate grace, too many people experience what Jarel Robinson-Brown describes as 'a famine of grace'.[19] The feast may be rich, but it has its limits.

Furthermore, if God justifies us and we are sanctified in response, then why do our sanctifications look so different? After all, our ethical developments are hugely inconsistent: some uphold White Supremacy, others fight against it; some ignore poverty, others expose and transform it; some say good things, but struggle to act on them, while others act without being clear what they would say. Yet you might think that if it is the same grace that acts on us all, we would all grow into deeper graciousness, but we don't – and we would not presume to judge the adequacy of others' agency, but we do. We might argue that the church can never be perfect, so it should not be judged for its failures – but actually that would cheapen grace, since there should be an expectation of transformation. But the church must also be gracious with itself as it must learn to be with others.

So what about an absolute emphasis on grace? The truth-in-process of divine openness, ever alert, receptive and welcoming, rather than indifferent and closed? There are, of course, difficulties here too. On the one hand, the liberal disposition that is attracted to grace can become an illiberal solidarity – a body of like-minded people congratulating themselves on their openness, even as they fail to engage with those who are inconveniently different. The presumption of grace can leave little room for those who are not similarly committed to a particular truth-in-hand version of it – which is odd, because it ought to foster graciousness towards all-comers. But the problem is that a certain sort of culture can be formed among the liberally minded that prizes the value of open-mindedness and does not know what to do – or how to relate – when confronted with different challenges. So the truth-in-process, aspiring to graciousness, is converted into an agenda, a conceit, a truth-in-hand that upholds a solidarity of the like-minded.

On the other hand, open-mindedness can create space for all-comers but can fail to confront the differences in power that maintain things a certain way. It can express acceptance without the necessary judgement. Welcome but without the demand for change. This is where the optimism of the liberal obscures the harsh realities of the world; a naivety that presumes we can be one big, happy family, if we simply try hard enough to be nice, overlooking the entrenched structures that work against the interests of so many. This is where the liberal mind dismisses 'original sin' too quickly,[20] whereas the reality is that systems of domination make it genuinely hard both to identify what we cannot see in ourselves and to address the very structures that work against grace. It is not about sin being passed through our biology, but recognizing how we are born into a matrix of inherited and reinforced structures which are unfriendly to the demands of truth-in-process and to the coming of Holy Anarchy. So, we cannot merely tell ourselves or one another to be generous or rely on a solidarity of liberals to change things. Rather, we need a capacity to expose and address the depths of injustice. After all, the open palm of divine love does not simply foster love for enemies, creating that space in which we may encounter difference and build solidarity among all-comers, but also exposes the ways of the world, their closed fists, systems of violence and oppression, and the need for real transformation.

A justice-focused approach to Christian identity therefore makes the point that orthodoxy is never enough; what matters is orthopraxis – right action. Agency exercised in the cause of justice. Of course, this in itself is also a belief-commitment: believing that the world is defined by structures of injustice and that it needs to be, and can be, transformed. It is, however, a belief-focus that is never satisfied with belief alone; it must be demonstrated in commitment to change. The difficulty here is the potential for a different sort of moral elitism, not one in which righteousness is given by justifying faith, but righteousness demonstrated by commitment to justice. It is not the commitment that is in question, but how people are to be judged. After all, Christians and churches certainly do fall short of their desire for justice; so how are we to account for this and deal with it?

In this regard, the insights of Aloysius Pieris and Mark Taylor offer a constructive way forward. For Pieris, it is the poor, of whatever religion, who are the appropriate judges of the churches' attempts to live out their calling. Liberation of the poor is, in any case, a true mark of God's reign coming on earth, so they are the ones with particular insight into churches' witness to God's reign.[21] Or, as Taylor argues, depicting the connections between all people in terms of a web, it is those on the outer edges or threads who have the role of drawing attention to what is happening.[22] They are the ones to call out injustice. They are the ones to keep the church honest. This is a powerful caution to any of us who, because of our privileges and power that place us closer to the centre, might be tempted to focus more on God's grace than God's justice. God's justice demands more change from us, it must be said, so no wonder we might opt for grace instead. And there are many aspects of Christian tradition, as I shall argue further in Part 2, that give voice to this bias towards those on the edges. In fact, even if grace is for all people, as its truth-in-process indicates, it does not come evenly, but highlights existing biases within our social order – the dynamics that leave many 'ruled over', whether by patriarchy, racism, economic injustices, ableism, discrimination against sexual and gender minorities, and human 'rule over' the Earth itself. God's grace illuminates these things and calls on us to partner with God in pursuing justice, the true outworking of boundless grace.

I will discuss further the relationship between grace and justice in Chapter 4, in the context of divine agency, but the essential point here is that truth-in-process should not be regarded as 'neutral', as though truth in one person's hand is to be treated much the same as any other's. Such so-called neutrality actually serves the status quo by editing the experiences of those with fewer privileges, thereby upholding domination. Instead, as I have begun to show but will develop further, the prioritizing of truth-in-process involves a necessary bias – or, rather, an intrinsic capacity to redress existing biases – because it alerts us to the dominant dynamics. It is what liberation theologies call 'the preferential option for the poor', or for any who suffer under prevailing systems. Whether in a world of wealth inequality, it is the poor themselves who see the truth-in-hand that rules; in a world of racism, it is the experiences of those with Global Majority Heritage that testify to these dynamics; in a world of patriarchy, homophobia, transphobia, ableism and ecological crisis, it is the voice of women, LGBTQI people, people of differing abilities – and of the Earth itself – which declare truth most tellingly.

Truth-in-process, far from being indifferent to these dynamics as though grace is neutral, is especially attentive to them. And *because* it is an open palm, it exercises no coercive power to force anyone to open up. In fact, to bully anyone into opening-up would be a further perpetuation of domination. Opening-up, or becoming more attentive to reality's pain and potential, is arguably 'easier', or at least safer, for those with status or self-assurance – though to be truly shaken is to have that status destabilized in pursuit of greater, and meaningful, solidarity. Therefore, the open palm of divine love, the graciousness of God, is not neutral, because of its intrinsic exposure of those vested interests safeguarded in fists and held at the expense of others, who remain closed for their own protection. This revelatory power, even if it shakes us open just a little, is what makes it possible for empathetic solidarities to emerge and grow, manifestations of Holy Anarchy.

The strong man, guarding his castle and his property, finds his false security exposed, illuminated, revealed (Luke 11.21), as the open palm alerts us to the biases in the 'System' that are the foundations of the fortress. A new solidarity becomes possible. A cry for justice. Something stronger, beginning with the weakness of an open palm, dethrones this false master. Mammon and all its strong men are destabilized. An alternative horizon dawns. We cannot serve them both, and yet we do.

What we see, then, is that the divine love of truth-in-process does not simply foster a neat or peaceful solidarity, but leads to uncomfortable solidarities in which newly shaken people recognize the distorting dynamics that have been at work, and commit to dismantling the systems of which they have been a part, in solidarity with those who have been crying out for change. How it does this, from a position of risky weakness, will be discussed further in Part 2. Essentially, it does not act as 'rule-over', but always as Holy Anarchy: truth-in-process's holiness consists in its unexpected capacity to defy domination, building solidarity instead.

This is truth, but not as we know it, precisely because it enables us to see the truths that are edited out by distorted systems of power. It quietly shakes us to the reality of the lies within which we operate: lies perpetuated by powers of domination, which favour vested interests over the multitude of other experiences. When we are given opportunities to witness the alternative truth of those multitudes, we see through the prevailing systems, and new possibilities open up before us. This is the power of Holy Anarchy: the horizon from which light shines and where the potential for new ways of relating to one another takes root. It represents an overcoming, even under the noses of the System, even in the shadows, even in the midst of conflicting notions of the apocalypse, the revelatory power of the open-palmed God. The truth-in-hand that holds things in place is illuminated and its overcoming is begun, enough to glimpse its undoing. This is the Christian story. This is Christian faith. This is the good news of salvation.

Stories of truth

The 1999 film *The Matrix* offers a powerful example of how the same story can be told in such different ways. In recent years, the Alt Right movement in the USA, a far-right network of White Supremacists and nationalists, has latched on to the 'red pill' scene in the film, even making the red dot an icon in their communication with one another. In the scene, the hero is invited to take the red pill, so that he will come to grasp reality as it truly is, seeing through the lie of the Matrix – which, it turns out, is only a computer-program within which people *seem* to live while their actual bodies are contained in pods. This scene captures the Alt Right's sense that we live in a world fashioned by the Establishment as they see it – that is, a multicultural socialist Establishment that has been denying Constitutional freedoms for years. This 'take' on *The Matrix* pays no attention to what the film's creators say; it is a perspective completely conditioned by the ideological truth-in-hand of racist nationalism. Meanwhile, the directors, two trans women, have given their account of it. As Lilly Wachowski explains, it was 'born out of a lot of anger and a lot of rage, and it's rage at capitalism and corporatized structure and forms of oppression', and the 'bubbling, seething rage within me was about my own oppression, that I [was forcing] myself to remain in the closet'.[23] In other words, we see here two starkly different interpretations: one in the cause of racism, the other in progressive causes of anti-capitalism and trans rights.

The same, of course, is true of Christian faith. It too has been interpreted in starkly different ways, made possible because of the 'risky' truth that dwells at the heart of things: the susceptibility of truth-in-process to the machinations of systems attracted to truth-in-hand. It is worth identifying how this tension has also interacted with cultural and intellectual developments, to help us see how the story has been told diversely through history. Of course, this is my own 'take' on those developments, from a White European perspective, even as I aim ultimately to illuminate how the contested, vibrant and interweaving takes arising from many contexts witness to truth-in-process more honestly and creatively.

Beginning briefly with what may be called the pre-modern epoch, it strikes me that a key feature of it was how people knew reality through belonging to the particular story of their particular community. They knew themselves to be storied people, defined by their social nature. Whether it was the world of Judaism, or of Hindu traditions, or of Christianity or Islam, the people's story was religious and political and cultural, bound together. Of course, not everyone belonged to it in the same way, and there certainly were tensions within stories, as well as between them, as different voices contested the truth-in-hand of those with power. There were dynamics that reflected the struggle between the two kinds of truth, with some voices in each tradition alert to the more expansive truth uncontained by particular words, even uncontained by the traditions themselves, and others who focused much more on their respective truth-in-hand. So, there were periods when traditions lived very peaceably with one another, and moments when they did not; but reality was encountered, known and lived through the all-encompassing lens of the story, with all its richness and ambiguities.

Then, in the West, came the so-called Enlightenment, not a moment in itself but a gradual shift in perspective. At its heart there was a particular conceit: that reality is best known not through the lens of a particular story, but by the careful use of human reason which enables us to rise above all such loyalties. The presumption was that reason allows us to see the world as it truly is, uncontaminated by the storied versions of reality. People were free to value such myth in the private sphere, but public discourse is for factual accounts of things, pointing us towards an ever greater grasp of universal truths, such as the universal freedoms of all people. This is the route to unfailing progress. After all, since human reason is a universal phenomenon, all people have access to its means and its benefits – though some people noticed that certain nations were quicker off the mark than others, so it was incumbent on those who had become civilized to share their wisdom and treasures with others. Nations began to colonize. Empires spread. It was for the good of the world as a whole.

What we see here is the dangerous inversion of the truth of things: those telling themselves they were doing good utterly failing to see the harm they caused; those believing their achievements were the pinnacle of progress totally overlooking what had been lost; but at the heart of it, those who thought that reason enabled them to step out of a story apparently ignorant of the dominating story that defined them. Modernity was not neutral, but very much agenda-driven. As Cameron argues, 'Christian men talked and wrote themselves into a position where they spoke and wrote the rhetoric of empire.'[24] Patriarchy, Whiteness, the 'subduing' of the Earth, and the reframing of biblical interpretation itself – these were all part of the exports of Empire.[25] As López further clarifies, 'There is collusion between the truth with a Capital T and the violence espoused by hegemonic forces that endeavor to cast out anything and everything that does not fit neatly within their fixed categories.'[26]

In other words, it *could* have been a story that truly affirmed truth-in-process, the alertness to the richness and complexity of the world – not as something to be conquered, exploited, absorbed into one's own truth-in-hand, but a realm where universal dignity might have fostered an ever greater solidarity of peoples in their diversity. But it was not. It was an era in which Whiteness became sovereign, the middle classes bolstered their power, telling themselves they were doing good while ascending on the bodies of slaves, and the Christian churches were at the heart of this – with a mission to save the world from its un-European-ness as well as from sin.

But there were always critical voices. Like Friedrich Nietzsche, alert to the will-to-power that dwells behind and within any supposedly neutral truth-claim. It is now something we see much more readily, but we still do not always see it when we should: how people telling us truths have an agenda. The thing is, we do not always want it to be true of the people whose authenticity we admire. And Sigmund Freud drew attention to the many layers below the surface: even where we think we are entirely rational, other instincts are at work. We are not brains on sticks, or certainly not rationality machines – but emotionally and psychologically complex. And Karl Marx: there are ideologies in play, shaping how we think, normalizing social structures that serve the interests of those who own things. In each case, as well, these insights speak of religion: its agenda, its unseen layers, its ideologies. After all, we are not entirely rational and free, but are caught up in webs of connection, for better and for worse; we are social creatures, formed by story and reformed by new stories. We are interdependent and interconnected, fragmented and broken, progressing and regressing, rising and falling.

So the postmodern sensibility begins to take shape. Gradually, though, different variants of it emerge. The following three are those identified by Peter Hodgson.[27] First, radical postmodernism focuses on the impossibility of any objective account; all stories are coming from somewhere; none has the means to judge all others definitively; the best we can do is live and let live, you with your truth and me with mine. As López puts it, 'rather than privilege ahistorical and overarching truth with a Capital T that reigns supreme above all other truth claims, we acknowledge the multiplicity of interpretations'.[28] What this leaves us with, in effect, is our multiple truths-in-hand, with no real possibility of a truth-in-process to help connect us. Of course, an individual truth-in-hand may nevertheless witness to such a possibility, but such a witness is always coming from a particular location, shaped by the distinctiveness of its contextual constraints, so should not profess to speak into other contexts. When one tradition does purport to speak across others' experiences, it tends not to be properly alert to the power differentials.

A counter-modern perspective insists, instead, that too much has been lost, because of both modernism and postmodernism. Confidence in the integrity of the original story is damaged when too much ground is ceded to the difficult questions raised by rationality or the suspicions that followed in its wake. It is preferable to rediscover, reclaim and renew the story of old, which does not mean it will inevitably be tribal or violent; in fact, it is *possible* to be a story that is truly distinctive by virtue of its commitment to alternative values. A truth-in-hand faithfully witnessing to grace, uncontaminated by modernism's deadening reductionism, its reconstruction of human life in individualistic and rationalist terms, reviving instead the human understood best in community, a human who desires and yearns to be who they are made to be. But often, this counter-modern approach does become tribal, even violent – reverting to religious 'fundamentals' which are not even as faithful to the story as the community believes. A desire for purity. Shunning modern embellishments. Resisting the ambiguities of interpretation and development. The very exemplar of truth-in-hand. Closed, but often seeking to impose itself on others.

But there is a third kind, the late modern or critical postmodern variant, which affirms the big story, the possibility of something that might be good news for all, while recognizing how such affirmations and endeavours have been abused and enacted so dangerously. So, it calls out the hypocrisies of modernism, its claim to be universal while benefiting White, western middle-class men; its aspiration to generate freedom and justice while entrenching imperial power and inequalities; its conceit that it is free from tribal stories while being forged within the most powerful one of all: global capitalism. What this entails is a deep alertness to the incompleteness of what we hold; a receptivity to the stories that have been silenced, or distorted, which may even reconfigure what we know; a love for neighbours and enemies which has the potential to foster an ever greater solidarity of the different.

In explicitly Christian terms, this means that whatever story we think we are holding, whoever 'we' are, needs to be held more loosely, that we might receive the multiplicity of stories, dialects and accents that come out of different experiences. Feminist theologies. Black theologies. Liberation theologies. Queer theologies. Dalit theologies. Disability theologies. Post-colonial theologies. These are some of the first few, as new voices – or, rather, ancient voices that have been silenced – enable the story to be told in diverse ways. And the idea of 'a' story, in the singular, is challenged. This is not to say that the big story becomes impossible – because the possibility of 'story' building the greatest 'solidarity' is real – but we recognize that my truth-in-hand can never be the whole of truth-in-process.

I realize, though, that I want two things to be held together: on the one hand, the profound complexity of reality, with its many kinds of diversity and, on the other, the audacious notion that the prioritizing of truth-in-process is the very truth of things! These can seem contradictory, acknowledging difference while asserting a particular approach is the heart of it, and an approach that will certainly not find universal approval. But actually, they are not contradictory; they are in tension, but they arise from the same foundation: that the truth-in-process of divine love erupts as Holy Anarchy!

That is to say, *of course* the story of Christian identity is diverse, because it arises from the risky state-of-affairs of divine attentiveness to the fullness of reality, with all its awkwardness, pain and potential. By virtue of reality's complexity, and God's alertness to it, no wonder the responses that emerge are awkwardly varied, not controlled by any single truth-in-hand; rather, they witness to the scandalous generosity-of-spirit of the divine life: acceptance on a grand scale. It would be much more convenient were there a command-and-control headquarters, telling all Christians what it is all about – and, of course, there have been, and still are, many efforts to convince us that there is. But that would be a poor reflection of the divine life and of the alternative horizon that beckons from the margins: a realm in which all such control is subverted by the an-archy of love. All such theological or political empires are humbled by the open palm biased towards anti-domination. Nonetheless, it is possible to assert, as I do, that Christian faith is best understood in these particular terms, because this affirms *both* the genuine solidarity-of-the-different that Holy Anarchy evokes, as a good reflection of divine openness, *and* that it is wholly legitimate to challenge certain versions of Christianity on the basis that they stray too far from Holy Anarchy.

That said, the caution remains important. It may be *possible* to hold the affirmation of diversity together with the particularity of my vision. I believe it is – and this book is an attempt to demonstrate this. I am cognisant, though, of the constant challenge: I run the risk of slipping into yet another unacknowledged empire. But in the following example, where I turn to G. W. F. Hegel, the philosopher who stands behind the work of Shanks, I address the risk and suggest Holy Anarchy is the answer.

Overcoming (1): Racism

I believe that anti-racism is intrinsic to the good news of Christian faith. It is only relatively recently that I would have thought to be so explicit about it. Now it seems so much more obvious. But why? The centrality of anti-racism is not simply because Christian faith regards itself as a universal story – an analysis of (and a promise for) the world, transcending all boundaries and distinctions. The fact that it generally presumes such universal scope is certainly a reason why it ought to be anti-racist, but more localized or particular traditions can also be genuinely anti-racist. So its catholicity of vision – embracing all-comers – is not the only or most important basis for energizing the commitment to anti-racism.

My proposals here are not an attempt to replace other approaches, but to complement them, on the basis of the particular foundations I have been identifying. Hopefully they represent a distinct contribution to a much richer conversation.[29] I have begun to outline, and will develop further in Part 2, the significance of the power-structures within which we live and have our being. Christian faith is directly concerned with their exposure and transformation: the principalities and powers that are being dismantled. Racism is one such structure, which has been conditioned in particular by the 'truth-in-hand' of imperialism: that is to say, when European nations believed their own propaganda, that their notion of civilization was worthy not only of being transported globally but of being imposed on others, they gave priority to their truth-in-hand as opposed to truth-in-process. Any sensibility to be alert to other voices was suppressed, as the truth-in-hand of imperial self-assurance dominated, and this was packaged and exported, backed up by state and commercial violence, with no interest in receiving the truths of other perspectives or experience. Even if it *told* itself that it was being 'open' by its desire to bring benefits to others, this was at best a half-truth; the realities of imperial expansion are well known, but in particular for our current discussion there was the presumption of White Supremacy at their heart, the fuel of racist mindsets, structures and behaviour. We shall return to the dynamics of Empire in Chapter 3, but at this point I am simply highlighting how the very structures of racism, which God's mission calls on us to dismantle, are shaped by the attachment to the interests of White Supremacy, a particularly life-denying form of truth-in-hand, edited truth, silencing the self-critical capacities of truth-in-process.

These dynamics can be understood in light of the threefold concerns that recur through this book. First, the power-structures that, in this case, uphold 'White privilege' – the often unconscious but sometimes explicit systems which, in a wide range of situations, give advantages to White people and uphold White Supremacy. It begins with the lust for power and it ends with the reinforcement of power. Editing history and shutting down other possible futures. Second, the norms that frame these systems, which make people take for granted that 'this is how things should be', are the norms of 'Whiteness' – constructed ideas, prejudices, groupthink that occupy our psychologies and social patterns, inherited from imperial history, and which filter out any efforts to hear alternative realities. Community identity is defined by these norms, so those who do not fit the norms of Whiteness are always 'other'.[30] And third, the editing of White history, generating a defensive reluctance to engage with criticism – this is 'White fragility' at work, the fear of being troubled by too much reality, since it might place unwelcome demands on us. Of course, these are not the only dynamics at work in social relationships; gender, class, sexuality, dis/ability also inform and shape our connections – they 'intersect' to create multiple forms of privilege and oppression, sometimes working across one another, sometimes compounding one another, but always meaning that some people have many more advantages in life than others. Intersectionality is therefore a vital way of making sense of these interactions, identifying how disadvantages are reinforced and where power resides.

To address this complex but striking reality is therefore not simply an optional extra, but goes to the heart of what Christian faith is for. This is because, echoing the discussion above, its focus is the prioritizing of truth-in-process in the cause of Holy Anarchy! Of course, I realize this is alternative language for the central thrust of Christian faith, discipleship and salvation, but I am attempting to reconceive the shaking power of divine love and the solidarity that it engenders. To prioritize truth-in-process is to break through the barriers represented by each truth-in-hand, including class, race, gender, sexuality, differing abilities and religious affiliation, in faithfulness to the alternative empire, God's kingdom, the kin-dom – or Holy Anarchy, a realm in which truth-in-process is given more weight, so dismantling the powers of domination. It is an alternative horizon that is coming, quietly, almost imperceptibly, in the midst of the mess, pain and potential of everyday living.

However, I need to wrestle with something, as I indicated above. For I am influenced by Shanks who himself acknowledges his indebtedness to the nineteenth-century philosopher G. W. F. Hegel. The problem is that Hegel said some appallingly racist things, which cannot even be excused as 'of his time' because not all his peers agreed with his view. So how can his ideas help to form the foundations of an anti-racist theo-politics? This is an important question: does his own approach undermine the progressive causes to which his ideas are put? But it is not just that his statements defied his own good intentions; his intellectual vision was itself an imperial project, constructing a worldview into which everything else must fit. This is why Shanks hopes that his own work is *neo*-Hegelian, a *new* kind of Hegel-informed thinking, not a replication of Hegel's errors.[31]

There are two issues here: first, returning to our earlier discussion about Christian faith, does appalling behaviour invalidate someone's contribution to Christian thought? The difficulty is that, if we only draw from thinkers and practitioners who were pure, we would have no resources, since all are corrupted one way or another. Sometimes people who got particular things terribly wrong can be right in other ways – but what matters is that the wrongs must not be whitewashed out of the picture. We must grapple with the whole of the reality, theirs and ours. It is right for us to reckon with the complexity of who we are, and the legacy that comes to us from others, not to deny it. So I do not wish to deny the racism of Hegel; it is part of his picture. But the more challenging issue is whether the models of Hegel are themselves affected in such a way that they cannot be re-purposed. Ironically, one of Hegel's own terms may help: 'sublation' (or *Aufhebung* in German), which means *to preserve and overcome*, both together. This enables us to preserve the brokenness of who he was, and of his model, rather than editing his truth, while overcoming it with the good news that this was not the whole story. In fact, Shanks argues that this is what his model involves: at its truest, it is not *meant* to be a project that claims to fit everything else within it, but is about openness to what we do not know. So Hegel needs to be opened to what he did not see, and his model needs to be interrogated for any latent imperial distortions – but even if this is not possible, it is possible to preserve and overcome it.

This is what truth-in-process involves: bearing the pain of reality as it is, but – through the power of empathy in the midst of the mess – also opening up the possibility of a new overcoming, whereby existing dynamics may be transformed. Neither the sin nor the goodness is to be seen separately as the whole story; rather, we aim to attend to the whole of reality. This *does not* ask those who bear the consequences of sin to accept that its 'preservation' can be naively held in tension with its future overcoming ('Bear with it, and justice will come eventually') – because sublation is *not* about maintaining a situation, but rather holding before us the *reality* of that situation, for all its awfulness, without preserving it in its current state. The element of 'preservation' is more specific: it is to reckon with that reality, particularly for those who would favour ignoring, excusing or romanticizing it, in order to prompt solidarity in the cause of the situation's overcoming.

In fact, it can be argued that Hegel's problem was that he was not 'Hegelian' enough; that is, he did not fully work through the implications of his vision, from which we draw the openness of truth-in-process. Rather, he withdrew into the cultural truth-in-hand that presumed European civilization was superior. Truth-in-process[32] punctures the lie of such presumption, drawing our attention to the reality and legacy of White Supremacy, imperialism and Christian exceptionalism. Space is opened up, by the power of Holy Anarchy, such that we who are inheritors of these legacies are enabled to learn from those whose suffering and wisdom have been crying out to us for centuries. But we were not listening. Now we can be allies with one another: White people may be allies with Black people who exercise their agency in pursuit of justice, and Black people may be allies (critical friends) with White people who must do the work of reckoning with their inheritance and dismantling its power. But of course it is not only the task of White people and Black people but of all people, since all are invested in the possibility of a world liberated from racism. The overcoming is close at hand; trust in it and believe that it is good news.

Overcoming (2): Anthropocentrism

It is not only in the structures and processes of racism that we can see the dominating power of truth-in-hand. It also goes to the heart of the ecological crisis. In particular, especially in the globalized culture engineered in western empires, it is the truth-in-hand of a very specific editing of reality: the notion that the human being is at the centre of the created order or, rather, at the pinnacle. This 'human-centredness', or 'anthropocentrism' (*anthropos* is the human), was clearly fuelled by Christian faith, all sorts of biblical resources seeming to support it, not least the 'dominion' that humans are given over nature in Genesis 1.

So the presumption has been: 'we' are the boss of nature, given the right to 'master' it, but also to exploit it for our own ends, because the Earth exists for us. It is necessary, then, to be a little more specific about this 'human' who is at the centre of things, because this abstract human is not representative of all humanity equally. Rather, it signifies the power and privilege of those who have driven the Earth-consuming economy. Those whose empires ravaged other lands, stealing not only young labour but also resources, and building a globalized economy on western foundations, according to rules that serve the interests of the wealthy. In this way, we see that racism and ecological devastation are part of the same story, suppressing the empathetic impulses of truth-in-process in order to feed the bellies and bank accounts of largely White western middle classes.

Eco-feminists[33] have identified too how this 'human' is far from abstract: it is bound up with patriarchy because anthropocentrism favours a particular kind of person. Maleness has been associated, again because of Christian faith, with 'spiritual things', while womanness has been viewed as representing 'the physical'; and Christian faith has generally given more weight to the spiritual over the physical. So, within this matrix, the exploitation of the Earth is not a concern, because what matters is our spiritual identity. Together, these factors generate a perfect storm when it comes to our stewardship of creation: we are given authority over it, according to the truth-in-hand of dominion; the status of the physical realm matters less than spirituality in any case; and the presumed right of empires to take from the Earth is legitimized by the gospel that spread with them.

As others have argued for many years,[34] the solution to the ecological crisis is therefore not merely economic, or about 'greening' our mindsets and behaviours; it also entails a theological revolution, a recovery of the 'ecology' of truth-in-process. But many of the contributing solutions remain locked in particular mentalities shaped by anthropocentrism.

Take the idea of good stewardship, for example: it is clearly preferable to 'dominion' because it directs us away from damaging the Earth towards nurturing it for the sake of future generations. But there is an argument that it still leaves us in a position much like a gardener in relation to a garden: we are responsible for tending it, but we are not part of it. In fact, neither are we the gardener, nor the Earth a garden, because the Earth is rather more complex, as an ecology of ecologies, interweaving with one another; there is even some truth in the notion that Earth will both survive and once again thrive, long after humanity cuts itself off from liveable futures. What, then, might it mean to recover our place 'among' nature, recognizing our co-dependency with others – 'majority creation' – on the rich web of life?

Similarly, there is an argument to have vis-à-vis 'the five marks of mission'.[35] On the one hand, they have contributed greatly to Christian re-commitment in terms of care for creation, since the fifth mark is to treasure its integrity through green attitudes and actions. On the other hand, since it is the fifth, it is tempting for churches to place it further down their agendas, with more overtly 'human' concerns coming first. As a student, Charles Jolly, suggested to me: what if the order of the marks of mission were reversed, so that everything else is rooted in the context of our place among creation?[36] What if the first sign of mission were the calling to understand and demonstrate the wonder and vitality of the whole Earth? What if our pursuit of justice, our care for those in need, our teaching and nurturing new believers, and our proclamation of God's kingdom flowed from this creation-centred mission? What if we destabilized the truth-in-hand of human-centred concerns, remembering that wherever Holy Anarchy comes, it comes not only to people but to overcome domination, not least our domination of life itself?

The big story of Christian faith touches on so many things, because it is meant to be profoundly holistic, not to be regarded as simply spiritual, as though spirituality can be separated from material life. Rather, it is embedded in the very stuff of life, in every ecology of life, every connection among all things, so cannot be reduced to any convenient truth-in-hand, any editing of reality, since it is concerned with responding faithfully to the truth-in-process of divine love: a scandalously uncontainable love. That is why, even though I could have begun by relating this to so many things, I chose to begin with two issues of such contemporary significance: racism and the ecological crisis. After all, the good news of the solidarity of the shaken, and of Holy Anarchy, is not just for the enrichment of some or the security of certain interests, but breaks barriers between all people and cherishes the integrity of all creation. Anything less is a diminution of divine love and purpose.

Conclusion so far: the 'other God'

What we have begun to glimpse in this chapter is that there are choices to make concerning the nature of truth, the nature of Christian faith, and indeed the nature of God. I will develop these themes in the subsequent chapters, but at the heart of the matter is a struggle – our original sin – as we confuse different notions of what is ultimately valuable or true. On the one hand, there is an edited version of reality, graspable 'in hand', which is manifest in patterns of domination, preserving vested interests, impatiently disregarding otherness, and engendering a sectarian form of solidarity. On the other hand, an alertness to what we have not yet appreciated, the persistence of otherness, the call for empathetic growth through encounter, a dethroning of domination, and the sustaining of unfinished solidarity. God is often widely co-opted in the service of the former, but there is another God, whose palm is open, waiting, evoking, at one with all of this struggle, lament and dreaming. On a quiet day, you can hear her breathing.

A hymn

The time of gloom is ending,
the former days are past,
the time of light is dawning –
the promised one at last!
Like harvest-time abounding,
like nations finding peace,
the yoke of burden breaking:
Oppression – You shall cease!

But, God, still shadows linger,
the former days persist;
the time of light is dimmer,
the hope obscured in mist.
God, strong men grasp at power,
and stoke the flames of fear;
the poor and hungry suffer:
God's freedom – You're not here!

But, God, your voice still echoes,
so gentle yet so firm,
inviting us to join you,

ignite our hearts to burn:
you heal our disillusion,
confound the mighty's schemes,
and through your word–flesh fusion,
fulfil rebellious dreams:

The time is now beginning;
the former days are past;
for you, great God of weakness,
speak through the least and last;
your fragile flame, your child's play,
your foolishness so wise –
you shake away the shadows,
you speak and we arise!

Graham Adams (2017)
Suggested tune: *Ellacombe* – or create another one
Based on Isaiah 9.2–4, and written originally in response to Donald Trump's
inauguration.

Questions to ponder

1 Can you recognize the struggle between 'truth-in-hand' and 'truth-in-process' – in yourself, in church or community life, and in the wider world? Can you think of examples?
2 Truth-in-process is basically about fostering greater empathy in the midst of every situation. Think of a situation known to you, or more than one, and imagine how greater empathy would change the world, step by step. It is important, though, to acknowledge where this raises difficult questions and what obstacles come to light.
3 Imagine if churches faced up to the reality of racism more directly, in the assumptions and structures so easily taken for granted, and were more intentionally committed to its overcoming, as a key mark of the gospel. How might this change our agenda?
4 Imagine if care for the Earth were regarded as the first priority of mission. How might this shift the focus of the church and generate a new understanding of what it is to be human?

Further reading

Andrew Shanks, *Faith in Honesty: The Essential Nature of Theology* (Farnham: Ashgate, 2005).

Race

Miguel A. De La Torre, *Decolonizing Christianity: Becoming Badass Believers* (Grand Rapids, MI: Eerdmans, 2021).

Willie James Jennings, *After Whiteness: An Education in Belonging* (Grand Rapids, MI: Eerdmans, 2020).

Grace Ji-Sun Kim, *Invisible: Theology and the Experience of Asian American Women* (Minneapolis, MN: Fortress Press, 2021).

Chine McDonald, *God Is Not a White Man: And Other Revelations* (London: Hodder & Stoughton, 2021).

James W. Perkinson, *White Theology: Outing Supremacy in Modernity* (New York: Palgrave Macmillan, 2004).

Anthony Reddie, *Is God Colour-blind? Insights from Black Theology for Christian Ministry* (London: SPCK, 2009).

Ecology

Steve Henrichs (ed.), *Buffalo Shout, Salmon Cry: Conversations on Creation, Land Justice, and Life Together* (Waterloo, ON: Herald Press, 2013).

Kiara Jorgenson and Alan Padgett, *Ecotheology: A Christian Conversation* (Grand Rapids, MI: Eerdmans, 2020).

Sallie McFague, *A New Climate for Theology: God, the World and Global Warming* (Minneapolis, MN: Augsburg Fortress, 2008).

Cynthia Moe-Lobeda, *Resisting Structural Evil: Love as Ecological-Economic Vocation* (Minneapolis, MN: Fortress Press, 2013).

Rosemary Radford Ruether (ed.), *Women Healing Earth: Third World Women on Ecology, Feminism, and Religion* (London: SCM Press, 1996).

Vinod Wesley, *Church and Climate Justice* (Delhi and Singapore: ISPCK and CWM, 2020).

Notes

1 https://www.cnbc.com/2021/08/02/3rd-police-officer-gunther-hashida-kills-himself-after-capitol-riot-by-trump-mob.html (accessed 6 January 2022).

2 https://www.washingtonpost.com/nation/interactive/2021/capitol-insurrec tion-visual-timeline/ (accessed 6 January 2022).

3 https://www.sojo.net/articles/terrorists-perceived-themselves-be-christians (accessed 6 January 2022).

4 https://www.sojo.net/articles/terrorists-perceived-themselves-be-christians (accessed 6 January 2022).

5 https://www.washingtonpost.com/nation/interactive/2021/capitol-insurrection-visual-timeline/ (accessed 6 January 2022).

6 https://www.whyy.org/articles/the-capitol-insurrection-was-never-about-the-election-it-was-about-white-supremacy/ (accessed 6 January 2022).

7 https://www.washingtonpost.com/politics/2020/05/08/very-fine-people-charlottesville-who-were-they-2/ (accessed 6 January 2022).

8 https://www.bbc.co.uk/news/world-us-canada-40943425 (accessed 6 January 2022).

9 For instance, the Revd Jesse Kearns referred to it in order to distinguish sharply between Christ's revelation, marked by the commitment to love our neighbours, and the events of the insurrection, events of division and death. See https://www.fccchico.com/response-to-epiphany-riots.html (accessed 6 January 2022).

10 In a speech at the White House on 5 August 2021: https://www.cbsn.ws/3jmGAEe (accessed 6 January 2022).

11 Joerg Rieger and Kwok Pui-lan, *Occupy Religion: Theology of the Multitude*, Washington DC: Rowman & Littlefield, 2010, p. 98.

12 See Andrew Shanks, *Hegel and Religious Faith: Divided Brain, Atoning Spirit*, London and New York: Bloomsbury T&T Clark, 2011, p. 3. In Shanks's earlier *Faith in Honesty: The Essential Nature of Theology*, Farnham: Ashgate, 2005, he employed the term 'truth-as-Honesty' rather than 'truth-as-openness' (p. 3).

13 There are similarities with John Caputo's distinction between the 'Unconditional' (that which cannot be contained) and the 'conditional' (how we do indeed claim to contain it); see, for example, John D. Caputo, *The Weakness of God: A Theology of the Event*, Bloomington, IN: Indiana University Press, 2006, p. 90. However, while Caputo regards the Unconditional, and not the conditional, as divine, this distinction does not apply so neatly to the two kinds of truth: as I will argue further, God may be more like truth-in-process, but God is not solely truth-in-process. See Chapter 4, p. 104.

14 Shanks, *Hegel and Religious Faith*, pp. 67–70.

15 See, for example, Al Barrett and Ruth Harley, *Being Interrupted: Reimagining the Church's Mission from the Outside, In*, London: SCM Press, 2020, chapter 3.

16 Shanks, *Hegel and Religious Faith*, p. 49.

17 Shanks, *Hegel and Religious Faith*, pp. 86, 88, 97.

18 Andrew Shanks, *A Neo-Hegelian Theology: The God of Greatest Hospitality*, Farnham: Ashgate, 2014, pp. 43–6.

19 Jarel Robinson-Brown, *Black, Gay, British, Christian, Queer*, London: SCM Press, 2021, p. 2.

20 See, for example, Shanks, *Faith in Honesty*, pp. 122–3; and Shanks, *A Neo-Hegelian Theology*, p. 116.

21 Aloysius Pieris, *An Asian Theology of Liberation*, Edinburgh: T&T Clark, 1988, pp. 196–201; Pieris, 'Interreligious Dialogue and Theology of Religions: An Asian Paradigm', *Horizons*, vol. 20, no. 1: 106–14 (especially 110); Pieris, 'Christ beyond Dogma: Doing Christology in the Context of the Religions and the Poor', *Louvain Studies*, 2000, vol. 25: 187–231 (especially 219–20).

22 Mark K. Taylor, *Remembering Esperanza: A Cultural-Political Theology for North American Praxis*, Maryknoll, NY: Orbis, 1990, p. 66.

23 https://www.hollywoodreporter.com/news/general-news/lilly-wachowski-

shares-how-matrix-franchise-was-inspired-by-rage-oppression-before-transition-1296914/ (accessed 22 December 2021).

24 Averil Cameron, *Christianity and the Rhetoric of Empire: The Development of Christian Discourse*, Berkeley, CA: University of California Press, 1991, p. 14.

25 Alejandro López, 'De-Imperializing God-Talk: Towards a Postcolonial Theo-poetics', *Journal of Hispanic / Latino Theology*, vol. 23, no. 1, article 13 (2021): 130–51 (or at https://www.repository.usfca.edu/cgi/viewcontent.cgi?article=1118 &context=jhlt pp. 1–22 (accessed 22 February 2022), as cited below referring to Willie Jennings, James Cone, Delores Williams as examples – and Mark G. Brett, *Decolonizing God: The Bible in the Tides of Empire*, Sheffield: Sheffield Phoenix, 2008, p. 2.

26 López, 'De-Imperializing God-Talk', p. 11.

27 Peter C. Hodgson, *Winds of the Spirit: A Constructive Christian Theology*, London: SCM Press, 1994, pp. 55–6, 59–61.

28 López, 'De-Imperializing God-Talk', p. 10.

29 For example, Anthony Reddie, *Theologising Brexit: A Liberationist and Post-colonial Critique*, Abingdon: Routledge, 2019; Chine McDonald, *God Is Not a White Man: And Other Revelations*, London: Hodder & Stoughton, 2021; and Barrett and Harley, *Being Interrupted*.

30 We see this in relation to the church, its complicity with – and reproduction of – such groupthink, as articulated by James Baldwin in the context of the lies told about Black people, how they 'are only a reflection of the lies the Christian Church has always helplessly told itself, to itself, about itself': James Baldwin, *Collected Essays: White Racism or World Community?*, New York: Library of America, 1998, p. 755.

31 Andrew Shanks, 'Introduction', in his forthcoming *Apocalyptic Patience: 'Mystical Theology', 'Gnosticism', 'Ethical Phenomenology'*, London and New York: Bloomsbury T&T Clark.

32 Hegel's term for this was 'Absolute Knowing', often misunderstood as though he meant 'the accumulation of all knowledge' (the manifestation of ultimate truth-in-hand), whereas he actually meant the disposition or way of knowing that is alert to the ecology of truth (the truth of truth-in-process); see, for example, Shanks, *Hegel and Religious Faith*, p. 7.

33 See, for example, Heather Eaton, *Introducing Ecofeminist Theologies*, London: T&T Clark International, 2005; Mary C. Grey, *Sacred Longings: Ecofeminist Theology and Globalization*, London: SCM Press, 2003; Rosemary Radford Ruether, *Integrating Ecofeminism, Globalization and World Religions*, Washington DC: Rowman & Littlefield, 2005.

34 For example, Lynn White Jr, 'The Historical Roots of Our Ecological Crisis', *Science*, vol. 155, no. 3767 (10 March 1967): 1203–7, reprinted in Roger Gottlieb (ed.), *This Sacred Earth: Religion, Nature and Environment*, New York: Routledge, 1996, pp. 184–93.

35 See, for example, Andrew Walls and Cathy Ross (eds), *Mission in the 21st Century: Exploring the Five Marks of Mission*, London: Darton, Longman and Todd, 2008.

36 Charles Jolly, 'How Do a Small Sample of United Reformed Churches Plan to Promote Care for Creation in their Missional Discipleship?', MA dissertation, Luther King House, 2019.

PART 2

Do Justice – Dismantle Domination

If Holy Anarchy is both the path and the destination, what are the obstacles along the way? In Parts 2, 3 and 4, I address three 'structural' challenges that impair, distort and overwhelm the progress of Holy Anarchy. They are different ways in which truth-in-hand is given disproportionate weight, as it dominates the impulse towards truth-in-process. The clenched fist over the open palm. As such, they edit reality. They close us down to one another. They obstruct empathy. They impede neighbourliness. Shanks calls them 'dishonesties', because they deny the truth of things in one way or another. We can think of them as expressions of False Order, against which Holy Anarchy must struggle. They are *false* because they are not attentive to the truth of reality as it is, but filter it, manage it, reduce it, contort it, in the interests of those with greater privilege. They are *order*, because they represent the structures of the status quo, its inertia, the sense it creates that 'this is just how things are', again for the sake of those who already benefit from prevailing dynamics. Holy Anarchy destabilizes their authority, shaking their hold over us, not through brute force but through the power of the open palm, an awesome kind of weakness, a strange kind of wisdom, an uncontainable wildness in the midst of the dough of life.

The first of these structures is Domination itself – both the will to dominate and the systems that embody it: psychological and social forces. Chapter 3 is largely a naming of these things, while Chapter 4 is an exploration of how God operates to dismantle them: the nature of God's power. This goes to the heart of the purpose of Christian faith, its alternative vision and mission dynamic, exposing and confronting idols, lamenting deeply and fostering hope in the midst of every struggle, and making possible a solidarity of all-comers.

3

Structures of Dominion and the Untame God

So all the people took off their gold rings from their ears, and brought them to Aaron. He took the gold from them, formed it in a mould, and cast an image of a calf; and they said, 'These are your gods, O Israel, who brought you up out of the land of Egypt!'
(Exodus 32.3–4)

My name is Legion

The central focus of Christian faith is the de-throning of power-structures that impede the flourishing of life in all its abundance. This means not just formal structures, like political or economic systems, but patterns of social relationships, habits and norms – and not only structures that seem to be 'external' to us, but structures within us, ideologies, mindsets and values. Both social/political and psychological/spiritual structures – anything and everything that denies breathing space to Holy Anarchy. Structures that co-opt us, which re-mould our values, re-casting them, so that what we desire are the structures themselves, like a golden calf – false gods who purport to set us free.

Of course, Christian faith is concerned with even more than this, but arguably all other aspects are related to this essential task. It would be foolish of me to imply that it has always been expressed in these terms. In fact, it is only quite rarely that it has been understood in this way. But as a number of theological movements have voiced, especially in the emergence of more radical approaches through the twentieth century, such as Black, liberation, feminist and postcolonial theologies, Life in all its fullness can never be possible without addressing the rulers, authorities and cosmic powers, as identified by Paul (Eph. 6.12) – the systems that prevail at large and that condition our existence.

First, though, it is essential to affirm that this insight is certainly not a postmodern invention. For sure, it has been rediscovered and given new impetus in postmodern contexts, as the multiplicity of voices – notably, crying for justice – that were suppressed and silenced during (and by) modernity have re-emerged. But such voices are there in the biblical witness: the cry of slaves, the agency of the dispossessed, the persistence of those struggling at the margins of life, their crisis demanding recognition and dignity and freedom but repeatedly met with religious and political indifference, cruelty and closure. God hears these cries.[1] The prophets hear them and speak truth to power. Again and again, from Amos to Ruth, from Mary to James, the experience of the poor and oppressed, the hungry and those deemed 'meek', was not only articulated piercingly, but was laid before the religious/political community, as though on an open palm: 'Look! Listen! Learn! And ask yourselves, "Who is your neighbour?"' And with compassionate intensity and unusual integrity, we witness in Jesus how God's solidarity took shape with those in debt, impurity, and on the edge of existence: the multitudes who followed him, the individuals who interrupted him, the 'wrong' people whom he put centre-stage.

These voices, throughout history and still today, express a disturbing truth that religion often massages and diminishes: that human civilizations live with a perpetual crisis. Religious traditions often seem conditioned themselves to focus on something rather more other-worldly: a vision of an afterlife, or a sanctuary from the wild seas around us. But the truth is that 'the good life' – a secure existence of plenty and protection – is enjoyed by a small minority, while most experience something much more precarious and painful. And civilizations are generally oriented towards futures in which not much will change, certainly not enough for the balance of power to tip significantly, even where big promises are made and trusted. We keep heading towards futures designed by those who already dominate, according to their 'truth-in-hand', their closed version of reality, with little scope for radically new possibilities. In fact, the 'System' teaches us, as we shall consider further below, that 'there is no alternative': this course of action is the only one really available to us, so make the most of it!

The fourth-century theologian St Augustine, however, put it starkly when he identified the key contrast that goes to the heart of the gospel: on the one hand, a reality shaped by the love of God, where life is experienced in all its abundance and, on the other hand, a reality shaped by 'the will to dominate'.[2] This contrast shows us that 'the love of God' is starkly different from domination, and yet far too often religious leaders and communities have been caught up with 'dominating', whether by enacting oppression themselves or legitimizing social systems that do; conditioned to perpetuate forms of community life that serve the interests of the powerful, rather than allowing space to open up in which new

possibilities may be born. We, by which I mean here 'those of us affil-
iated to religions', have been co-opted by these dynamics, even though
the very essence of Christian faith, for example, exposes such idolatrous
powers-that-be and offers an alternative horizon where deserts flourish,
the hungry are fed, the outcasts find security, and justice and peace kiss
each other. Religion has manipulated, neglected or silenced this message
and mission, for fear that if it is allowed to blossom, who knows what
structures might crash down around us – and within us! It could be …
anarchy. Which is precisely the point: Holy Anarchy!

The story of the person known as the Gerasene demoniac, encountered
by Jesus, is an episode that demonstrates the interaction between psychological and social/political forces (Mark 5.1–20). It occurs immediately
after Jesus has suggested that he and his friends should 'go across to
the other side' of the Sea of Galilee; that is, away from the predomin-
antly Jewish side to the largely Gentile side. This represents a challenge
to their socio-political identity and security. No wonder a storm arose for
them: whether symbolically internal or physically external, it represents
the turmoil of the prospect of facing 'the Other'. So here we have one
dimension of psycho-social structures: the way in which communities live
with a constructed sense of boundaries, of who is in and who is out, and
the difficulty of stepping out of one's truth-in-hand reality. Then, having
overcome this awkwardness, they are confronted with another: a man
'possessed' by a demon, chained and living among the tombs, to represent both his affinity with death and his uncleanness. But nothing had
the power to restrain him. And he speaks, or rather the spirit within him
speaks: 'My name is Legion.' A clear signifier of Roman imperial force.

This is one of a handful of very explicit references to the presence of
Rome in the territory of the Gospels. The 'spirit' that possessed him was
the spirit of military occupation, 'possessing' him at various levels – his
land, his people, his own psyche. After all, as I will argue further in the
following section, 'Empire' is fundamentally concerned with colonizing
people's minds, not just their land and resources. And here we see the
damage that it does. The man is in turmoil, nothing can restrain him,
because the presence of foreign armies has an effect on people beyond the
particular places where they march. The repercussions of military power
reverberate through the people, in their public spaces and in their internal
lives. It generates fear, because of the violence they do, the threat of more
and the rumours of it. It instils anger and resentment in people, but also a
sense of helplessness, a grieving over the freedoms that could have been.

In that short phrase, 'My name is Legion', we see how systems become
persons and persons become systems, and how perpetrators 'possess' the
lives of their victims. Systems of oppression are both political and deeply

personal, touching people's sense of their own identity, often turning them towards self-destruction. Even if the people involved are merely 'obeying orders', they are still active contributors to a system of horror – and Rome itself was not concerned when soldiers acted out of their own volition, raping and terrorizing to keep people in their place. So the dynamics are complex: the leaders of Empire colonize the minds of the agents of Empire, so that soldiers know what to do even without being told exactly, and the soldiers colonize the minds of the colonized by creating an atmosphere of terror. The structures oppressing the people are therefore both psychological and political.

Mark, in his telling of the story, understood these dynamics and exposed them. This was a subtle act of transgression, even Holy Anarchy, as the message conveyed is not exactly explicit; rather, he fosters an echo of it, so those with ears to hear might tune in. We miss the point if we read it simply as the story of Jesus healing a troubled individual; in fact, such an 'individual' reading ends up reinforcing the structures that continue to do violence in our world – because silence in the face of them inadvertently gives them legitimacy. So if we believe such systems of oppression and violence are illegitimate, then we must pick up on the cues to call them out.

As identified by Ched Myers, a biblical scholar and activist, there are indeed several cues in the story to help us hear the denunciation of systems of psycho-social oppression and violence.[3] The fact that Mark has moved the geography of Gerasa to the lakeside would have jolted his initial audience to ask what is happening here. Also, at the time he was writing, around AD 70, Gerasa had already been the site of a violent suppression of the Jewish Uprising, so the story echoes this post-Jesus history. And he packs the episode with military allusions, not only Legion, but when Jesus transfers the 'spirit' to a herd of pigs, he dismisses them like a troop and sends them as though into battle – into the lake, echoing also the Egyptian army's drowning in the sea of reeds in Exodus. In other words, Mark is touching our own psyches, and our politics, through these metaphorical battle-cries against the power of imperial occupation. Jesus' miracle is a denouncing of those forces and liberates the unnamed man – who represents the wider community colonized by force – to discover a new identity, as a proclaimer of good news under the nose of Empire, the good news of life set free from the tombs of violence.

The forces, then, that stand in the way of Holy Anarchy are interactive forces, dancing between our internal lives and the external realities of structure, policy and brute force, and tying these things together. Part of their cunning, as Shanks identifies, is that all sorts of people get caught up in the dance[4] – even those who suffer the consequences can find themselves defending the system, and even those who attempt to see through it can be unwittingly complicit with it. The progress of Holy Anarchy is therefore not straightforward at all. The Powers of Domination, as Wink names them, are painfully resilient, both psychologically and politically, and we are born 'into' them, like an all-consuming matrix – as in *The Matrix* which we discussed in Chapter 2. So we cannot easily hold them at bay, as though they are simply external to us, because they are also part of us and we are part of them.

This is why Walter Wink speaks of 'engaging' the powers, rather than 'demonizing' them,[5] because to demonize them is to demonize ourselves and our neighbours, as well as our enemies, whereas to 'engage' them is to reckon with the complexity and ambiguity of their presence and power. It is not that their effects are unclear, because there is nothing ambiguous about deep poverty, racism, exploitation and violence, but how we pinpoint responsibility and identify ways forward is more complex. The System likes it that way, because we can allow ourselves to be overwhelmed by the complexity, paralysed by the impossibility of getting it exactly right. But Holy Anarchy is not about waiting for purity before we act; rather, it enables us to live constructively with the mess, recognizing that our actions will not be perfect, but that action is nevertheless required.

This is the truth-in-hand that confronts us: the will to dominate and the structures that dominate. *Arche* in the face of and suppressing *An-archy*. Politically and economically supreme, too often religiously justified, but never so absolute as to silence the small seeds bursting through the cracks. As Rieger puts it, there is always a surplus that cannot be contained.[6] It represents solidarity with every hurt and the possibility of transformation.

The Empire within: colonized (un)consciousness

The 2010 Theology Statement of the Council for World Mission (CWM), entitled 'Mission in the Context of Empire', refers (p. 4) to the definition of Empire developed by the Globalization Project, a partnership between the Uniting Reformed Church in South Africa and the Evangelical Reformed Church in Germany. The definition is as follows:

We speak of Empire, because we discern a coming together of economic, cultural, political and military power in our world today, that constitutes a reality and a spirit of lordless domination, created by humankind yet enslaving simultaneously; an all-encompassing global reality serving, protecting and defending the interests of powerful corporations, nations, elites and privileged people, while imperiously excluding even sacrificing humanity and exploiting creation; a pervasive spirit of destructive self-interest, even greed – the worship of money, goods and possessions; the gospel of consumerism, proclaimed through powerful propaganda and religiously justified, believed and followed; the colonization of consciousness, values and notions of human life by the imperial logic; a spirit lacking in compassionate justice and showing contemptuous disregard for the gifts of creation and the household of life.

As also in the 2004 Accra Confession of the World Communion (formerly Alliance) of Reformed Churches (WCRC), which also offers a critique of Empire, it is important to recognize that this understanding of 'Empire' is a theological judgement. It is not as such a description of particular historical empires – like the Greek, Roman, Ottoman, British, French, Russian or American empires – though those specific geo-political entities do indeed reflect and embody aspects of this broader term. So the Accra Confession describes Empire as 'the coming together of economic, cultural, political and military power that constitutes a system of domination led by powerful nations to protect and defend their own interests' (paragraph 11), to show that this is not simply about one city- or nation-state colonizing others, or one extract of history, but is a broader trajectory.

It is important to distinguish between the specific geo-political entities of individual empires and the broader and deeper state of affairs called 'Empire', because people are often quick to point out that particular empires 'did some good'. While the haste to emphasize these positive aspects may betray a significant degree of defensiveness about imperial history, it is nevertheless important not to dismiss this argument altogether. Even empires can bring some benefits, whereas the theological category of 'Empire', represented by symbolic Babylon, the Beast, is more straightforwardly 'the antithesis of Holy Anarchy'. The negation of what God intends. The definitions given by WCRC and CWM intend to impress on us that this deeper kind of Empire is the very system that obstructs the progress of Holy Anarchy; it is the system in reference to which 'the kingdom of God' *is the alternative*. That said, Empire manifests itself in much that individual empires have done. Even if some good was done, the very structures of domination that they represent inflict harm on others. Those of us of colonizer heritage do not like hearing this, precisely because the Empire in its particular historical forms has always deployed propaganda effectively, so we like to think of those forms as civilizing, a view held also by many who have been colonized, because the reality of widespread violence, exploitation, grand theft, inequality, racism and prejudice, which were intrinsic to imperial dynamics, has been obscured from us or purportedly reframed as the unfortunate by-products of better intentions.[7]

In terms of the connection between Empire and particular empires, the longer definition above argues that it is very much a reality embedded in the particular norms and processes of global capitalism, naming corporations, greed and consumerism, which, in the context of the longer historical narrative, are relatively recent features of the imperial system. But again, those features are not limited to the boundaries of an individual geo-political empire because global capitalism transcends borders. Empire, after all, cannot be confined by such borders, even if its presence is not always as discernible as we might imagine. That is to say, it can disguise itself even in the claims of anti-Establishment insurgencies (such as Trumpism), or it presents itself as benign, even while imposing itself on others and overriding their agency. In this way, it is more far-reaching than we appreciate, not only occupying land, economies and social structures, but burying itself in hearts, minds and souls.

Other terms may be used for it, however: like Wink's 'Domination System', capturing the sense in which social relations and practices are framed by a system in which powers of domination are in charge.[8] They are both spiritual and political entities, being both about our deepest identity and the very structures that govern our practical dealings with one another. Or Elisabeth Schüssler Fiorenza's 'kyriarchy',[9] meaning 'rule-over by a lord, or by lords' – any dynamic of lordship, including patriarchy but broader than that, reflecting also racialized structures, class structures, and our 'Dominion' of the Earth. In some respects, the notion of Dominion may even be a helpful alternative to the language of Empire, since it avoids the confusion between theological Empire and historical empires, while still alluding to the religious/spiritual/idolatrous roots of the very system. I will sometimes use it synonymously, but the use of 'Empire' is quite widespread among scholars and activists, so it is appropriate to be familiar with it.

Nonetheless, the CWM Theology Statement is also clear: the mission of God has *always* occurred in a context of Empire. So it is not only defined by these particular economic dynamics, but is a system constantly re-forming itself, manifested in multiple contexts, though consistently as a structure of domination, in which an elite issues propaganda, backed up by political and military force, to inculcate in the multitudes a sense of the inevitability, legitimacy and goodness of how things are. We see, then, how Empire prevailed in various forms through the biblical witness – Egyptian, Babylonian, Assyrian, Greek and Roman. We see how Israel was confronted with options and chose different approaches in particular

moments: whether to go with the flow of Empire, or to resist, or to imitate it. We see how the early church too had to choose, and how some
of its early radicalism was tamed in the light of an overbearing imperial
presence. As Wes Howard-Brook argues, though, in the context of the
book of Revelation, the Empire did not use violence as much as we often
imagine – or, at least, it could rely on people's fear that it could be used
more; the greater cause of obedience being the sheer seductiveness of the
imperial project.[10] So people went along with it, and still do, because it
affects us at a level that we cannot always put our finger on – not simply
a matter of fear, nor of intellectual assent. But a matter of the heart, the
psyche – even the spiritual.

Our obedience, or at the very least acquiescence, is the result of systematic propaganda. Shanks defines propaganda as 'the work of a gang
addressing a herd ... to help consolidate the herd ... At its most singularly
effective, and least benevolent ... fusing the herd into a mob.'[11] He refers
there to the 'mob' especially in the light of totalitarian regimes, where
propaganda catalyses groups of people, and not only state agencies, to
intimidate others to fall into line. But of course mobs are active in all sorts
of systems, including liberal democracies – whether in the public form of
insurrections against election results, or as online trolls or schemes of
disinformation and conspiracy theories; anything reactionary that seeks
to uphold the interests of those threatened by Holy Anarchy. But much
more insidious and powerful is Empire's propaganda in itself, having its
widespread impact even without the involvement of a mob. As Shanks
explains, 'it charms ... with alluring promises'[12] – for example, seducing
us with the gospel of consumerism while threatening us with the costs of
not succumbing to such norms; so it binds us together by exploiting our
fears; and it enthuses us with the assurance of ultimate victory. In effect,
it creates an 'us versus them' world, of those who play by the rules and
win, and those who reject our 'way of life'; they are even constructed
as 'enemies of humanity'[13] – people who think they know better than
the 'market', or who want to undermine it altogether. Of course, people
often notice that many who play by the rules do not in fact 'win' at all,
but we are taught to see this as the exception and to trust that the goods
will come in the end.

The definition of Empire used by CWM captures this well, not only
in terms of the propaganda – ideas that are religiously justified, beliefs
and values that ultimately cause us to worship things such as money,
an idol – but in terms of the 'colonization of consciousness'. It is such a
powerful phrase, but as with one or two other phrases in the definition
I want to qualify it a little, and suggest that this proactive Empire does
not only colonize our *consciousness* but also our *unconsciousness*. For,

as I said above, we are not fully aware of what is going on and how we are affected by it. Incidentally, I would also adapt the notion of 'lordless domination'. It is named, I suspect, in order to assert that there is only one Lord and that any authority over Empire is a false lord. But there are two problems with this: first, that even if the prevailing structures of Empire do not have one single lord – but, rather, a network of rulers in boardrooms and governments – its system of domination is not exactly 'lordless'. Kyriarchy is real. People know the effects of living under lords, however 'false' we may deem them to be. Second, if we reconfigure 'the kingdom of God' as Holy Anarchy, the point is that lordship itself is to be subverted. After all, as I shall argue further shortly, even where we *feel* that we are loyal to *the true Lord*, we run a real risk of upholding systems of domination, often in his name. Lordship itself is false, detracting us from the true nature of divine power. The broader point here, though, is that the cunning of Empire, created by us – as the statement emphasizes – simultaneously enslaves us, as we find ourselves 'captivated' by its grandeur and its promise.

Nestor Miguez, Joerg Rieger and Jung Mo Sung suggest that Empire promotes itself as good and just, the only true source of peace;[14] its intentions are to *become* transcendent, present everywhere, and that this will be the foundation of our security and welfare. That what it offers us is too good to refuse, so it is no wonder that we accept it – though, of course, who is the 'we' here? Who gets to decide whether to be colonized by Empire? It is clear that those who decide never speak for the many, only the few.

But the system that emerges nevertheless colonizes us in multiple ways, against the will and interests of the multitudes. For instance, working with the ideas of Anibal Quijano, Walter Mignolo speaks of 'the colonial matrix of power', a complex of interweaving dimensions.[15] Specifically, there are four forms of control:[16] control over the economy; over systems of authority; over constructs of gender and sexuality; and over subjectivities and claims to knowledge. This gives further detail to the wide-ranging assessment of Empire articulated in the CWM definition. Another way of categorizing the comprehensive nature of our colonization is in terms of the anthropological, the psychological, the socio-political and the religious/theological, none of which can be neatly separated from the others, but that again reflect the multifunctional operation of Empire. For instance, the anthropological issue is that Empire reconstructs our human identity, as Moe-Lobeda identifies.[17] In my terms, this is according to the agenda of its particular truth-in-hand, its edited distortions of the fullness of human life within the wider web of life. So, for Moe-Lobeda, Empire refashions humanity as *Homo economicus*, defined principally in terms of economic agency and worth, *Homo consumens* – that is, our capacity for consumption – and *Homo dominans*, reflecting our dominion over the Earth. We see there how our psyches are reconstructed too: our 'worldview' and our sense of what is possible are conditioned by economic assumptions, goals and interests.

Segovia also captures this comprehensive situation, as follows: 'the reality of empire, of imperialism and colonialism, constitutes an omnipresent, inescapable and overwhelming reality'.[18] But it is telling that these, or similar, insights come also from less explicitly theological quarters. For example, Max Weber, a sociologist writing in the early part of the twentieth century, argued that 'the capitalistic economy of the present day is an immense cosmos into which the individual is born, and which presents itself to him, at least as an individual, as an unalterable order of things in which he must live'.[19] Even there we see that capitalism is not merely a way of doing economics, but 'an immense cosmos'. He also judged its relationship to material goods to be a 'reversal' of how humanity is naturally inclined to be – that is, rather than subordinating the acquisition of goods to a prior concern for our material needs simply to be met, capitalism causes the meeting of needs to be subordinated to the prior concern for acquisition in itself; and 'at the same time it expresses a type of feeling which is closely connected with certain religious ideas'.[20] In particular, he suggested that the Protestant notion of salvation generated a capitalist work ethic, so capitalism accelerated in Protestant countries. There are arguments contradicting the details of these claims[21] – but what he and his critics agree on is that religious and economic ideologies influence each other.

Much more recently, Kathryn Tanner developed this in her analysis of finance capitalism.[22] She suggests that the past has an overbearing hold on us, whether because of the investments of an elite, the contracts of workers or the debts of debtors, binding us to commitments even if they harm our wellbeing, while urging us to be increasingly efficient, so creating an inescapable treadmill effect;[23] whereas, by contrast, Christian faith allows for disruptions from the past, the impact of grace to set us free, and make new futures possible. Therefore, she seeks to show how particular commitments of Christian faith can subvert and remodel the norms of economics.[24] The liberation theologian Jung Mo Sung also offers a critique of neo-liberalism, the particularly dominant manifestation of capitalism (though more than an economic model) that urges states to refrain from interfering in the market and to privatize as many assets as possible. This is directly pertinent to the immediate discussion of the religious/economic interplay, because he explicitly identifies an idolatrous theology present within such economics.

In short, Sung identifies theological language and intent in the very discipline of economics and its specific embodiment in neo-liberal global capitalism. He identifies how Friedrich von Hayek, arguably the high priest of such a model, effectively retells the Adam and Eve story to judge humanity's misplaced belief that it knows better than God;[25] he deemed such delusion to be present in governments' efforts to correct the market. Whether on the basis of an implicit theological underpinning or even its explicit references to religion, Sung suggests that neo-liberal economics functions as an *idolatrous* theology, with a false god.[26] Its 'God' is the market itself, which the system believes should be free to be what it is; and, on that basis, 'sin' consists of our misguided efforts to restrain the market, as though we could know better than 'God'. As in many theologies, Sung explains, there are even 'necessary sacrifices'[27] in this model: those who suffer because of human sin, neo-liberalism actually believing that the poor are disadvantaged when humans interfere with the freedom of the market, and promoting this version of reality despite all the evidence to the contrary. In neo-liberal theology, salvation comes when we let the market be the market – and it will deliver the goods. So Sung suggests key themes of Christian theology are evident but distorted in neo-liberal economics, and that its damaging effects cannot be addressed without reckoning with this idolatry.

It is important, though, to underscore the interplay here: between religion and economics, notions of God and of the market. That is to say, it is not simply that religious ideas flavour our sense of the market, or encourage economic activity as though it is religiously justified or deemed to be religious activity – how we are devoted to it, how it functions as a religion (which John Cobb names 'economism'[28]), how it is regarded as saving us. It is also that economics re-forms religion and theology. Of course, it conditions us at multiple levels, not only because our lives are measured by economic performance but because we see the world through capitalist lenses: determining whether things or activities are valuable enough, efficient enough, cost-effective enough; reducing even relationships and our commitments to transactional norms, whether we 'gain' something from them or what we are expected to 'give'. And this also infiltrates religious sensibilities and practice: whether our particular preferences are met, whether things can be afforded – but also how God is viewed, as a deliverer of goods, supplying what we demand and demanding what our faithful obedience can supply; conditioning us to focus on growth (spiritual or numeric); and engendering in us a sense that results come from investing ourselves, applying ourselves, bearing the costs and expecting the return.

Such norms may be framed in terms of relationship – a personal relationship with God – exemplified by God's costly self-giving on the cross, but so often even this seems somewhat transactional, like a payment made to deal with our debt. As Moe-Lobeda further argues, the notion of 'personal relationship' is stripped of its interpersonal, political and ecological dimensions.[29] Of course, religious faith must not be 'reduced' to any single dimension, for even where Empire has its grip on us, faith signals what cannot be contained. So I would expect any of us to push back against the claim that imperial economics have entirely refashioned faith and God. Nevertheless, because powers of domination are all-pervasive, including in our unconsciousness, we should reflect on how they affect even what is most precious to us.

God of the crucifiers or the crucified?

How, then, would I understand the roots of this interplay, between Empire and God, in particular the predominance of economics? I suggest the distinction between the two kinds of truth is helpful here, since Empire holds tightly to its particular truth-in-hand, with little room for the empathetic openness of truth-in-process. This way, its vested interests are secured. Shanks suggests that the tension between the two kinds of truth is reflected in a civil war within us:[30] a 'Changeable aspect' of the self is open to truth-in-process, apprehending reality for all its subtlety and awkwardness without expecting it to confirm any preconceptions, so enabling us to receive others' experiences, learn through them, and develop deeper solidarity. But this aspect of ourselves is humbler, so it often defers to, or can be subdued by, the more assertive 'Unchangeable aspect', or 'the Rigidity-Principle', which encounters reality, filters it, massages it, or conditions it to fit with what it supposes we already know or need to know.

This (un)civil war within us is the psychological context that external systems can easily exploit; specifically, Rigidity-Principles in our sociopolitical structures feed our anxiety about the difficulty of reality and urge us to close down, defend borders, bolster our security, but – more importantly – serve the vested interests of those with privilege. There is interplay between the personal/psychological and the political/structural. However, this psychological conflict (described here in mythic terms) is not experienced in the same way in all cultures; in fact, the respective weight given to each 'aspect of the self' and each kind of truth can vary greatly, according to a whole web of cultural, spiritual and political factors, but – at the very least – the particular way in which rigidity prevails is the basis for imperial ambition and the colonization of others' consciousness. For the colonizers presume they are the civilizers, giving little credence to alternative narratives, therefore possessing more and more psycho-logical territory. This power runs through politics, economics, culture, education,[31] religion and more.

It is, though, a genuine interplay: between external structures exploit-ing the tension within us, and the tension within us feeding and bolstering the external structures. This takes us back to our previous discussion of so-called anti-Establishment movements and God (in Chapter 2), because this interplay very much affects our notion of God. After all, if truth-in-hand prevails, and not just any truth-in-hand but specifically the truth-in-hand committed to 'good order' and the boundaries between insiders and outsiders, then the 'God' we believe in reflects such con-cerns. It is a god who will command some to lord it over others, men over women, White over Black and Brown, straight and cisgender over LGBTQI; a god who will claim to be non-political while excusing the status quo; a god who will ordain the exceptional status of one nation or another, of imperial ambition, of the inevitability and legitimacy of global capitalism. This is indeed the 'God' who reigns. But it is a 'false Lord God', strong but an illusion, projected by our internal Rigidity-Principle;[32] a god who confirms what we already suspect, on the basis of what those with privilege maintain: that certain rules are required to restore and preserve the good life – rules that favour particular groups – and a god whose goals match those of the external structures.

So Rieger and Kwok suggest that the greatest issue in theology is not whether or not people believe in God, but whether their model of God upholds or resists Empire. All too easily, where Empire prevails, God is co-opted as its legitimizer.[33] In Walter Brueggemann's terms, we are children of a 'royal consciousness', which determines that this is how things should be, whereas the alternative is 'the prophetic imagination' which calls forth a different reality.[34] But the false Lord God has his grip on things – so when Jesus dared to resist and do a new thing, in the cause of divine truth-in-process, the guardians of the imperial God called Jesus a blasphemer, discrediting him, seeking to silence him, ultim-ately even crucifying him. This was the will of the false God, exposed by the moral bankruptcy of such an action. Jesus died in solidarity with all who suffer at the hands of regimes and religion that demand sacrifice in the name of good order. He died in solidarity with every Changeable self, subdued by structural Rigidity-Principles. He died for the cause of divine generosity-of-spirit that the System sought to close down. He died at the hands of False Order while manifesting the alternative horizon: Holy Anarchy!

But where does the church stand, in the light of the cross? The church has generally spoken in defence of it, as the means by which good order is restored. It was willed by God, so cannot be questioned; it is the way in which God healed the wound between us, conquering forces of death and sin, and putting us right with him. We have defended it even though it has meant contorting ourselves to do so; ill-at-ease with the inevitable paradox of love coming through such horror. The problem is that, while celebrating Christ Crucified, we find ourselves on the side of the cruci-fiers,[35] as though they were enacting God's will. In so doing, we have risked excusing other violence,[36] as though it too is divinely ordained. We, the church, have stood behind those who have used the cross – demanding correct belief in it – as the means of establishing insiders and outsiders, holding it high at the front of armies and as a legitimation for imperialism. We have done this without knowing what we do. We have been conditioned by the false Lord God projected through the interplay between anxious psyches and privileged systems. There had been little room for alternatives. Or little scope to hear them, even when they spoke up. Meanwhile, Jesus called forth forgiveness, as a remarkable witness to the awesome weakness of divine love, which is even *for* those who would crucify it. But how can this reckon with the real harm done by such a false 'God' and his followers? How can such generosity-of-spirit hold Empire, including in its religious manifestations, to account? How can such weakness take on the might of Dominion, its violent truth-in-hand, its truth-as-possession, its colonization of lands, economies and psyches?

We will come to this question of justice in the next chapter, but the final point in this section is to acknowledge that, in the face of such crucifying systems, underpinned by a false 'God', the challenge is to *imagine* alter-natives that begin, however imperfectly, to overcome the colonization of our (un)consciousness. The problem is so stark because, within the constraints of Empire and its logic, 'the imagination becomes virtually atrophied and unable to conjure up anything outside the conditions of the symbolic system in which it finds itself, incapable of venturing beyond the limit of the dominant reality'.[37] Because the structural Rigidity-Principles colonize our psyches so successfully, 'the ability to imagine otherwise, to envision an alternative, to draw from the reservoirs of creativity will yield nothing but excessive reiterations of the same'.[38] This is the challenge that Holy Anarchy must address.

A hymn: Kings shall shut their mouths

'My servant shall be lifted,
    exalted up on high';
and kings shall shut their mouths up –
    no longer free to lie.
His form shall be rejected;
    he'll bear no regal crown,
but though he'll die in silence,
    the noise will be profound.

The governor will question,
    'So what is truth, you say?',
indifferent to the answer,
    but keen to get his way:
to coax the crowd's submission,
    'We have no king but yours',
securing Rome's position,
    upholding Untruth's cause.

So nailed for all to witness –
    'anointed' crucified,
a light for all the nations,
    'King of the Occupied';
his kingdom, unlike empires
    which rule through force and fear,
illuminates their falsehoods.
    Let those with ears now hear:

For this, the king rejected,
    is how the truth is known:
not brandishing a weapon,
    nor clinging to its throne,
not waged by strong religion
    that tames the wild and weak,
but in the empires' voiceless
    through whom God dares to speak.

Graham Adams (2020)
Suggested tune: *Passion Chorale*
Isaiah 52.13—53.9 (especially 52.15), John 18.28—19.30

The Empire throughout: powers of domination

The structures of Empire are certainly not only economic in nature. They also affect dynamics of gender and sexuality, race and ethnicity, dis/ability and age, religious and cultural identities, and so on. Intersectionality is the approach that acknowledges how these different dimensions interact with one another. For example, Person X may be disadvantaged by gender but not by race, while Person Y may be disadvantaged by race and dis/ability, but not by gender. The task is not to put people in a hierarchy of privilege as such, according to how many dimensions affect them. After all, the issues are rather more complex than that, since, in any single scenario, one particular disadvantage can have more weight than others. Even so, where someone experiences multiple dimensions of disadvantage, this certainly does greatly affect their freedom to flourish in relationship with others. Meanwhile, the System's attraction to truth-in-hand causes us to make trade-offs between different factors, setting the various modes of oppression against one another (whether race versus gender, dis/ability versus age, and so on), or encouraging 'whataboutery' where people do not attend to the issue before them, but ask 'what about …?' in order to detract from the immediate situation of injustice. Attempts to divert attention come out of defensiveness, anxiety over being confronted with realities that feel either too big to address, or small enough to present us with the inconvenience of making changes. And Empire encourages these anxieties and diversions, entrenching the ways in which one group is set against another, dividing excluded voices from one another in order to rule over them all.

It is an issue in the global relationships between churches. Where one church seeks to be attentive to LGBTQI communities, another may be more alert to economic challenges; or where one is slow to engage with its structural racism, it may profess instead to be attentive to the challenge of ecological care. But each may claim the superiority of its position because of the insidious legacy of imperialism: for instance, where some churches in the Majority World prove more resistant to the dignity of LGBTQI communities, there is often a colonial back-story to this in which the binaries and boundaries of earlier colonizers superimposed psycho-social structures on the 'indecent' fluidities of Majority World cultures.[39] That is to say, if we can speak of 'mission Christianity' as that form of Christianity that went hand in hand with colonial projects,[40] often well-represented today among various American Pentecostal traditions and megachurch theologies that continue to be exported globally, it is the western/industrialized cultures driving such a model that conditioned the colonized to accept and reinforce rigid concepts and practices. But it is also legitimate to call out 'Empire' wherever its dominating dynamics arose – because, as a structure of dominion, it is not limited to the particular geo-political projects of certain nations, but reigns in every instance of, say, patriarchy, exploitation and exclusion.

In the face of any single issue, it may be tempting to set one group against another, but it is vital that we attend to warnings from within liberation theology. Ivan Petrella, for instance, expressed concern that liberation theology was building silos, rather than bridges, between the different constituencies.[41] Anselm Min, too, argued that there needs to be a solidarity among the various liberation causes – gender, race, disability, sexuality, class, ecological.[42] As Keun-Joo Christine Pae explains, Marcella Althaus-Reid had also cautioned that liberation theology was becoming too 'decent' in its desire to get a wider audience;[43] what it needs instead is to build wilder coalitions of multiple perspectives, each rising up against one form or another of domination. And Robinson-Brown's intersectional approach roots this longing for a solidarity of solidarities in a British context.[44]

Having said, though, that the structures of Empire are concerned with many more things than economics, I return to the economic realm because it is arguably the most potent driver of the current matrix. So, for example, while the sexualized and gendered dimensions of poverty must be addressed,[45] the sheer prevalence and insidiousness of global capitalism in our psyches and systems must be reckoned with. For Moe-Lobeda, its pervasiveness means that it functions as 'hegemonic vision', colonizing life to such an extent that it is seen as 'natural'.[46] It becomes hard for us to 'see' through the mask, which presents the 'System' as good, to recognize instead the real connection between the privilege of the few and the suffering of the many.

This requires the honing of our perceptions, to perceive the reality of such injustice, but our perception is constructed, or distracted, by the power of 'moral oblivion'.[47] That is, a socially constructed order that conditions us to be oblivious. It has eight ingredients, she suggests: first, an emphasis on privatized morality, so even where we see issues, we are urged to find personal and privatized solutions rather than addressing the public structures. Second, the history of possession is retold so that the inheritance of what is owned is seen in terms of blessing, to deny the grand theft by nation against nation. Third, the emotions of denial, guilt and grief are fostered at the expense of really facing up to the demands for change. A sense of entitlement reinforces our denials; grief takes up more of our energy, so there is less space for transformative action. Fourth, the further emotions of despair and hopelessness create an atmosphere of powerlessness, as though 'we' are the powerless. Fifth, we unconsciously conform; it is, after all, so much easier to do so. Sixth, corporations invest heavily in propaganda to maintain public moral oblivion. The seventh ingredient is the uncritical belief in growth, as though it is the only way to climb out of our crises; and the eighth is that moral oblivion is embedded in practices: our consumer habits are shaped to keep the show on the road.

Interestingly, John Weeks, an economist, confirms many of these in what he regards as 'fakeconomics'[48] or market myths. They begin with the notion that 'there is no alternative',[49] to which we return below. He goes on to illuminate how, despite people's common experience of market failures, where the System has not delivered as expected, people are urged to see regulation of the market as bad – this is the cognitive dissonance we are urged to live with.[50] After all, competition is celebrated as inherently virtuous. If our experience is otherwise, this is a matter of our own ignorance, since economists know best – we have simply not got enough of the big picture. Of course, if we still persist in doubting the System, its trump card is that we would not want communism – the classic false dichotomy that allows no room for a whole host of other options. In fact, to question the distribution of wealth is seen as anti-scientific, because obviously the System is entirely logical, and to redistribute would be merely sentimental.[51] As everyone knows, according to these market myths, our transactions are entirely voluntary, so the System cannot be blamed for the trouble that people find themselves in! And the great big lie is that, even if we do not see it right now, its efficiency will ultimately deliver for all – so we should be patient.[52]

As I have summarized previously in more depth,[53] Rieger and Kwok identify several lies within the System, three of which are particularly significant: the first is the very notion of individualism. The problem is not merely that we are encouraged to act as self-sufficient individuals, making our own futures in competition with one another, but that this construction of a self-sufficient individual is in fact a lie. This is because people achieve what the System encourages, not in a vacuum of individual skill or hard work, but on the basis of distortions in the web of relations; distortions that serve the interests of the few but impede the development of the many. So when religion purports to encourage us away from individualism, to act in community, it affirms good values but fails to address the underlying issue: the structures of dominion embedded in class, gender, race and global positioning. The appropriate response to this is proper class analysis and an understanding of our interdependence, as in Paul's vision of the body of Christ, so poorly manifest in church or society; a vision where greater attention is paid to the least, the indecent, yet those who feed the very mouths that condemn them.[54]

This leads, second, to the lie that it is the poor who act as parasites by drawing resources downwards. The truth is that the 1 per cent at the top are the parasites, drawing resources upwards. Politics and theologies that pay more attention to the sins of the poor than to the structural sin legitimized by the rich must be transformed. What is needed is a theology 'of the multitude' which affirms the agency of the many, without reducing it to mere economics, or romanticizing it for its resilience, but which reckons with the fullness of reality: the generational disadvantages entrenched by multiple structural challenges and intersectional dynamics, as well as all the ways in which those with more wealth, security and social status depend on the work – and poverty – of the multitudes.[55]

The third lie is inseparable from this; a lie peculiar to religion: the notion that all of these issues can be resolved if only more people believed in God. It takes no account of times when the church had the numbers but defended structural injustices. It pays no meaningful attention to non-theistic activists. It over-simplifies the question of solidarity, as though 'like-mindedness' secures justice, whereas what is needed is a piercing analysis of the prevailing models of power, both in society at large and in religion.[56] The missionary and theologian Lesslie Newbigin was right that even supposedly secular societies have their own 'religious' commitments: a mythos or idol of one kind or another, which attracts our devotion.[57] But religion itself is also infected by such things: so belief is not intrinsically the path to justice. For instance, as Rieger and Kwok identify, religious faith can emphasize transcendence as a means of affirming something 'higher' than the norms of the current system, but such an emphasis can too easily become other-worldly, diverting our attention from injustice on the ground. Alternatively, God's immanence can be emphasized, to impress on us God's commitment to the challenges of life, but this can too easily baptize things as they are, with the affirmation that 'God is everywhere' insufficiently addressing the 'partisan' solidarity of God, in the midst of those especially oppressed or excluded.[58] As Rieger and Kwok note, it is no coincidence that Rome regarded the early Christians as 'atheist' for their devotion to a crucified peasant – a non-god if ever there was one![59] But churches have often failed to appreciate this ironic insight: that we do indeed follow a God who subverts prevailing models of power, in society and in religion. Our theism is indeed revolutionary, affirming the *theos* as a 'non-god' in Empire's terms; for our 'kingdom' is also revolutionary: Holy Anarchy is at hand!

But as Gerald West identifies, churches struggle to make such an analysis. In terms of the 1985 Kairos Document from South Africa, we are not well accustomed to resisting 'state theology' – the theologies of the prevailing structures, whether in government, business or culture at large – because we are ourselves in the thralls of 'church theology', a supposedly non-contextual form of Christian theology that 'relies upon a few stock ideas derived from Christian tradition and then uncritically and repeatedly applies them to our situation'.[60] Too often, and too easily, our 'church theology' adopts a political neutrality, restraining the gospel's critique of oppression and so basically allowing the status quo to prevail. As the Kairos Document itself indicated, where we refuse to take sides with the oppressed, we take sides with the oppressor (Kairos, 1985, p. 13). It is an insight we also see in the work of the trailblazing Black theologian James Cone: 'While pretending to be concerned about the universal character of the human condition, oppressors are in fact concerned to justify their own particular status in society. They want to be oppressors and Christians at the same time.'[61] In other words, in the face of these structures in which we are embedded, it is not really attractive, especially to those of us who benefit from them, to act in subversive solidarity with those harmed by them. It is not attractive, and the overbearing power of the system seduces us to fit in, but the gospel calls us to dance to a different tune. What, then, is the tune we are called to dance to?

From TANA to TASA

At one level, the first contexts for 'postcolonial' perspectives were obviously those where colonizing empires had imposed themselves, their worldviews, and their practices on the lands, psyches and lives of colonized subjects. For those of us of 'colonizer heritage', colonialism was something that happened 'over there', and postcolonialism was the re-emergence of experience, stories and insights to challenge what had been done 'over there'. So its focus could be regarded as those of hybrid identities that were formed where a powerful narrative – that is, an imperial narrative backed up by wealth and military force – had a distorting effect on the narratives of the Majority World. In response, voices began to reclaim the right to be. Critiques of Empire illuminated exactly what had been done to people and planet. Stories re-emerged which retold the dominant narratives but in transgressive ways, subverting the colonialism and neo-colonialism of imperial presumptuousness and imposition. That is to say, the primary contexts of postcolonialism were those that 'received' Empire, and who were now rediscovering who they were, what had been lost and what the future might be, in the light of this resurgence of suppressed identities. Implicit in this was the challenge to the colonizers: how would we 'receive' these re-emerging insights?

But there was much more to it than that. As Arif Dirlik recognized, postcolonialism presents the former colonizers with as much of an identity challenge as it does for the colonized.[62] Not only the question of 'who on earth did we think we *were*?', but also 'so who are we *now*?' Musa Dube confirmed this, seeing the 'postcolonial subject' as being present at both ends of the colonial project.[63] Perhaps it is no surprise, then, that western concerns have often dominated postcolonial debate.[64] As with liberation theologies, postcolonial approaches have found themselves in the thralls of western tentacles, potentially calming the scandalizing potential of postcolonial energy.

However, the insight that Empire is not simply something that happens 'over there', but that former colonizers are also colonized by a system of dominion, opens up the issues in a different way. It does not mean that 'we are all colonized in similar terms'. Even if some constituencies within Britain – for example, working-class communities – have good reason to find common cause with exploited labour in former colonies, opening up the possibility of solidarity across other divisions, it still does not mean that colonialism affected the different groups equally. But where a focus on particular geo-political empires can encourage the delusion that 'colonialism happened far away', and that it therefore does not concern 'us' very much, the alternative focus on Empire as theological judgement can help to highlight the way in which we are all entangled in structures of control and propaganda. Of course, on the one hand, even geo-political empires were very much colonizing the minds of those in the motherland – whether Rome, Britain or America – so people ought not to claim 'it is nothing to do with us'. But to recognize how powers of domination operate behind and extend beyond any single geo-political structure is to see more sharply the prevalence of what we live within.

The resources of postcolonial critiques and theologies are hugely helpful to illuminate for us the ways in which powerful narratives overwhelm and distort weaker ones, whether far away or closer to home; whether along lines of nationality and 'race', or in terms of class, gender, sexuality, dis/ability and age. Patterns of domination of every kind can be seen more clearly as a result of postcolonial wisdom, so it is no wonder its strategies are applied in so many spheres now. But a shift to the language of 'decolonial' may be even more reconstructive, as we recognize that we are not in a 'post' colonial environment, since Empire remains all-pervasive. Rather, what we need is decolonial insight and action – naming the structures of oppression, deconstructing them, and opening up alternative patterns that can enable us to become increasingly disentangled from imperial tentacles.

At the heart of this challenge is a shift from TANA to TASA. Instead of TINA (There Is No Alternative), I call it TANA (There Are No

Alternatives), which recognizes that it is plural possibilities that have been denied, so to affirm the move to TASA (There Are Several Alternatives).[65] On the one hand, strategically this can seem to be a frustrating solution to Empire, because it may appear more sensible to bind our multiple streams of resistance into a clearly defined alternative: either Empire or This Way. But on the other hand, there are good anti-imperial reasons for multiplicity itself.

The first argument for TASA is concerned with ambiguity, a theme that recurs through this book. As Miguez, Rieger and Sung explain:

> Christianity, when it came to power, became an enemy of ambiguity, like all authoritarian logic, and thereby has constituted orthodoxies and heresies. Even the so-called 'liberation Christianity', with multiple manifestations, has often also fallen into this trap.
>
> Ambiguity – this possibility that a thing could also be something else, that an expression could be understood in different ways, that an action could be interpreted diversely and produce effects beyond the intended, the expected and unexpected – is an unavoidable reality of the human condition, and not the worst. It is a condition of our language, of our thought itself, of our action, and, which is hard for us to accept, of our ethics ...
>
> It is worth remembering that the main enemy of Jesus was not impurity but injustice. Jesus placed himself in the midst of the impure, of the Galilean semi-gentiles, of the impure prostitutes, of the ambiguous publicans, opposite the univocal intolerance of the Pharisees. What he seeks in their midst is the 'Kingdom of God and His Justice', and not the kingdom of abstract purities.[66]

So TASA is a mark of Holy Anarchy, a means by which the alternative horizon takes shape, because any uniformity would be a closing-down of reality according to the priorities of False Order and a denial of the multiplicity of life in all its awkwardness. We return to this in Chapters 5, 6 and 7.

Upolu Lumā Vaai argues in effect for TASA on the basis that TANA, or 'onefication' as she calls it, directs people and systems towards 'one answer'. In particular, that 'one answer' tends to pull apart the connections between economy, ecology and oikumene.[67] Oikumene is the word from which we derive 'ecumenical', as in the church's ecumenical movement, the movement towards togetherness and unity. It might seem odd that 'onefication' could do damage to ecumenism if ecumenical endeavours are about upholding the unity of the church, but – as I shall explore further in Chapter 6 – the oneness or unity of the church should be appropriately anarchic. The argument against onefication makes the point: economy, ecology and oikumene properly belong together, as the whole 'household' of God (the root of all three is the Greek word *oikos*, for house or household), but Empire divides them, with an economic realm supposedly divorced from its impact on ecosystems, and churches insufficiently engaged to hold it to account. What is needed[68] instead is a 'whole of life' imperative, affirming the interconnectedness and flow between all things; a 'we are' imperative, emphasizing the collaborative possibilities of deeper solidarity; and a 'relational time' imperative, recognizing the power of slow progress, the patience required to build connections and make good decisions, as distinct from patterns of frenetic urgency.

TASA, therefore, is about living constructively with our ambiguities, the impossibility of controlling exactly what we mean and what we do; affirming the richness of life within a diverse household, our connectedness and mutual interdependence; and resisting those, whether political, economic or religious, who would push us towards 'one answer'. After all, even Holy Anarchy is not one answer – it is, in Rieger and Kwok's terms, more akin to 'polydoxy',[69] in which one another's orthodoxies are brought into dialogue, not to iron out the differences but to engender a deeper solidarity of solidarities. Kwok's gathering of material concerned with civil disobedience in Hong Kong, reclamations of selfhood from colonial desire, interreligious solidarity and peacebuilding, and earth care, altogether demonstrates this interweaving of multiple movements.[70]

The undomesticated *oikos* and the untame God

The image of the *oikos*, the homely basis of economics, ecology and ecumenism, is instructive because it reminds us that relationships between churches are not only relationships between particular church traditions. They are, or are called to be, expressions of a movement – the ecumenical movement – which is itself a response to the reconciling activity of God. The God whose palm is open, inviting relationship and connection between a multiplicity of experiences and stories, evoking in us empathy towards those who suffer at the hands of closed-fist systems, and beckoning us to witness to an open horizon where relationships are healed. In other words, whenever we are 'ecumenical' we must also be engaged in the quest for economic justice and ecological justice, seeking fullness of life for all.

To celebrate the household of life, whether within the ecumenical movement or beyond it, is to affirm the connections between all aspects of life. But it is also to recognize the systematic forces that delimit our sense of the house: the imperial forces that tell us to take our alternative visions home with us; the expectations impressing on us that such audacity belongs to the private realm, speaking only of promises of an afterlife. We must surely, after all, appreciate that our claims to an alternative household are misguided; there already is an overarching structure, an Empire that gives us all the security we need, an economy that affords us the goods we desire, a temple in which we may worship the market, or a de-politicized version of our own god(s). No other 'household' is necessary, apart from the households of nation, or local community, or family.

It is as though there is a tension between different visions of the house. The imperial vision is nicely groomed, neat and tidy; everything has its place; the borders are defined, and the functions of each room are well known. There is little space for anything poetic, anything that might push ambiguously or subversively against such a vision, except that it fosters sentimentality in us, nostalgia for an edited time when we 'all' lived in safety: so it is only a poetry of cliché, purity and manicured beauty. It is a house in which certain people know how to live well, whereas many others would feel lost, ill-at-ease, alien. Meanwhile, there is another vision, of a house or a household, that is less domesticated, more unruly; a wilder space where an unexpected coalition of people make their home, not easily, not without tension, and sometimes moving the walls, redesigning the architecture, reframing the space to make room for newcomers. It is a house or a home that does not define its borders too closely, because the tenants – or they may be the owners; no-one quite knows – recognize how interdependent they are on the wider environment, where roots and streams and clouds intermingle. It is a vision of an *oikos* which is undomesticated, always pushing against its containment within more restrictive patterns of living, allowing room for the untame God to erupt through the cracks.

As Alejandro López suggests, 'Whereas the theo-logos is always ready to offer explanations of God, a theo-poiesis is about experience, transformation, and movement with God',[71] referring there to Silas Krabbe.[72] *Poiesis* is the process of bringing something into being, and is the root of our word for poet and poetic. Citing Faber,[73] López affirms, 'The "poet" is the God of an ever-becoming world in which there is nothing but becoming.'[74] This matters, because when we try to conceive of reality other than Empire, we need imagination, because the structures of the Rigidity-Principle are so all-pervasive and overbearing and the colonization of our (un)consciousness is so thorough. There is just this little surplus that has not been contained. We have been tamed, domesticated, and split from our deep connectedness by powers of domination that divide and rule; but a seed of hope, multiplied many millions of times, bursts forth, like *poiesis*. In the face of these challenges, theology must try and try again to 'construct paths and praxis towards an otherwise of thinking, sensing, believing, doing, and living',[75] remembering that, as Stacey Gibson reminds us, 'imagining is an act of liberatory adventure since it feels borderless, boundary less, and free of the constructs that bind. To imagine is to transcend.'[76]

In that poetic spirit, Jung Mo Sung speaks of 'the transcendental imagination of a society free from oppression and alienation', one that acts both as a judge of what 'the dominant rationality cannot see and does not allow to be seen' and 'as a force that motivates people to struggle for a more just human society'.[77] Even then, as we struggle to conceive of a different household, not ordered according to prevailing economic patterns, or patriarchy, or kyriarchy of one kind or another, but shaped quite differently, there is the possibility of anticipating something different. Anticipation, Sung suggests, is not the same as resistance, by which we still react to the tunes of Empire; anticipation instead is 'a capacity to go beyond the logic of the Empire, experiencing in advance the future that can surprise us'.[78] It is this capacity that we explore in Chapter 4.

A hymn: It came as poem (the Lamb that roared)

The people wanted soldiers
so hope might come as curse,
to smash the occupation –
but change turned up as Verse:
the poetry of yeasting,
the parabolic sword,
no match for *Pax Romana**
and yet this Lamb still roared.

Although it claims possession
of mind and heart and soul,
the Empire's grip has limits –
it can't control the whole:
the surplus lives as Poem
for those with ears to hear,
resisting final closure,
declaring what is near:

This dream of re-creation,
this threat of life set free,
disturbing tame religion,
confounding how we see:
it won't succumb to cliché
where purities abound,
but glimpsed in seeds' potential,
it ruptures solid ground.

Where empires grow by violence,
where systems blame the last
and close down other futures
by editing the past,
the Poem can't be silenced,
though quietly it dies,
and dances through the fissures
to teach us how to rise!

Graham Adams (2021)
Suggested tunes: *Thornbury, Cruger* – or create another one
Pax Romana is 'the peace of Rome' secured through military violence; if it's
easier to replace this with 'crucifixion', the meaning still works.

Questions to ponder

1 'My name is Legion': In how many different ways can you identify
   the presence of 'Empire', whether in the wider world or your local
   community, whether in terms of the legacy of a particular historic
   empire or the system of domination that colonizes us at many
   levels?
2 The Empire within: How helpful do you find the notion of 'Empire',
   or 'the Domination System', or 'kyriarchy', as a key way of analys-
   ing the world as we know it? And can you think of examples of how
   it 'colonizes' our hearts and minds?
3 God of the crucifiers or the crucified: How easy is it to identify
   ways in which our sense of 'God' is affected by the structures and
   dynamics of 'Empire'? For example, do you see the dangers in 'God
   of the crucifiers'? Perhaps I have overstated some things; if so,
   how?

4 The Empire throughout: In what ways do the critiques of the economy resonate with you – for instance, the ingredients of moral oblivion identified by Cynthia Moe-Lobeda, or the market myths outlined by John Weeks? And how much do you think these things condition how we see things *beyond* directly economic actions?

5 From TANA to TASA: Do you see how we can so easily be constrained within a world of 'no alternatives'? What alternatives would you like to imagine and create?

6 The undomesticated *oikos* and the untame God: In what ways does the vision of two houses speak to you – a neat and tidy imperial house with clear boundaries, and an alternative house where all-comers may make their home? How much do you think God has been 'tamed'?

Further reading

Akala, *Natives: Race and Class in the Ruins of Empire* (London: Two Roads, 2018).

Jione Havea (ed.), *Doing Theology in the New Normal: Global Perspectives* (London: SCM Press, 2021).

Richard A. Horsley (ed.), *In the Shadow of Empire: Reclaiming the Bible as a History of Faithful Resistance* (Louisville, KY: Westminster John Knox, 2008).

Nestor Miguez, Joerg Rieger and Jung Mo Sung, *Beyond the Spirit of Empire* (London: SCM Press, 2009).

Cynthia Moe-Lobeda, *Resisting Structural Evil: Love as Ecological-Economic Vocation* (Minneapolis, MN: Fortress Press, 2013).

Joerg Rieger, *Christ and Empire: From Paul to Postcolonial Times* (Minneapolis, MN: Augsburg Fortress, 2007).

Joerg Rieger and Kwok Pui-lan, *Occupy Religion: Theology of the Multitude* (Washington DC: Rowman & Littlefield, 2010).

Jung Mo Sung, *Desire, Market and Religion* (London: SCM Press, 2007).

Kathryn Tanner, *Christianity and the New Spirit of Capitalism* (New Haven and London: Yale University Press, 2019).

Bud Tillinghast, https://www.subversivechurch.blog/ (accessed 22 December 2021).

Notes

1 Jacques Ellul, trans. Geoffrey W. Bromiley, *Anarchy and Christianity*, Eugene, OR: Wipf and Stock, 1991, p. 39: 'The biblical God is above all the one who liberates from all bondage.'

2 See Andrew Shanks, *Faith in Honesty: The Essential Nature of Theology*,

Farnham: Ashgate, 2005, p. 53, noting Augustine's use of the term '*libido domin-andi*'.

3 Ched Myers, *Binding the Strong Man: A Political Reading of Mark's Story of Jesus*, Maryknoll, NY: Orbis, 1988, pp. 190–4.

4 Andrew Shanks, *A Neo-Hegelian Theology: The God of Greatest Hospitality*, Farnham: Ashgate, 2014, pp. 113–15.

5 Walter Wink, *Engaging the Powers: Discernment and Resistance in a World of Domination*, Minneapolis, MN: Augsburg Fortress, 1992, p. 10.

6 Joerg Rieger, *Christ and Empire: From Paul to Postcolonial Times*, Minneapolis, MN: Augsburg Fortress, 2007, p. 9.

7 See, for example, Akala, *Natives: Race and Class in the Ruins of Empire*, London: Two Roads, 2018; Kehinde Andrews, *The New Age of Empire: How Racism and Colonialism Still Rule the World*, London: Allen Lane, 2021; and Sathnam Sanghera, *Empireland: How Imperialism Has Shaped Modern Britain*, New York: Viking, 2021.

8 Wink, *Engaging the Powers*, p. 10.

9 Elisabeth Schüssler Fiorenza, *Jesus – Miriam's Child, Sophia's Prophet: Critical Issues in Feminist Christology*, London: SCM Press, 1994, p. 14.

10 Wes Howard-Brook and Anthony Gwyther, *Unveiling Empire: Reading Revelation Then and Now*, Maryknoll, NY: Orbis, 1999, pp. 254–6, 268: 'that's how the seductiveness of Babylon really works … it's simply the air we breathe'.

11 Shanks, *A Neo-Hegelian Theology*, p. 89.

12 Shanks, *A Neo-Hegelian Theology*, p. 91.

13 Nestor Miguez, Joerg Rieger and Jung Mo Sung, *Beyond the Spirit of Empire*, London: SCM Press, 2009, p. 92.

14 Miguez, Rieger and Sung, *Beyond the Spirit of Empire*, pp. 70–1.

15 Walter Mignolo, 'Decolonizing Western Epistemologies/Building Decolonial Epistemologies', in Ada María Isasi-Díaz and Eduardo Mendieta (eds), *Decolonizing Epistemologies: Latina/o Theology and Philosophy*, New York: Fordham University Press, 2012, pp. 27–8.

16 Walter Mignolo, 'Introduction', *Cultural Studies*, vol. 21, nos 2–3 (2007): 156 (155–67).

17 Cynthia D. Moe-Lobeda, *Healing a Broken World: Globalization and God*, Minneapolis, MN: Augsburg Fortress, 2002, pp. 110–11.

18 Fernando F. Segovia, 'Biblical Criticism and Postcolonial Studies: Toward a Postcolonial Optic', in R. S. Sugirtharajah (ed.), *The Postcolonial Bible*, Sheffield: Sheffield Academic Press, 1998, pp. 55–6.

19 Max Weber, *The Protestant Ethic and the Spirit of Capitalism*, London: Unwin University Books, 1930, p. 54.

20 Weber, *Protestant Ethic*, p. 53.

21 See, for example, J. M. Blaut, *The Colonizer's Model of the World: Geographical Diffusionism and Eurocentric History*, New York and London: Guilford Press, 1993, and Chris Harman, *A People's History of the World: From the Stone Age to the New Millennium*, London: Verso Books, 2008.

22 Kathryn Tanner, *Christianity and the New Spirit of Capitalism*, New Haven and London: Yale University Press, 2019.

23 See also Jeremy Rifkin, *The Zero Marginal Cost Society: The Internet of Things, the Collaborative Commons and the Eclipse of Capitalism*, New York: Palgrave Macmillan, 2014, p. 276.

24 Tanner, *New Spirit of Capitalism*, p. 7.

25 Sung, in Miguez, Rieger and Sung, *Beyond the Spirit of Empire*, p. 81, citing Friedrich von Hayek, 'The Pretence of Knowledge', https://www.nobelprize.org/prizes/economic-sciences/1974/hayek/lecture/ (accessed 11 January 2022).

26 Jung Mo Sung, *Desire, Market and Religion*, London: SCM Press, 2007, p. 21.

27 Sung, *Desire, Market and Religion*, pp. 17–19.

28 John B. Cobb Jr., 'Liberation Theology and the Global Economy', in Joerg Rieger (ed.), *Liberating the Future: God, Mammon and Theology*, Minneapolis, MN: Augsburg Fortress, 1998, p. 32.

29 Moe-Lobeda, *Healing a Broken World*, pp. 105f.

30 Andrew Shanks, *Hegel and Religious Faith: Divided Brain, Atoning Spirit*, London and New York: Bloomsbury T&T Clark, 2011, pp. 50–1.

31 For example, Willie James Jennings, *After Whiteness: An Education in Belonging*, Grand Rapids, MI: Eerdmans, 2020.

32 Shanks, *Hegel and Religious Faith*, p. 50; Shanks, *A Neo-Hegelian Theology*, p. 113.

33 Joerg Rieger and Kwok Pui-lan, *Occupy Religion: Theology of the Multitude*, Washington DC: Rowman & Littlefield, 2010, p. 96.

34 Walter Brueggemann, *The Prophetic Imagination*, Minneapolis, MN: Fortress Press, 2001, p. 37.

35 See Shanks, *A Neo-Hegelian Theology*, p. 114.

36 Wink, *Engaging the Powers*, pp. 13ff. ('The Myth of Redemptive Violence'), pp. 146–7 (the violence of 'God'), p. 201 (violence as 'Christian'); James Alison, *Living in the End Times: The Last Things Re-imagined*, London: SPCK, 1997, pp. 23–4, 42.

37 Alejandro López, 'De-Imperializing God-Talk: Towards a Postcolonial Theopoetics', *Journal of Hispanic / Latino Theology*, vol. 23, no. 1, article 13 (2021): 130–51 (or at https://www.repository.usfca.edu/cgi/viewcontent.cgi?article =1118&context=jhlt, p. 12, referring to the work of Rubem Alves, *Tomorrow's Child: Imagination, Creativity, and the Rebirth of Culture*, Eugene, OR: Wipf & Stock, 2011, p. 25. See also Zetta Elliot, 'Decolonizing the Imagination', *The Horn Book Magazine*, 2 March 2010: 16–20 – how the colonized find themselves with an imagination that is not authentically theirs.

38 López, 'De-Imperializing God-Talk', p. 12.

39 For example, Adriaan van Klinken and Ezra Chitando, *Reimagining Christianity and Sexual Diversity in Africa*, London: C. Hurst & Co. Publishers, 2021, highlights African contributions to justice for LGBTQI people and decolonizes queer theory.

40 Anthony G. Reddie, *Theologising Brexit: A Liberationist and Postcolonial Critique*, Abingdon: Routledge, 2019, pp. 38, 56 n.1, 64, 66–70, 91.

41 Ivan Petrella, *Beyond Liberation Theology: A Polemic*, London: SCM Press, 2013, p. 84. He speaks of the danger of 'monochromatism', where different kinds of liberation theologians 'suffer from a limited range of vision'.

42 Anselm Min, *The Solidarity of Others in a Divided World: A Postmodern Theology after Postmodernism*, New York: T&T Clark, 2004, pp. 70–3, 226–30.

43 Keun-Joo Christine Pae, 'Indecent Resurgence: God's Solidarity against the Gendered War on Covid', in Jione Havea (ed.), *Doing Theology in the New Normal: Global Perspectives*, London: SCM Press, 2021, p. 184, summarizing an

argument in Marcella Althaus-Reid, *Indecent Theology: Theological Perversions in Sex, Gender and Politics*, London and New York: Routledge, 2000.

44 Jarel Robinson-Brown, *Black, Gay, British, Christian, Queer*, London: SCM Press, 2021.

45 Pae, 'Indecent Resurgence', p. 184.

46 Cynthia D. Moe-Lobeda, *Resisting Structural Evil: Love as Ecological-Economic Vocation*, Minneapolis, MN: Fortress Press, 2013, p. 86.

47 Moe-Lobeda, *Resisting Structural Evil*, pp. 85–104.

48 John F. Weeks, *Economics of the 1%: How Mainstream Economics Serves the Rich, Obscures Reality and Distorts Policy*, London: Anthem Press, 2014. See also Steve Keen, *Debunking Economics: The Naked Emperor of the Social Sciences*, Sydney: Zed Books, 2001 (revised 2011); Norbert Haring and Niall Douglas, *Economists and the Powerful: Convenient Theories, Distorted Facts, Ample Records*, London: Anthem Press, 2012, chapter 4.

49 Weeks, *Economics*, p. 3.

50 Weeks, *Economics*, pp. 55–8.

51 Weeks, *Economics*, p. 12.

52 Weeks, *Economics*, p. 59.

53 Graham Adams, 'Justice is the Heart of Faith: Truth in a World of Propaganda', in Vuyani Vellem, Patricia Sheerattan-Bisnauth and Philip Vinod Peacock (eds), *Bible and Theology from the Underside of Empire*, SUN MeDIA MeTRO, 2016, pp. 34–5, citing Rieger and Kwok, *Occupy Religion*.

54 See Rieger and Kwok, *Occupy Religion*, pp. 63–7.

55 See Rieger and Kwok, *Occupy Religion*, pp. 61–3.

56 See Rieger and Kwok, *Occupy Religion*, pp. 83–8.

57 Lesslie Newbigin, *Gospel in a Pluralist Society*, Grand Rapids, MI: Eerdmans, 1989, p. 221; Newbigin, *A Word in Season: Perspectives on Christian World Missions*, Grand Rapids, MI: Eerdmans, 1994, p. 150; Newbigin, *Foolishness to the Greeks: The Gospel and Western Culture*, Grand Rapids, MI: Eerdmans, 1986, p. 115.

58 See Rieger and Kwok, *Occupy Religion*, pp. 71–4, 87, 98.

59 See Rieger and Kwok, *Occupy Religion*, p. 89.

60 Gerald O. West, 'Reopening the Churches and/as Reopening the Economy: Covid's Uncovering of the Contours of "Church Theology"', in Havea (ed.), *Doing Theology in the New Normal*, p. 83.

61 James H. Cone, *God of the Oppressed* (rev. edn), Maryknoll, NY: Orbis, 1997, p. 136.

62 Arif Dirlik, 'The Postcolonial Aura: Third World Criticism in the Age of Global Capitalism', *Critical Inquiry*, vol. 20, no. 2 (1994): 337 (328–56).

63 Musa W. Dube, *Postcolonial Feminist Interpretation of the Bible*, St Louis, MO: Chalice Press, 2000, p. 16.

64 Dirlik, 'The Postcolonial Aura': 337; Gerald O. West, 'Doing Postcolonial Biblical Interpretation @Home: Ten Years of (South) African Ambivalence', *Neotestamentica*, vol. 42, no. 1 (2008): 150 (147–64); Anne McClintock, 'The Angel of Progress: Pitfalls of the Term "Post-Colonialism"', *Social Text* 31/32 (1992): 86 (84–98).

65 Shanthikumar Hettiarachchi, 'Avowing Religious Identity and the Religious Other: A Postcolonial Perspective', in Elizabeth Harris, Paul Hedges and Shanthi-

kumar Hettiarachchi (eds), *Twenty-First Century Theologies of Religions: Retrospection and Future Prospects*, Leiden: E. J. Brill, 2016, p. 206.

66 Miguez, Rieger and Sung, *Beyond the Spirit of Empire*, pp. 186–7.

67 Upolu Lumā Vaai, '*Lagimālie*: Covid, De-Onefication of Theologies, and Eco-Relational Well-being', in Havea (ed.), *Doing Theology in the New Normal*, pp. 211–12.

68 Upolu Lumā Vaai, '*Lagimālie*, pp. 213–15.

69 Rieger and Kwok, *Occupy Religion*, p. 128.

70 Kwok Pui-lan, *Postcolonial Politics and Theology: Unraveling Empire for a Global World*, Louisville, KY: Westminster John Knox, 2021.

71 López, 'De-Imperializing God-Talk', p. 20.

72 Silas C. Krabbe, *A Beautiful Bricolage: Theopoetics as God-Talk for Our Time*, Eugene, OR: Wipf and Stock, 2016, p. 18.

73 Roland Faber, 'Process Theology as Theopoetics', Lecture, Kresge Chapel, Claremont School of Theology, 7 February 2006.

74 López, 'De-Imperializing God-Talk', p. 21.

75 Walter Mignolo and Catherine Walsh, *On Decoloniality: Concepts, Analytics, Praxis*, Durham, NC: Duke University Press, 2018, p. 4.

76 López, 'De-Imperializing God-Talk', p. 15, citing Stacey A. Gibson, 'Sourcing the Imagination: Ta-Nehisi Coates's Work as a Praxis of Decolonization', *Schools*, vol. 14, no. 2 (2017): 266–75.

77 Sung, in Miguez, Rieger and Sung, *Beyond the Spirit of Empire*, p. 131.

78 Sung, in Miguez, Rieger and Sung, *Beyond the Spirit of Empire*, p. 131.

4

Awesome Weakness and God the Child

The nursing child shall play over the hole of the asp,
and the weaned child shall put its hand on the adder's den.
(Isaiah 11.8)

Is not my word like fire, says the Lord, and like a hammer that
breaks a rock in pieces?
(Jeremiah 23.29)

Holy Anarchy is at hand: decolonizing consciousness

In Chapter 3, we focused on the imperial systems of oppression, particularly manifest in the prevailing economic structures, but also active in racialized relationships, gender and sexuality, dis/ability and age, and the damage we do to the ecosystems of the Earth. It is possible, of course, that not everyone experiences reality in terms of 'systems of oppression'. To some people, this can seem like heightened rhetoric, while life carries on comfortably enough, freely enough, pleasantly enough. I recognize this experience myself, but this is because I am significantly a beneficiary of the status quo. But I also recognize, however fleetingly and partially, the presence of Holy Anarchy in our midst. Even from the edges of my vision, even through the cracks in the glass, even as a whisper often drowned out by louder propaganda, it wakes me up a little. It shakes me open. It alerts me to alternatives that do not serve my interests, at least not as I understand my interests from within the structures that possess me.

These alternative voices, which 'redescribe reality',[1] are deeply embedded throughout the witness of Scripture. The ancient prophet Amos declared words of warning 'two years before the earthquake' (Amos 1.1), signalling the shaking power of what would come:

'The Lord roars' (1.2),
'Seek the Lord and live, or he will break out' (5.6),
'Alas for you who desire the day of the Lord!' (5.18).

And again and again, systems of oppression and exclusion are brought under judgement:

From Micah:
'Your wealthy are full of violence' (6.12);
To Isaiah:
'Ah, you who join house to house, who add field to field, until there is room for no one but you' (5.8);
From Jeremiah:
'Oppression upon oppression, deceit upon deceit!' (9.6);
To Habakkuk:
'Alas for you who get evil gain for your houses, setting your nest on high to be safe from the reach of harm!' (2.9).

Of course, we may be tempted to suggest that these denunciations belong in the past, in their particular contexts – as some exhortations certainly do. But there are too many experiences today that confirm the need for these judgements. Too many places where the poor are exploited, excluded, stigmatized, starved, because of the very systems that prevail, whether legal or illegal. Too many situations where the demand for profit justifies inhumanity. Too many cries from the Earth as humans are caught up in patterns of destruction. Too many groups, communities, peoples who are dehumanized, denied their place at the feast of life, damaged by distorted social relations.

The first thing that Holy Anarchy does, once we begin to attend to this alternative horizon, is to help us see more fully the reality of the world as it is. It makes it possible for us to identify our colonization, and how it impacts asymmetrically on people, relationships, communities, and the planet, with some of us benefiting hugely without realizing the cost to so many. Simultaneously it offers us a glimpse of our decolonization. So Jeremiah's words of hope, originally for Israel, can speak across times and places (31.3–5):

I have loved you with an everlasting love ...
Again I will build you, and you shall be built, O virgin Israel!
Again you shall take your tambourines, and go forth in the dance of
 the merrymakers.
Again you shall plant vineyards on the mountains of Samaria; the
 planters shall plant, and shall enjoy the fruit.

But of course, such a vision of renewal brings forth new conflicts, as one people's liberation can come at the expense of another's, one nation's decolonization can leave another dis/possessed. Which is why Holy Anarchy is best expressed as a solidarity of solidarities, as we come to see how one injustice is entangled with another, how liberation movements need one another, how intersectionality offers us insight into the complexity of the dominating matrix that divides us and 'rules over'.

To be alerted to these connections is to affirm what so many have declared: that no-one is free until all are free; that justice is realized nowhere until it is realized everywhere.[2] It does indeed begin, in seed-sized moments, in movements buried by stronger forces, in childlike adventures that defy the overbearing systems of control. It does indeed begin. And every beginning is real. A real step towards the horizon. An expression of what is anticipated. A surging forth against the walls of the tomb that confine. A joining-in with the dance of the merrymakers.[3] But its realization cannot be complete until the solidarity within one movement connects with the solidarity of another, and another, and another. Until Empire falls, and the angels say, 'Fallen, fallen is Babylon the great!' (Rev. 14.8).

Holy Anarchy, then, appears as an alternative horizon, a crack in the System, beckoning to us. It enables us to see reality as it is, but not all at once, since there are so many layers and dimensions to be revealed – so we will be shaken open, again and again. It enables us to see by illuminating things in the light of the alternative: a vision of our decolonization, where justice and peace kiss each other, where the hungry are fed, the oppressed are set free, those who are downtrodden by the systems of dominion are given room to breathe, to rise, to live life in all its fullness. It enables us to see the limitations of any single solidarity, but without dismissing the rightful 'identity politics' of those whose dignity has been denied; so it does not presume to 'open up' those who need safety and companionship, but rather addresses and subverts the closed fists that have made people vulnerable. It does not romanticize vulnerability, or poverty, or fragility, but it helps us to see how, in the experiences of such things, God's presence reveals the truth of reality: that it is a world of 'archy' being beckoned towards 'an-archy', of a holy kind. God's awesome weakness wreaks holy havoc to make possible a world free from domination.

It exposes us to the colonization of our (un)consciousness, the propaganda that conditions us to see the world in imperial notions of black and white, insider and outsider, civilized and uncivilized, pure and impure; notions that have shaped religion too. It alerts us to the harm done by religious and political Establishments, and opens up alternative paths. For instance: reparation, to address the legacies of entrenched injustices; reconfiguration of our identities as oppressors engage in *metanoia*, repentance, radical reorientation, learning to be newly human, through openness to the reality of others' dehumanization – and thus reconciliation that is not at the expense of justice, but through it.

In other words, Holy Anarchy turns the world upside down; its vision is all-encompassing; its aspiration and anticipation are far-reaching; its capacity to bring about change is unyielding. And yet, and yet it remains an alternative horizon, too rarely witnessed in the real dynamics of everyday life. It may be 'at hand', but more than that is needed. So what is God doing?

The kingdom of chaos: butterflies and children

The thing is, God is an open palm. Perfect truth-in-process. Alert to the complexities, ambiguities and awkwardnesses of reality. But not neutral. It is not merely about receiving reality just as it is. Without question, without concern. It is rather about exposing reality just as it is. Drawing attention to the prevalence of dynamics that differ from its open palm. The widespread power of closed fists. The systems that opt for the rigidity of truth-in-hand. The structures that exploit our internal rigidity-principles, closing us down to one another's realities. In particular, it alerts us to the asymmetrical effects of such structures: the ways in which a few benefit from them at the expense of the many.

Holy Anarchy, the realm or state of affairs that is shaped by virtue of divine truth-in-process, is therefore double-edged. Like an open palm with two sides. The first side is simply generous, towards all-comers. Even towards those who do not attract generosity, because God has room for those who are enemies of one another, even the enemies of such generosity. Such is the extent, the ridiculous and impossible extent, of divine love, that it does not close down even in the face of *archy* – patterns of domination. Even those of us participating in such systems are 'received', held, even somehow loved, not at all because of what we do – but we do not necessarily know what we do. We are caught up in these systems, sometimes unconsciously, sometimes consciously, often in complex circumstances, trying imperfectly to disentangle ourselves while also finding new reasons to remain embedded. And in the face of all of it, despite how it seems to us, God *is* love. Grace is grace, and cannot close itself down.

Were this the only side of the open palm, grace would always trump justice. We would be left with things as they are, and only really the *offer* of an alternative. An alternative in which grace itself would be the defining mark. But this is still very much a good alternative, since grace can change hearts and minds and lives and structures. After all, the perpetual

offer of an open palm can inspire *metanoia* even in the harshest of hearts.
People can change as a result of grace, extended to them when it makes
no sense. It may be rare that grace does change such harsh hearts, but it
can happen and sometimes it does. But that is not the whole story. Grace
and justice need each other. So, there is another side, or another edge.

It is the side that upholds justice. It is the critical edge. While receiving
even the worst that the powers of domination can do, like an open palm,
it also exposes them, for all that they do, and makes possible their subversion and transformation. This is because, although God is perfect
truth-in-process, so seeks to understand reality for all its awkwardness,
contradictions and pain, God is not *only* truth-in-process. God also knows
truth-in-hand. That is to say, God holds firm to certain values, as distinct
from other values. God is God of justice, and of peace, and of healing.
God is love. Steadfast love. Each of these realities can only be articulated and recognized because of truth-in-hand: claims to, and assertions
of, their ultimate worth. This means that God is truth-in-process, the
perpetual graciousness extended in hospitable generosity towards all of
creation, and God is truth-in-hand, values of justice, peace and healing.
In fact, even the claim that God is truth-in-process requires the use of
truth-in-hand, a claim to a particular state of affairs.

This is where language struggles, or at least the metaphor of the open
palm takes us only so far. Of course, as a metaphor, it works *because* it is
not the whole truth: it hooks into a sense in which God 'is' like this, while
playing creatively with a sense in which God 'is not'. And all language
for God has this paradox within it: God is father, God is mother, God is
judge, God is king, God is shepherd, God is midwife, and so on. All play
with an 'is' and an 'is not'. But a reason why we are struggling to capture
the *justice* of God, together with the *grace*, is because of the question of
divine *power* – which will lead us shortly to other metaphors. The difficulty is, though, if God *is* the truth-in-hand of divine justice, then how
does the divine roar against injustice manifest itself? Where is 'the day
of the Lord' that brings upheaval to those who complacently enjoy their
comforts? What does it mean to speak of God as the doer of justice, if
injustice remains on such a scale? It is the same question as above: Holy
Anarchy may be 'at hand', but more than that is needed, so what exactly
is God doing?

The thing is, when we speak of God as *truth-in-hand*, as well as truth-
in-process, it gives an impression of a God who can seize things, take
control, enact change in the world; a God who may be a velvet glove
of grace, but within it is the iron fist of justice. I certainly maintain that
God is both grace and justice, that God holds within the divine life
certain paradoxes in dealing with creation, through which all-comers are

included while simultaneously exposing and subverting the worst that they do – the worst that *we* do. But I also incline towards truth-in-process as the more important image for understanding the divine life, though it is indeed a palm with two sides: openness and criticality. It is more important as an image of the divine life because it holds at bay the view of God as seizing and controlling; but it still leaves us with the question: how, then, does God act?

In terms of the structures of oppression and exclusion, it is vital that God acts by illuminating the reality of things. The image of the open palm acts as a mirror in which we see reality more fully, according to the 'preferential option' of such alertness, which attends especially to those experiences more widely silenced by the systems of domination. Illumination may seem like minimal action, but it is the basis of all that follows. So, even as God's openness receives reality for all its injustice, scandalously including those whom the world would exclude according to one measurement of justice or another, God's critical edge also exposes the *truth* of asymmetric power relations: the domination, exploitation and alienation exacted on people because of imperial structures and dynamics. At one and the same time God loves us and denounces the very systems that cut us off from one another. There is room for us, while there is also judgement on our dominions that give little room for so many. It is, then, a shaking experience, a shaking encounter: to be held in the divine palm is also to be exposed, while for those who have been laid bare by the 'System', they are clothed with mercy. And as for the millions who are complicit while also resistant – that is, a mix within ourselves of entangled and disentangled – the encounter with Holy Anarchy is *metanoia* and embrace; justice and grace; challenge and healing.

All this, from an open palm with two sides. But is it enough? Is it enough that reality is illuminated, that any encounter with Holy Anarchy should shake us open a little, however partially, so making possible new ways of being? Is that all God does – revealing and making things possible?

There are three theological strands that inform this vision, which I aim to hold in creative tension. The first is Shanks's model, in which God is primarily the revealer; God acts through shaking us open.[4] Revelation is about not only recognizing God more directly, but the nature of reality more fully; so when God self-reveals, through the cracks in the world around us, God does not only assert God's presence, but alerts us to the reality of the matrix. And through alerting us to divine life, in solidarity with us, and to the brokenness of the world, God makes possible our desire for, and commitment to, deeper solidarity with one another. Not only with those 'like us', but all-comers, as God is in solidarity with all-comers. *Within* this God, who is open to reality in all its awkwardness, there is the potential for self-change – after all, if it is the changeable aspect *of ourselves* that is inclined to truth-in-process, this must be derived from, or a reflection of, the changeable aspect *of the divine*. So, God's own encounter with reality may lead to change within God. But this is not a question that Shanks pursues as such. His focus is the way in which God's empathetic openness evokes such empathetic openness in us, such that we participate in the deepening and broadening of an ever-greater solidarity.

However, process theology does ask that question about change within the divine. It is a second influence for me. It is, in fact, intrinsic to the divine nature that the open palm, if you like, is the basis for change. God certainly does evoke change in others or, in the language of process theology, *lure* us towards change. Never coercing, never controlling, but persuading by virtue of the divine love towards us that inspires a response. This is significant in terms of the nature of God's power: evoking, luring, *possibilizing*, but not determining, making-happen, even 'doing' as such. More of that shortly.[5] But the depth of God's relationality with all of creation, bound up with every atom and every light particle, means that God is not only evoking change but receiving it within the divine life, such that God is in process along with the cosmos. There are parameters to this, given by process theology's 'dipolar' framing: an absolute and unchanging condition of Love, but a relative and changing dynamic of love-in-practice. So, God cannot change into hate, or into control, or into domination. But God's engagement with a dynamic creation evokes *within God* new ways of engaging lovingly with us. That is to say, the relational depths between God and the cosmos run impossibly deep, such that we are indeed co-workers and co-creators with God, remaking our reality and God.

Incidentally, this is not the same as saying that every process within the natural world is a God-shaped process. God may be present within the depths of life, but not everything that happens is God's will. Far from it. Much that happens is not God's will, which is why Jesus invited us to pray for it: that God's will *be done*. This struggle is because of the nature of God's power, and the risk of divine truth-in-process: unintended consequences can follow even from the good that is evoked. God does not 'control' outcomes, not even where a particular event reflects divine hopes. After all, not only are we as human beings entangled in a complex set of relations, in which we do not have as much control of things as we sometimes like to imagine, but all of nature is an intricate web in which the connections between causes and effects can be all too elusive. God's will may be done and undone simultaneously. Even Holy Anarchy can lead unexpectedly to 'archic' consequences, where people misread or misuse the freedoms it affords, re-presenting faith in the hands of those whose vision is 'pure' truth-in-hand.

In the light of such tensions, evolution is an illuminating test case. Is it as God intends or not? It is a complex question. On the one hand, evolution (by natural selection) reflects the dynamic involvement of God, 'risking' a creation that continues to create itself, leading to such daring diversity and intricate beauty even as a result of the chaos of chance manifest in environmental changes and genetic mutations. It testifies to a God who delights in such striking variety, but who does not control it; potentially evoking in us such delight and knowing ourselves to be just a part of such a rich web of creaturely neighbours. But on the other hand, it is savagely wasteful with millions of lives, all too capricious and cruel, and has led human beings to such distortions as social Darwinism, in which 'survival of the fittest' is misconstrued as a hierarchy of the strong. It is possible that evolution is a *distorted* reflection of the divine will, or that it both is *and* is not what God intended. In any case, it makes no sense to reject it, but neither can it be simply baptized as God-given.[6] Rather, God *could* be intending to enable us to cherish the diversity that evolution has birthed while mitigating the waste it involves. We cannot stop predators claiming their prey, but we can refrain from the destruction of biodiversity.

How exactly the God of process theology relates to particular issues such as evolution is, in certain respects, profoundly unanswerable. The same is the case for any model of God, though within any theological worldview we seem compelled to try to pin things down with a truth-in-hand assertion. However, process theology testifies to the limitations with fixed notions of God. It even allows for its own models to be re-examined. From A. N. Whitehead through to Catherine Keller – who specifically holds process theology together with 'theopoetics', so affirms that God-talk is necessarily creative – it is an approach which maintains that how we view God cannot be finished.[7] We simultaneously say too little and too much. In other words, by its very nature process theology is not 'an end' but a way of holding open new possibilities. The creation of metaphors continues; God is still becoming, as I explore below.

In this quest for ongoing interrogation of God-models, Keller shares a commitment with John Caputo, my third influence. He is working with the postmodern deconstructionist approach of Jacques Derrida.[8] Caputo's theology is a contribution to Radical Theology, whose ancestry includes 'Death of God' theologies such as that of Thomas Althizer. Incidentally, Shanks also finds common cause with the death of false gods,[9] so distinguishes between God and 'God', where the latter is the false Lord God, the projection of our Rigidity-Principle. As we saw in Chapter 3, it is such idolatries that lie at the foundations of God-of-the-crucifiers, justifying violence in the name of religion and Empire in the name of God. For our current purposes, Caputo's approach is focused on two issues, very much related to those matters: whether God is 'being' or 'event', and whether God is strong or weak.[10] These concerns intersect powerfully with Shanks's and Keller's, who also affirm God's power is weak, even if awesomely weak, as I see it – but Caputo offers something distinctive: the 'promise' of the weak God, 'the power of powerlessness … which is a way of making the impossible possible'.[11] That is, it is not only that such a God *possibilizes*, or makes possible, the stuff of Holy Anarchy, by virtue of evoking in us an alertness to and desire for that alternative horizon; it is also that God is the event of 'the possibility of the impossible'; 'the weak force of the "perhaps"'.[12]

God's *possibility* is one way of explaining how Holy Anarchy can be celebrated by a whole host of people, including many who are not theists – an issue we address more explicitly in Chapter 7. After all, what matters most is Holy Anarchy itself – 'your will be done, on earth as in heaven' – not the language we give it, the reasoning behind it, or the imperfect representations of it in any single community. It is about a solidarity of solidarities, and their shakenness towards deeper and broader solidarity. And the primary reason why Caputo steps back from the 'actuality' or 'being' of God is because such things, which he calls 'onto-theology' (where 'ontology' is the concern with *being*), are too easily aligned with the idolatry of divine strength.[13] A powerful God, capable of any action, is not only a moral conundrum in a world where so much transformation is needed but missing, but also the basis for dangerous religion, presuming to act in the name of such a God.

To conceive alternatively of God as 'event', or a 'happening', is to free God from the boundaries of being, opening up different space in which God 'becomes'. It is, of course, elusive. It is, in a sense, beyond words. Unconditional.[14] It is resistant to credal formulation, or at least as creeds tend to be known. It points, or alludes, to something more like an open palm, where not only is God waiting to receive reality, in a spirit of generosity, but reality awaits the becoming of God. It is a mutual openness – and also a mutual criticality, as the 'God'/God who (be)comes may need constant reconstruction in light of the alternative horizon. In other words, any model of God, just like any version of reality, cannot be the whole story; in fact, any such notion that 'this' is God will be at least partially idolatrous, just as any claim that 'I' or 'we' have grasped reality is delusional, as though our truth-in-hand is the very truth of things. Instead, the God who becomes, or is in the event of becoming, is the God who makes possible what structures of oppression would obstruct: the happening of Holy Anarchy!

To use another metaphor that 'captures' this imperfectly, I need to refer fleetingly to Chaos Theory/Complexity Theory, two overlapping theories from within mathematics. At their basic core, they identify how even the smallest input to a complex system can be the instigator of disproportionate change. So Chaos Theory is often characterized as the Butterfly Effect, in the sense that even a butterfly fluttering its wings can logically be the 'cause' of a hurricane-event in another part of the world, because all things are connected intricately, even if unpredictably. Other theologians have identified how this may explain God's involvement in 'chance', in the processes and dynamics of creation and the cosmos as a whole,[15] which relates to our earlier discussion of evolution. But my point here is simply to sit with the metaphor of the butterfly: that this is the very nature of God's activity, an open palm, a state of possibility, only as fragile as a butterfly, yet which has a disproportionate and unpredictable impact within the webs of relations. In other words, God is a chaos-event,[16] the true basis of Holy Anarchy.

The point, within Complexity Theory, is that once a small input begins to effect change, as ripples through the System, there's no going back. The System can never be the same again. Even if the System finds new ways to manifest its control, so the small event may not have changed things for everyone; nonetheless, the small event did indeed give rise to meaningful change. This is why, even if God's power is weak, it is awesomely weak. The event of God's becoming may seem minimal, 'only' illuminating the harshness of reality rather than directly transforming it, but the event can give rise to multiple possibilities – some of them unwanted, because of the risks and unintended consequences of truth-in-process, but some may be the basis of justice, peace and healing.

God as chaos-event, the God of awesome weakness, illuminates reality and critiques it according to the alternative horizon – and, in such happenings, Holy Anarchy, which is at hand, comes closer.[17] Caputo describes it as follows:

> The event that takes place under the name of the kingdom of God is an anarchic field of reversals and displacements. So rather than identifying the highest entity or nominating the supreme governor who everywhere brings order, my anarchic suggestion is to think of the name of God as the name of a disturbance or a holy disarray. That is what I call 'sacred anarchy' … In the kingdom, weak forces play themselves out in paradoxical effects that confound the powers that be, displaying the unsettling shock delivered to the reigning order by the name of God.[18]

And furthermore:

The kingdom of God is a domain in which weakness 'reigns', where speaking of a 'kingdom' is always an irony that mocks sheer strength ... [it is] the provocative and uplifting weakness of God, a sublime weakness that, however weak, should not be underestimated.[19]

Or, in Thomas Jay Oord's terms, this power is neither a matter of omnipotence nor of impotence, but is 'amipotent' – the potency of love.[20] Contrary to those who regard such a model as too weak, as though the power of love is unrecognizable, I would argue that love – or the empathetic openness of divine truth-in-process, or the amipotent nature of awesome weakness – is not ineffectual, or impotent, but is indeed different from the brute force of traditional notions of power. Its potential to effect change is real. But like any kind of power, it comes with risks. Where the risks in traditional models are concerned with its potential misuse or how its non-use leaves us wondering why, the risk in the amipotent model is its apparent fragility, its capacity for unintended consequences, and indeed its failure to effect the desired change. But if the end to which Holy Anarchy orientates us is a realm of non-domination, then the means of pursuing it must also be non-dominating, so the will of awesome weakness cannot be imposed, or even guaranteed; rather, it evokes the possibility, connecting with and inspiring co-workers through whose solidarities such a goal may emerge.

A final metaphor at this point helps to underscore what is happening here: it is the model of childlikeness. As I will consider further in Chapter 5, we are used to conceiving of God in adult human terms, not least, I am sure, because it conveys a certain degree of power, or specifically conjures up an image of power-over. But several biblical motifs point towards the childlikeness of God – or what I call the embodiment of God the Child in Jesus and his relationships. Naming him 'the Son of God', or 'God the Son' incarnate, is saying something about his *childness* in relation to the 'Father/Mother'. So, although he 'grew', physically and in wisdom, he remained a child in relation to 'God the Parent'.

But I am making an additional point. After all, in Mark's Gospel, Jesus says, 'Whoever welcomes one such child in my name welcomes me, and whoever welcomes me welcomes not me but the one who sent me' (9.37). In other words, in a child, presumably any child, welcomed in Christ's name, it is not simply the child or Christ who comes to us, but God; that is not to say that a child 'is' God, but that God comes to us in the childness of a child. Moreover, it is to little children that the kingdom belongs, and it is 'as a little child' that we must receive it and thereby enter it (Mark 10.15).

The chaos-event of God's nature, God's power, God's love, is both like a butterfly, fluttering to effect a hurricane-event far away, and like a child. Like an open palm, or a wild-child, daring, risking, taunting its adversaries to 'bring it on', this awesome weakness is too quickly underestimated, judged to be ineffectual, even as it slips into the cracks in the fortress and makes possible the subversion of such structures of domination.

In Christ, God the Child is embodied, like the firstborn of God's own childlikeness, wrong-footing the systems that expect to face a worthy adversary, a man of war; but here they are: butterflies and children and communities who are used to being belittled, but possibilizing what ought not to be: *Holy Anarchy is at hand!*[21]

A hymn: Compare God's domain

Compare God's domain
with mere mustard seeds:
see how much they change
to shelter and feed.
Praise God who begins
with what's tiny and small:
expansively focused
with love that's for all!

So welcome a child! –
in whom God's revealed.
Attend to the small,
till fractures are healed;
for when no-one's valued
by stature or power,
the world's re-created:
let's welcome that hour!

Receive this new world
which comes in the least –
in those still obscured
like seeds and like yeast.
Receive it like children
who chase what's ahead;
who risk and who question
till everyone's fed.

Come, play the great game
like Christ, God the Child,
re-making the rules
with love that is wild!
Spread branches of nuisance,
for habits must burst!
May adults grow downwards,
the last become first!

Graham Adams (2018)
Suggested tune: *Hanover* – or create a new one

God's becoming: small is beautiful

'The day of small things' (Zech. 4.10) is an elusive image; those who despise it will rejoice! This paradox in itself is not unusual, because it is a twist we find also in the Beatitudes (Matt. 5.2–12, Luke 6.20–26). But the idea of a 'day' of small things is certainly intriguing: imagine a whole day dedicated to, or filled with, or defined by 'small things'. It could be a day when a list of minor tasks is fulfilled, which can feel very satisfying; or, on the other hand, a day full of trivialities, the mundane things that need to be done but which distract from what 'really' matters. Small things can be precious conversations, a new discovery, finding something lost like a treasured coin, or sowing a seed that has the potential to grow into something far greater. From some perspectives, they may be things that are despised – as a world of strength, scale, grandeur, wealth, status, power tends to demean what is already small and apparently weak. But from other perspectives, small things can be the basis of rejoicing: every small act of kindness, each immeasurable memory of a loved one, a fleeting encounter or nugget of wisdom that can give disproportionately more than we might expect. And, of course, the gospel of divine truth-in-process also teaches us to regard despised things as loved by God.

We noted above how God's agency, God's power, may be best understood in terms of smallness: the chaos-events of butterflies, like seeds, like yeast, like childlikeness effecting unexpected transformations. The nursing child who plays at the hole of the asp, the weaned child with their hand over the adder's den; an open hand, risking, venturing, reimagining. So as Jarel Robinson-Brown asks, 'can [the church] become small like its Lord?'[22] Here I develop this a little further.

In reflecting on the Covid-19 pandemic, Jim Perkinson suggests that we have witnessed how 'a dwarf has downed a monster';[23] that is to say, a microscopic virus has humbled the grandeur of imperial civilization –

and we do not even know exactly what a virus is! Perkinson argues that civilization was too 'big', its values were all wrong, and the tiny virus exposed this. He is not implying that God caused or blessed the virus, though even in such a trauma God's solidarity-in-the-midst can shake us open to what otherwise might remain concealed, inviting us to attend to reality and reconfigure our social relations. As Arundhati Roy suggests, the pandemic represents a 'portal' through which we have been invited to step, to a different world,[24] but the evidence suggests we are barely attentive to the portal, let alone venturing through it. But Perkinson is also viewing the dwarf/monster framework as an analogy for God's agency, notably in Jesus: specifically, that Jesus is a 'down-sizer', not a destroyer, exposing and subverting large-scale spiritual power – like the 'strong man' of the temple – which he regards as exploitative, and redistributing its goods for the sake of liberation. God the Child disrupts the System, mocks the Giant, re-wilds wherever False Order claims its territory. God the Child *possibilizes* Holy Anarchy!

Furthermore, in relation to the pandemic, Kuzipa Nalwamba notes how Covid drew attention to society's dependency on those who are especially vulnerable and precarious, as I noted previously – those on the frontline in schools, hospitals, shops, transport, 'exposing themselves to infection' to keep civilization going.[25] In structural terms, they may be 'little people', but their significance, and risk, and collective power, is huge. She cites Ngugi wa Thiong'o who captures the competing forces at work within our lives; that is, over our very bodies: 'Our lives are a battlefield on which is fought a continuous war between the forces that are pledged to confirm our humanity and those determined to dismantle it.'[26] In other words, the Strong may destroy us, but the collective power of awesome weakness is no force to be dismissed. It is truly wild.

However, this is not at all about idealizing smallness or vulnerability. Even if they constitute the very means through which God reveals truth, that does not make them always beautiful. After all, small things can be destructive things too (like viruses, or split atoms), and destructive things can be minimized, as though they are small when they are in fact huge: like racism reframed as 'banter', or barriers to access and participation for people with dis/abilities reframed as 'not enough of a priority to justify the effort or cost'. These instances of belittling real struggles show us that the System likes to control the narrative about how issues are quantified and measured.

Smallness and vulnerability are also sites of rage, grief, despair, hopelessness,[27] which cannot be beautified or whitewashed. In fact, such raw reality demands our attention. Volker Küster cites Miguel de la Torre's theology of hopelessness to remind us that we must not 'passively wait' for Easter Sunday, but must 'struggle for justice' on Holy Saturday, acting in the midst of hopelessness and fuelled by it.[28] In such contexts, as Küster notes, people are forced to navigate and even choose between different kinds of evil, such as whether to risk being infected by Covid or to starve, a reality that pushes back against any attempts to tidy up our sense of smallness, as though clear ethical options are always available in every 'small' moment of decision.[29]

So when Angelica Tostes and Delana Corazza speak of 'finding hope in the midst of chaos', they are clear that this is not about 'the promise of future paradise' but is about 'concrete and touchable things' – where 'the sacred and the profane mix' in the midst of real questions, real actions, however small they are in the face of large-scale challenges.[30] What they celebrate is the Quechua concept of *sumak kawsay* (quality life, or living well), or *buen vivir* (good living), realities that cannot be easily translated, but that draw on the wisdom of ancestral traditions of indigenous cultures in Latin America to affirm 'a community-centric idea of harmony', threatened by imperialism.[31] And the threat is real, heightened by 'Coronashock', which has intensified processes that were already pushing people further into hunger and poverty.[32] In the face of such forces, it is solidarity among the poor that has sustained life – such as the solidarity campaign *Periferia Viva* (Living Periphery).[33] Such actions cannot be romanticized, because they express the struggle for survival, but they must be acknowledged.

So in the face of structures of domination, it is in the wildness of 'small things', pushing against the status quo, that hope may be found and practised: in the midst of vulnerability, chaos, struggle. The System, though, demeans such things, patronizing smallness, impressing on people the inadequacy of what is little. Whether it is the experience of being a minority, from a UK Minority Ethnic background/with a Global Majority Heritage in settings dominated by 'Whiteness', or from LGBTQI communities in an unsafe space; whether it is a matter of the inaccessibility and indifference faced by someone with a dis/ability or a neuro-divergence, experiences of 'smallness' are often unsettling and disempowering. And they are obviously compounded by any intersectionality between different 'minority' experiences. I have written elsewhere about the way in which the System 'measures' people against norms and standards, even if the intention is to quantify how much support they need. Any such world-of-measurement reduces us all to objectified and edited versions of ourselves; but specifically in relation to dis/ability, the effect is to misconstrue 'small' changes in a person's situation as mere tiny steps, whereas the truth, being relational, is that tiny steps can in fact be huge leaps.[34] So it is, too, with the chaos-event of any small act, as embodied in the life of, say, a dis/abled child, or a solidarity campaign on the peripheries: without romanticizing such situations, as though this is always the case or intrinsically beautiful, there dwells the potential for small, wild things to give rise to expansive possibilities.

As in the ministry of God the Child, smallness can be the very locus in which God's abundance is realized. A scattering of seed leads to the day of jubilee (Mark 4.8), and a mere mustard tree becomes a sanctuary for outsiders (4.32). So, if we apply Julian of Norwich's insights to a post-Covid world, as Michael Mawson does, we may contrast the prevailing narrative of scarcity, which detracts from the wealthy's obscene hoarding, with a narrative of abundance: her 'unruly God-talk' opens up the possibility of a reconfigured social world, a vision of the expansive solidarity of God-with-us and of us with one another, not least for those who experience 'actual scarcity and oppression'.[35]

Missional trajectories: signs, foretastes and agents of Holy Anarchy

As indicated in Chapter 3, the mission of God (sometimes known in its Latin form as the *missio Dei*) always occurs in the context of Empire, the Dominion, or Domination System. This all-pervasive system resides in social structures, patterns of interpersonal relationships, notions of race and ethnicity, gender and sexuality, dis/ability and age, religion and our engagement with the Earth. It is a challenge for us to discern it, because we live within it, but Holy Anarchy wakes us to its prevalence, exposes its asymmetrical dynamics, and beckons us to subvert and transform it.

Consequently, we may conceive of mission – our participation with God in the *missio Dei* – as social practice through which we continually discern and seek to fulfil God's 'anarchic' purposes for creation, even under the nose of Empire, as we engage with and work to transform its very structures of oppression, exploitation and exclusion. These purposes are significantly demonstrated in the ministry of Jesus, and in his social embodiment of God the Child, who shows us the awesome weakness of God and its capacity to evoke disproportionate and wild subversions of the System.

Of course, this relies on some assumptions. First, that mission is best understood in terms of the mission of God – that is, that it is first of all God's nature and concern, before it is the church's or mine. God is missional, God has purposes, which can be summarized as Holy Anarchy, the anti-kingdom of heaven-on-earth, the ever deepening and broadening solidarity of the shaken among all creation. As Andrew Kirk puts it:

'[Mission is] when people of faith seek to understand and fulfil God's purposes in the world, as these are demonstrated in the ministry of Jesus Christ.'[36] Even though I argue that Holy Anarchy is demonstrated beyond the ministry of Jesus, and occurs not only when people of faith seek to understand God's purposes, it is nevertheless helpful for those who consciously seek to engage in it to root it first of all in *God's* purposes, not our own. In other words, God has a vision, extended to us through the grace and justice of divine truth-in-process, the divine palm open to reality in all its awkwardness, pain and potential, exposing it for its injustice and brokenness, and alerting us to the alternative horizon, a realm in which life in all its fullness may flourish. As such, it is a vision that incorporates the healing of the nations, justice for all at the feast of life, peace between all peoples, and ecological integrity.

Second, not only are these purposes extended to us as an alternative horizon in our peripheral vision, but God calls us to participate as co-workers, co-creators. And, in Kirk's terms, to understand God's purposes and how Jesus demonstrates them we have the resources of our faith – not least the parables of the alternative empire, the kingdom, or Holy Anarchy. They show us that this alternative realm *is* alternative; it is different from the norms of Empire.

As noted above, we see that it is glimpsed in seeds, mustard seeds, seeds of a wild bush regarded as a bit of a nuisance, and yet when it grows it becomes home to strangers, outsiders, birds of the air. It is like buried treasure, hidden but precious; not a great palace, or impressive city, but underground yet, even so, worthy of all that we can give: a new *oikos* untamed by the fortresses of dominion. It's like yeast, barely visible, imperceptible and yet hugely transformative, mixed in with the dough of everyday life – a chaos-event that grows bread, a feast to break and share. And it's what we receive as children do – that is, those at the bottom of society's pile, the little ones, the least; but also those who play and adventure, those who take risks, those who push at the boundaries, those who haven't yet been socialized fully into the ways of Empire, those who ask, 'why, why, why?', daring to believe an alternative world is possible.

In other words, these parables tell us crucial things for mission: that small things are significant; small acts of kindness, defiance, compassion, justice. They all matter. They are graced by the God of truth-in-process who receives them all and affirms that such small things can effect great change. They tell us, too, that taking risks for a greater cause, playing by different rules, even under the nose of Empire – these are like seeds of an alternative reality. And offering hospitality to birds of the air, strangers and outsiders, even while Empire seeks to impose its borders on others, to exclude and exploit – these are marks of Holy Anarchy in our midst, its solidarity-building capacity, its domination-subversion, however small each act of defiance may be. Here, in any of these things, we begin to see God's purposes and how to fulfil them.

And the church is called to be a sign, a foretaste and an agent of these things,[37] in order to share in growing Holy Anarchy. A sign: discerning Holy Anarchy and helping to direct people towards its manifestations, proclaiming, 'There! That's it!' To do so is to acknowledge that we are not this alternative reality in ourselves, completely. We can never entirely encapsulate it, but even so we can point to it – even pointing to other communities that also partially demonstrate it, being as gracious as an open palm, so we may celebrate wherever it is being realized, thus helping each other to discern it, recognize it, celebrate it, whoever is pursuing it, and whatever name they give it. Because wherever it is, in whoever's name it is built, it is always good news.

But to be a sign, to discern and declare God's alternative empire, is to evangelize and teach with a difference. To evangelize, to witness to God's good news, is to tell the story of our colonization and offer an alternative: the possibility that we may 'come out' of Empire,[38] disentangle ourselves, however gradually and awkwardly. This witness is demonstrated as we build communities committed to undoing the grip of imperial power, in solidarity with any who are alert to the conditioning of Empire. It is not a tribal evangelism, as though cutting people off from the world's diversity or from engagement in the very midst of life; but is anti-tribal, challenging forces that divide to rule. Of course, the call to belong to particular, rather than generic, communities, ones in which all-sorts can find a place of belonging, is part of the good news, since the good news is social. Declaring and demonstrating the good news of ever more catholic, ever wider and deeper solidarity among all-comers, and a solidarity of solidarities, cutting across other loyalties, in confrontation with hierarchies, divisions and exploitation. So, to evangelize, to witness to the grace and justice of divine truth-in-process, is a call to alertness – to affirm God's alternative empire, Holy Anarchy, as a space in which reconciliation between all peoples, at one with the Earth, is possible.

It is also a call for us to be a foretaste of Holy Anarchy, to give people a flavour of this great feast; again not claiming to be the whole thing, but audaciously affirming that we should resemble our vision, even partially. Our relationships, our worship, our care for each other, how we do community with one another, how we make decisions together – these things should be yeast, seeds, treasure, so that when people encounter us they encounter a glimpse of a community that differs from Empire; but gracious enough with itself when it fails. A community seeking to embody Holy Anarchy, however imperfectly.

To be a foretaste, a glimpse of it in our corporate life as churches, is also to celebrate this alternative horizon in our worship – where our desires are reoriented (as we explore further in Chapter 8). Where we learn not to love Empire, but to love God's alternative purposes. Purposes that are religious but also economic, political, ecological. So the priorities of our communities shift, and we attend to the least in our midst, and focus on the big picture around us.

Therefore, it is also calling us to be an agent of this alternative empire, this Holy Anarchy – to work for it, to build partnerships with whoever is pursuing it, furthering the cause of justice, care for creation, the reconciliation of all things, by exposing wherever the System resists such generosity-of-spirit, such rage in the face of injustice, such love in the face of fear, and transforming the dynamics of Empire, right under its nose.

And to be an agent, to work concertedly for this new realm, is to pursue justice in the face of racial injustice, gender injustice, economic injustice; peace in the face of violence; and healing in the face of prejudice and of the exploitation of the Earth. It is to treasure our common home,[39] our great big neighbour, and encourage neighbourliness, and be encouraged by others to be neighbourly, as we aim to become an ever greater, ever deeper, ever broader solidarity of solidarities.

This is what I mean when I speak of mission as social practice, through which we continually discern and seek to fulfil God's purposes for all creation, as we engage with and transform the social practices and structures of Empire. This is the all-encompassing and challenging process of witnessing to and working for Holy Anarchy, beginning with ridiculously small acts which may have disproportionately great effects.

Uncivilized habits: the wild marks of mission

Empire likes religion to be civilized – namely, to be civil to those who it deems to be civilized. Nice and respectable. Well behaved. Playing the apolitical game, so not to rock any boats. Ideally, directing people as individuals to an other-worldly paradise. If possible, specifically justifying Empire itself, whether implicitly as the status quo – even allowing a degree of faith-based charity to soften the struggles for those around the edges – or explicitly taking the side of Empire in face of critical outsiders, mingling God-talk with Empire-talk and blessing prevailing norms.

It is also quite happy for religion to be wholly other – that is, to be uncivilized, to be uncivil to imperial civilization. That way, Empire has a convenient enemy to define itself against. The enemy may imitate Empire, purporting to have its own absolute vision of how things should be, leading to conflict, sometimes violent – so such religious movements should never be romanticized; but their history may be understood as uprisings against Empire, perhaps drawing on distortions of their tradition but in order to expose and confront the delusions of Empire itself. There are movements within all major traditions that testify to this conflict: Christian nationalisms, rising up against border-crossing imperialism that was ironically fuelled by mission-Christianity; militant neo-Islamic jihadism,[40] rising up against the imperial West; specific forms of Jewish Zionism (but not all forms), legitimizing the colonization of Palestine; Hindu nationalism and those Buddhist models that also confront the ongoing legacies of colonialism. In each case, Empire can demonize them as political distortions of true religion, as though religion ought never to be critically political.

There is, though, an alternative which Empire does not appreciate: religion that is civil to the uncivilized. Of course, that may not be its only characteristic, but commitment to solidarity among those demeaned and demonized by the System is an expression of the truth-in-process of divine love: the empathetic openness to those who have been shut out. The exact implications of this are not straightforward; I will consider them further in Chapter 7, but more simply at this point I affirm that to witness to Holy Anarchy is to defy Empire's expectations of civilized religious categories.

It is about being noticeably wild, rather than domesticated. Untamed rather than 'respectable'. For the church, called to be a sign, foretaste and agent of Holy Anarchy, there will always be a degree of wildness in our DNA, even if the impetus for this impertinence is the apparent fragility of an open palm, the awesome weakness of butterfly-sized chaos-events. After all, if we are to expose the structures of oppression, exploitation and exclusion in which we are embedded, we will not always be popular. We will challenge the claims of civilization to be good news, alerting people to the depths of the System's bad news for so many people, even as the System obscures such realities with propaganda.

So the wildness that runs through our missional calling involves the discipline of discernment, drawing on the resources of our faith to help us identify the very structures that do not want to be exposed. The market myths. The scapegoating of the poor and of refugees. The claim that hard work alone will lift people out of poverty. Such lies need exposing, even if this defines us as wild.

It will also be wild to aim to embody a different kind of community. I will address this much more in Part 3, but here I note simply that it is surely impertinent to claim to be a different quality of community, right under the nose of Empire; to claim distinctiveness even as we too are colonized by the same forces. What will set us apart, in alliance with others committed to such solidarity, will be our determination to be with those marginalized by the System, to locate ourselves among such stories and to listen to them, bear them, be changed by them. This is difficult, not only for middle-class churches that may be cut off from such realities, or may view them only through partial lenses, but also for churches in the margins that may themselves feel weary and overwhelmed. But the good news is that to be wild in this way, at one with the stories marginalized and exiled from polite society, can simply begin with being real, being honest, acknowledging the connections among us, the interdependence, the mutual giving and receiving, and of course the pain, represented and heightened through a trauma such as a pandemic, but always present. We can hear and share stories.

Wildness will also affect our readiness for engagement across borders, to those on the edges of Empire, but also other communities which in themselves can feel cut off. To be truly ecumenical, in the sense of fostering a household of life for all, in which conversations can touch on economics, ecology and so much more,[41] and relationships with other faith communities can be fostered. This may be wild, because it could be unsettling for Empire, as it has the potential to build a solidarity of solidarities, cutting across other loyalties but making it possible for smaller groups to build collective power that can effect change.

It may be helpful to relate these developments to the widely valued 'five marks of mission', as noted also in Chapter 2 in relation to ecological care. This can give rise to a reconfiguration of our missional tasks, in light of the challenge to expose and subvert Empire in which we are embedded. As in Chapter 2, I reverse the normal sequence – so first, our task is to discern the damage done by Empire to the integrity of creation, to hear its groans, to act in solidarity with it and with all who are especially at the forefront of its damage, working for its renewal and its freedom from exploitation. Second, this leads us into discernment and subversion of the very social structures that justify, perpetuate and expand patterns of oppression, exploitation and exclusion – systems of domination, in terms of economic class, racialized identities, sexuality and gender, dis/ability, age, religion and culture. And third, while engaging with these systemic challenges we must aim to care for those especially bruised by the System, those struggling in pain, isolation, grief, weariness, as well as in poverty, debt, homelessness, precariousness.

Fourth, as we seek to be an alternative community, we must foster our capacity to discern how we are colonized, teaching one another the skills of alertness and decolonization, growing in faith, hope and love in solidarity with each other, and baptizing people into such solidarity, whether as infants or adults, each with a part to play in witnessing to the grace and justice of God. And fifth, we must witness to the good news of the alternative horizon, the reality that, through all such tasks, is closer at hand, but that comes to us first as gift, as invitation, unconditionally for all people, inspiring us to respond; so we witness to Holy Anarchy that exposes, subverts and transforms the things of Empire, even through the power of chaos-events, the small seeds of childlikeness in our very midst.

In these tasks, the wildness of our mission is expressed and furthered, as we seek to witness to God's mission, Holy Anarchy, close at hand, but often imperceptible; seemingly too small to make a real difference, yet it shakes the very foundations of the System such that the System tries to silence it.

This is the Lamb that roars.

Five marks of anti-imperial mission

1 Hear the groans of creation to discern the damage done to it by the structures and practices of Empire. Expose, subvert and transform these patterns.
2 Hear the cries of the oppressed, exploited and excluded to discern the harm caused by the structures and practices of Empire. Expose, subvert and transform these patterns.
3 Attend to the needs of those bruised by such systems of domination, in all their forms (economic, racial, gendered, sexual, ableist), and to all who are grieving, wearied and unwell.
4 Build community in which we learn together how to decolonize our (un)consciousness and commit to an alternative solidarity that has room for all.
5 Witness to this alternative solidarity in the stories we tell, believing in the good news of Empire's subversion at the hands of God's awesome weakness.

A *hymn: Slaying giants*

We are faced with Goliaths at large in the world:
all the giants deflecting the stones that are hurled;
the injustice persisting in spite of our prayer,
all the systems denying the fruit of our care.

'Let us go,' Jesus says, 'to the other far side' –
to whatever is stranger, from which we might hide:
but this call on our courage engenders a storm;
whether peace comes or not, still our faith must reform.

While such chaos may tempt us to seek out the calm,
to be faithful to God is not always a balm:
for the giants oppressing the weak must be faced;
though our smallness consumes us, our daring is graced.

So in faith let us rise on the waves that are wild,
finding peace in the hope that is shaped like a child;
let us face down the giants dismissing our cheek
as we build what is new with what's laughably weak.

Graham Adams (2021)
Suggested tune: *Stowey* – or create your own
Based on the story of David and Goliath and Mark 4.35–41.

Questions to ponder

1 What helps you to see the world as it really is, the extent of our colonization by systems of domination, while also seeing the presence of an alternative horizon close at hand?
2 I suggest God acts like an open palm, revealing to us the truth of the world, exposing its distortions and, in every butterfly-sized chaos-event, making new things possible. In what ways does this resonate with you or challenge you?
3 What are your experiences of the power of small things?
4 If mission is social practice in which we discern, subvert and transform the things of Empire, in what ways does this overlap with mission as you know it, and in what ways does it not?
5 How could we be wilder in our mission?

Further reading

Jonny Baker and Cathy Ross, *Imagining Mission with John V. Taylor* (London: SCM Press, 2020).

John D. Caputo, *The Weakness of God: A Theology of the Event* (Bloomington, NY: Indiana University Press, 2006).

Jione Havea (ed.), *Doing Theology in the New Normal: Global Perspectives* (London: SCM Press, 2021).

Catherine Keller, 'Process and Chaosmos: The Whiteheadian Fold in the Discourse of Difference', in Catherine Keller and Anne Daniell (eds), *Process and Difference: Between Cosmological and Poststructuralist Postmodernisms* (Albany, NY: State University of New York Press, 2002).

Catherine Keller, *Face of the Deep: A Theology of Becoming* (Abingdon: Routledge, 2003).

Andrew Shanks, *A Neo-Hegelian Theology: The God of Greatest Hospitality* (Farnham: Ashgate, 2014).

Notes

1 Walter Brueggemann, *Redescribing Reality: What We Do when We Read the Bible*, London: SCM Press, 2009.

2 For example, James Cone, *God of the Oppressed* (rev. edn), Maryknoll, NY: Orbis, 1997, p. 135.

3 Dance is a motif for Brian Edgar in the context of the playfulness of life in God's alternative realm, not simply as something in the future, but something that we are invited to demonstrate now: *The God Who Plays: A Playful Approach to Theology and Spirituality*, Eugene, OR: Cascade Books, 2017, pp. 116, 119f. I return to 'dance' in Chapter 8.

4 Andrew Shanks, *God and Modernity: A New and Better Way to Do Theology*, London and New York: Routledge, 2000: 'God as the one who shakes' (p. 15); 'the shaking away of that which conceals' – that is, revelation (p. 36).

5 As we see in John D. Caputo, *The Weakness of God: A Theology of the Event*, Bloomington, IN: Indiana University Press, 2006, p. 91: 'God's power is invocative, provocative, and evocative, seductive and educative, luring and alluring, because it is the power of a call, of a word/Word, of an affirmation or promise.'

6 See, for example, Celia Deane-Drummond, *Christ and Evolution: Wonder and Wisdom*, London: SCM Press, 2009, pp. 24–30.

7 With thanks to a Facebook discussion among a Radical Theology Discussion Forum for helping to illuminate these dynamics, especially the clarificatory insights of Luke B. Higgins, 21 February 2021.

8 See, for example, John D. Caputo, *What Would Jesus Deconstruct? The Good News of Postmodernism for the Church*, Grand Rapids, MI: Baker Academic, 2007.

9 See Andrew Shanks, *Theodicy beyond the Death of 'God': The Persisting Problem of Evil*, London and New York: Routledge, 2018.

10 Caputo, *The Weakness of God*, pp. 2–5, 7.

11 Caputo, *The Weakness of God*, pp. 90, 96.

12 Caputo, *The Weakness of God*, pp. 88, 105.

13 Caputo, *The Weakness of God*, pp. 7–8, 87–8, 90–1.

14 Caputo, *The Weakness of God*, p. 90.

15 See, for example, Sjoerd L. Bonting, *Creation and Double Chaos: Science and Theology in Discussion*, Minneapolis, MN: Augsburg Fortress, 2005.

16 See, for example, Catherine Keller, 'Process and Chaosmos: The Whiteheadian Fold in the Discourse of Difference', in Catherine Keller and Anne Daniell (eds), *Process and Difference: Between Cosmological and Poststructuralist Postmodernisms*, Albany, NY: State University of New York Press, 2002. For her, 'chaos' is 'a boiling ocean of incessant relatedness' (p. 65) and 'the border along which creativity takes place' (p. 66).

17 This approach is also, arguably, an example of what Edgar invites, in terms of *theology* as playfulness: *The God Who Plays*, pp. 60, 71.

18 Caputo, *The Weakness of God*, p. 14.

19 Caputo, *The Weakness of God*, p. 14.

20 Thomas Jay Oord, *Open and Relational Theology: An Introduction to Life-changing Ideas*, Grasmere, ID: SacraSage, 2021, p. 81.

21 Adrian Thatcher also uses the term 'God the Child', but specifically as the basis for the rights of children: see 'Theology and Children: Towards a Theology of Childhood', *Transformation*, vol. 23, no. 4 (October 2006): 194–9, especially 196–7. He suggests, by virtue of the incarnation, 'God the Child represents all children before God'. This could imply that God's receptivity to any of creation's dignity, pain and potential depends on incarnation, whereas for me the chaos-power of God's intrinsic 'childness' exposes all domination and evokes even the smallest events of Holy Anarchy – and, in Christ, this 'childness' is embodied.

22 Jarel Robinson-Brown, *Black, Gay, British, Christian, Queer*, London: SCM Press, 2021, p. 159.

23 James W. Perkinson, 'Coronavirus Cacophony: When the Dwarf Rebukes the Giant', in Jione Havea (ed.), *Doing Theology in the New Normal: Global Perspectives*, London: SCM Press, 2021, p. 228.

24 Arundhati Roy, 'The Pandemic Is a Portal', *Financial Times*, 3 April 2020, https://www.ft.com/content/10d8f5e8-74eb-11ea-95fe-fcd274e920ca (accessed 7 January 2022).

25 Kuzipa Nalwamba, 'Vulnerability: Embodied Resistance During Covid', in Havea (ed.), *Doing Theology in the New Normal*, p. 153.

26 Ngugi wa Thiong'o, *Devil on the Cross*, Portsmouth: Heinemann, 1987, p. 53.

27 See, for example, Calvin L. Warren, 'Black Nihilism and the Politics of Hope', which first appeared in *The New Centennial Review*, vol. 15, no. 1 (Spring 2015), http://www.docplayer.net/48679084-Black-nihilism-and-the-politics-of-hope-calvin-warren.html#show_full_text (accessed 7 January 2022): 'political theologians and black optimists avoid the immediacy of black suffering', p. 30; 'ultimately, we must hope for the end of political hope', p. 32; and Karen Bray, *Grave Attending: A Political Theology for the Unredeemed*, New York: Fordham University Press, 2020, p. 7: 'we might theologically rethink the neoliberal narratives of redemption which keep us chained to our misery, while promising us we will, through them, be happy and free'.

28 Volker Küster, 'Interpretation Against: What if Not Punishment?', in Havea (ed.), *Doing Theology in the New Normal*, p. 125, citing Miguel de la Torre, 'Embracing Hopelessness', lecture, 'The Center for Prophetic Imagination' confer-

ence, 21–22 September 2018, https://www.youtube.com/watch?v=oCoRFMe_vgQ (accessed 7 January 2022).

29 Küster, 'Interpretation Against', pp. 126–7.

30 Angelica Tostes and Delana Corazza, 'Spiritualities in Resistance: Latin-American Social Movements and Solidarity Action', in Havea (ed.), *Doing Theology in the New Normal*, p. 54.

31 Tostes and Corazza, 'Spiritualities in Resistance', p. 55.

32 'Latin America Under CoronaShock: Social Crisis, Neoliberal Failure, and People's Alternative', *Tricontinental*, 7 July 2020 (www.thetricontinental.org/dossier-30-corona-shock-in-latin-america/ (accessed 18 November 2021).

33 Tostes and Corazza, 'Spiritualities in Resistance', pp. 58–9.

34 Graham Adams, 'Glimpses of God's Dis/Abled Domain: Rising Up against Empire in Small Steps/Huge Leaps', in Jione Havea (ed.), *Dissensions and Tenacity: Doing Theology with Nerves*, Lanham, MD: Lexington, 2022 (forthcoming).

35 Michael Mawson, 'Speaking of God: Unruly God-Talk with Julian of Norwich', in Havea (ed.), *Doing Theology in the New Normal*, p. 205.

36 J. Andrew Kirk, *What Is Mission? Theological Explorations*, London: Darton, Longman and Todd, 1991, p. 21.

37 David Bosch, *Transforming Mission: Paradigm Shifts in Theology of Mission*, Maryknoll, NY: Orbis, 1991, p. 374.

38 Wes Howard-Brook, *'Come Out, My People!' God's Call out of Empire in the Bible and Beyond*, Maryknoll, NY: Orbis, 2012.

39 Encyclical Letter *Laudato Si'* of the Holy Father Francis on *Care for Our Common Home*, 24 May 2015, https://www.vatican.va/content/francesco/en/encyclicals/documents/papa-francesco_20150524_enciclica-laudato-si.html (accessed 7 January 2022).

40 Paul Hedges, *Understanding Religion: Theories and Methods for Studying Religiously Diverse Societies*, Oakland, CA: University of California Press, 2021, p. 362.

41 Al Barrett and Ruth Harley, *Being Interrupted: Reimagining the Church's Mission from the Outside, In*, London: SCM Press, 2020, pp. 142ff.

PART 3

Walk Humbly – Embody Community

In Part 2, I explored the first task of the church, according to the evocation of Holy Anarchy – to discern, engage and seek to transform the powers of domination that deny fullness of life. The big vision, we could say, is to subvert these structures, according to the awesome weakness of God. Though it is a big vision, it is demonstrated through the smallness of childlikeness. This implies that the church presumes to be different from the prevailing ways of the world. After all, if we claim to know what is wrong with the world, we should at least offer an alternative. Here in Part 3 I consider what it means for the church to assume such a calling, especially since it is not renowned for the integrity that this calling demands. It often seems no different from the world – in fact, sometimes worse and more damaging. In the light of those versions of Christianity that have justified crusading violence, inquisition by torture, mass enslavement, colonialism and more, surely the church cannot claim the moral high ground. And even where it has dissented from such behaviour, it remains complicit with unnoticed or unexamined systems, its apparently gentler forms acquiescing to insidious forces and frameworks. So what exactly is the nature of this imperfect church, entangled with domination yet purporting to overcome it? How can we better reflect and embody the vision that we claim to pursue?

At the heart of this vocation is the insistence that the church is not *in itself* the alternative reality, but that it seeks to embody it *provisionally*. We are not Holy Anarchy, but we mean to be shaped by it and to grow into it. This requires us to recognize our limitations. But two dangers could flow from this distinction, between the goal and our partial embodiment of it: first, it could be a way of excusing our shortcomings rather too swiftly. That is, it could allow us to say, 'We know we're not as good as our ideals, but that's because we don't have to be; in fact, we never will be' – which is an evasion of responsibility for what we do and for failing to learn. So the church must dare to be a community of self-examination, reflecting critically on its exclusions of so many people and belittling of various concerns. Second, though, this distinction between 'the church as it is now' and 'Holy Anarchy that is not yet' could also be misleading, implying that the ultimate goal of Holy Anarchy is a stable state in which everything is reconciled and resolved. But Holy Anarchy is not like that. In Chapter 2, we considered 'sublation', an unfamiliar word for a subtle truth: each aspect of reality, each voice coming out of experience, each truth-in-hand, is both *preserved* and *overcome* in the dynamic of truth-in-process. What this means is: the 'final' point is not a single point at all, but a way of being, in which the ambiguities, awkwardness and asymmetries of life are addressed through a commitment to deeper solidarity that involves ongoing learning and transformation. This is about being as attentive as possible to the contextual realities of each moment and place, not dismissing or distorting them, but bringing them into further engagement with other voices, questions and hopes. So Holy Anarchy is not a place where things are 'finished'; after all, it is glimpsed here and now, in the cracks and along the borders, opening up new possibilities. Therefore, the church's flawed embodiment of Holy Anarchy is not simply a work in progress; it also points to a central truth about Holy Anarchy: it too is in motion.

Part 3 is therefore concerned with the 'unfinished' and 'unfitting' calling and nature of the church: not a 'settled-state' community that can take its own place or status for granted, but alert to ever new insights and horizons. In Chapter 5, the focus is the Christ-shaped nature of this dynamic, as the relationships of Jesus with others illuminate how the body of Christ may conceive of itself. Chapter 6 develops some of these dimensions particularly with regards to the ways people or experiences would not 'fit' were the assumptions and boundaries of church too settled.

5

Structures of Purity and the Unfinished God

'But to what will I compare this generation? It is like children sitting in the marketplaces and calling to one another, "We played the flute for you, and you did not dance; we wailed, and you did not mourn." For John came neither eating nor drinking, and they say, "He has a demon"; the Son of Man came eating and drinking, and they say, "Look, a glutton and a drunkard, a friend of tax collectors and sinners!" Yet wisdom is vindicated by her deeds.'
(Matthew 11.16–19)

Look, a glutton and a drunkard

It may be apparent by now that this vision of Holy Anarchy that I am pursuing is one in which the ambiguities of life are to be reckoned with and not neatly ironed out.[1] There are ambiguities in our motives, our lack of consistency, the tensions within our religious commitments, but also the ambiguities in the world at large, in the structures around us, which work for good but also do harm; even of course in the violence and beauty of nature. Life can be read in different ways, and when we try to cut out some of these complexities, we deny aspects of truth and thereby silence certain experiences. On the one hand, these ambiguities may be viewed as the creases that give life a certain texture, making us all interesting, and indeed strange, to one another; but, on the other hand, such a view can itself overlook or excuse the very real pain that is part of the picture. After all, sometimes we are impatient with ambiguities, or dismissive of them. When things don't seem to 'fit' with our assumptions or desires, or where a situation can be 'read' in quite different ways, we can find it frustrating and we opt for a version of reality that excludes these alternatives.

Our attraction to truth-in-hand can make us want things sorted, categorized, ordered. But Holy Anarchy – the clue is in the name – is not like that, because any tidying-up tends to be done in the interests of those with power and privilege. (Once again, this is not to 'romanticize' chaos, which in particular forms is obviously deeply harmful especially to people lacking in power. But false order is no less harmful, and chaos, as I am arguing, can be not only a state out of which creative possibilities emerge but also the very subverting of false order, in the interests of those most in need of such change.) Holy Anarchy, then, reverses the priority, away from the control of truth-in-hand and towards the potentiality of truth-in-process: sheer empathetic attentiveness to the multiplicity of life. Domination may bring order, even if it is a false or premature order. But Holy Anarchy allows for the freedom and creativity of life in its fullness. As argued by leading queer theologian Marcella Althaus-Reid, 'God becomes chaos',[2] which is to say that God confronts such systems of order, creating space for 'indecency'.[3]

This notion of 'indecency' can sound very strange to many in the church. It can feel counter-intuitive to what we are often conditioned to have in mind: a community of good order, respectability, high morals, even if we also realize that forgiveness for shortcomings should be among those morals. But an episode like the one in Matthew's Gospel, noted above, draws direct attention to the 'indecency' of Jesus' friendships and challenges us to think both about him and about us as his body. Notice the ambiguities, or tensions, that are part of his story. On the one hand, he recognizes that John was criticized by the religious authorities for being too austere, too ascetic, too purist, apparently refraining from certain kinds of enjoyment and being slurred as a result: 'He has a demon'. On the other hand, Jesus 'the Son of Man' finds himself being called a 'glutton and a drunkard' because he does quite the opposite, eating and drinking with all the 'wrong' people. So the first ambiguity is this tension between purity and impurity, or indeed decency and indecency, as Jesus, also strongly associated with John, represents an emerging movement which holds these things together creatively. He personally leans towards impurity, or indecency, as understood by the authorities, while pointing out their seemingly middle-of-the-road hypocrisy. They criticize the clowns to the left of them, the jokers to the right – but what does it mean to be stuck in the middle with them? Walking a tightrope of caution and judgement, a sense of superiority over the 'radicalism' of John and Jesus.

For Jesus, it is not about holding to the domineering centre-ground, from which people can be pushed out to the margins. No, to be part of his story is to hold the tension between purity and impurity, to reconfigure what they mean rather than resigning ourselves to the fact that such terms and such judgements must be made by the people in the middle with the power. After all, Jesus is not accepting the notions of purity and impurity promoted by the authorities, the religious and political Establishment. For them, the purity of John represents a radicalism that reflects badly on their own status and behaviour, and the impurity of Jesus represents a laxity that defies their authority and points seditiously to a new religio-social order. No wonder they sought to demonize both John and Jesus, to slur their names, to urge people to distance themselves from these provocative leaders. Meanwhile, for Jesus, these neat categories of pure and impure were themselves lies fuelled by the insecurity of the dominators. He instead advocated a new vision of im/purity.

The second ambiguity, then, is in terms of where Jesus locates himself. With tax collectors and sinners. That is, with those 'beyond the pale', 'beyond redemption', those whose lifestyles placed them outside of the covenant. (In first-century Palestine, the category of 'sinners' was not applied to all people, as later Christian tradition would apply it, but was directed at those regarded as the worst of the worst – which was where Jesus located himself.) Jesus, who also proclaimed 'Blessed are the pure in heart', placed himself with those regarded as impure. Why? To show that the presence and purpose of Holy Anarchy unsettles religious assumptions about where to be and with whom to be. His body is with impure bodies. Perhaps this suggests that the very purity of himself and to which he calls us is not a purity of separation, but a purity of engagement and solidarity. This is, as I indicated in Chapter 1, the way in which 'holy' functions in Holy Anarchy too: the holiness of presence *in the midst* of the mess and ambiguity of life.

This is why Jesus compared his generation to children in the marketplaces, who played but others did not dance, or wailed and others did not mourn. Such children want their friends to join in, or anyone to join in, but the game isn't happening; people are ignoring the cues – instead of engagement and solidarity, there is separation and indifference. This is what the religious authorities have conditioned. A world in which people dare not go to the 'wrong' places, be with the 'wrong' people, join in with the 'wrong' games, because any such (mis)adventures will render them impure. Indecent. Unholy. But for Jesus, it would be exactly such joining-in that would reflect the presence of Holy Anarchy at hand. And the effect of such solidarity with the impure was not simply that they may have felt respected, at least more than usual, but that he would have been regarded as indecent and shamed as a result. This is also how the purity code worked in terms of the woman who reached out and merely touched his cloak (Mark 5.27). As a result of her own impure status, it would have been believed that Jesus became impure too – which is precisely why the disciples became nervous; in contrast, Jesus not only praised her defiant initiative, saying, 'Daughter, your faith has made you well', but effectively and publicly showed that he was not worried if people assumed her shame had passed to him. This is the risk of engagement. This is the risk of Holy Anarchy. This is what we are called to be and to do: people who risk upsetting expectations that hold us in a certain place; people who put our holiness at risk through engaging in the 'wrong' kinds of solidarity; people who recognize that life is not best lived when petrified of these ambiguities, but lived in the midst of them, like playful street children.

A hymn: Taking her lead

What a friend we have in Jesus –
Christ, who made two daughters well:
one, enjoying social status,
one who suffered living hell.
On his way to help the leader's,
he felt power seep away:
for the lowly dared to touch him,
though she should have stayed away.

In a culture marked by honour,
bleeding meant she was unclean
and should honour certain boundaries,
rarely heard and barely seen.
But through desperation, yearning,
she defied her given role.
Jesus should have cursed her for it,
but he yearned to make things whole.

What a friend she had in Jesus,
taking on the shame she knew,
then commending her defiance,
and he paused to see it through:
so the other daughter faded
while he let himself be shamed,
but his purpose was to change things,
so the barely-seen were named.

Daughter! Rise like resurrection!
See, the first shall be the last,
and in social re-creation
roles shall be defied, re-cast.
Interrupted by an outcast –
she who took initiative –

Jesus stopped and reimagined:
take her lead that all may live!*

Graham Adams (2018)
Based on Mark 5.22–43, and indebted to insights in Ched Myers, *Binding the Strong Man: A Political Reading of Mark's Story of Jesus* (Maryknoll, NY: Orbis, 1988)
*I regret that this hymn, written for a particular service, still accentuates Jesus' heroism in his willingness to be shamed in solidarity with the unnamed Daughter, rather than foregrounding her own defiant faith, but even if it is too subtle, the sense remains that the under-the-radar woman takes the initiative and Jesus takes his lead from her.

Who do you say that I am? The agency of others

It is important to acknowledge two things at work in what I have outlined so far in this chapter: first, what I call 'social christology', and second, how this opens up for us a vision of what it means to be church. Social christology is simply a way of looking at the person of Jesus, which refuses to view him as an individual in a vacuum. So often, whether unconsciously or because of a particular agenda, Christians regard Jesus' identity as a straightforward 'given', something that just 'is' – this *is* who he is – and all of the data or stories about him are read as though they point to the answer that we already know. That he is God and human wrapped up together. That he was saviour and is alive today. That such an identity was established out of time, and implanted in history for all time. This is who he is. But to do social christology is to believe that, as a fully human being, his identity is not simply given but grows in and through relationships and encounters with others; that he 'becomes' through such a process; and that this means other people contribute to our understanding of who he is. By that, I do not simply mean that other people subsequent to him help us to look back and interpret him, though that is certainly true. I also mean that the people in his immediate context shaped him. He would not be whom he became, *were it not for them*.

So I have argued previously, in *Christ and the Other*, that we should affirm three broad networks of people who contributed to his 'becoming' – those within his own tradition, but whom others might have overlooked or marginalized; those in other traditions, but who were otherwise held at bay because of dynamics within his tradition; and those who were beneath the radar of any such formal traditions, because of their socio-political oppression. All three dynamics apply to us in our locations too. There are examples of all such networks playing their part in his story of engagement and solidarity – and there will be examples for us in ours. What this shows us is two things: that he was more receptive and empathetic than many were, in receiving such contributions to his identity, since he tended to validate what people brought to him – their touch, their faith, their questions, their pain, their longings; all of these shaped the sense in which he 'became' Christ. Also, it shows us that the 'agency of others' matters within Holy Anarchy; it is not a one-way street of grace flowing out to those on the margins, but is a dynamic interaction in which the seemingly pure and the apparently impure give and receive and the categories are reconfigured through the process.

In other words, Holy Anarchy not only messes with assumptions about who is in and who is out, and defies expectations about the nature of purity and impurity. It also shakes up any system's presumption that certain people are the givers and others the receivers. I call this 'mutual humanization':[4] the sense that we are all 'other' to one another in different respects and can contribute to the 'becoming' of one another, but that special attention is to be paid to the contribution of those particularly 'othered', whose experiences bring insight, challenge and change to the table; and as those of us with more privilege learn to be changed, there is a solidarity in which we become more fully human in and through such relationships, not merely as a nice or respectable process but, to coin a term, as an 'upside-downing' of the prevailing Domination System. True an-archy. This is also articulated in terms of the three economies in *Being Interrupted*, so that the church learns not simply to 'count in' nor only to 'give out', but to be interrupted by the gifts and agency of others.[5] Their assets, insights, struggles and gifts help to reshape whom we presume to be. So this is not only about social christology in itself, but about the implications for the church, as we too learn how to be 'pure' not through separation but through engagement and solidarity. We become more deeply im/pure.

It is significant, then, in an episode most clearly concerned with Jesus' 'identity' (Mark 8.27–29), that he does not simply tell them 'the answer'. Rather, he asks them questions – first, 'who do people say that I am?' because he wants to hear other people's answers; he demonstrates empathetic truth-in-process through such willingness to receive the insights of others, which see in him John the Baptist, Elijah or 'one of the prophets'. But then Jesus asks, 'but who do you say that I am?' because he shows an interest in the agency of his friends, for all their faults. And this is an important model for us, as the body of Christ in our own contexts. Can we dare to ask what names others would use of us? Would we be seen as one of the prophets – or perhaps many would not know what language to use? Perhaps we would be seen as people who think they are pure but actually demonstrate such impurity? Maybe the ambiguities there would not be recognized so affirmingly, but rather we would be called hypocrites. Many churches certainly have been. It is not difficult to see why. I will turn to our collective hypocrisy and the need for honesty in Chapter 6. Others, though, may view us as do-gooders, people who try to interfere in the ways of the world, bringing our other-worldliness to issues we do not properly understand. Some say, 'Stay out of politics'; others, 'You are not political enough' – and it will depend on the politics of the people and the politics of the church. For others, we represent danger, since religion is at the root of so much violence, ignorance, prejudice and division. For some, we may be simply irrelevant. Some are interested in Jesus, but not the culture of the church or the metaphysical conundrums of 'God'.[6] So we find ourselves caught up in conflicting ambiguities as we listen to the names used of us.

My point, however, is not to try to capture all of the many names for the church, but to identify the importance of listening as an expression of engagement and solidarity; an expression of what it means to be church. For if we cannot begin with a real quality of listening, how can we presume to act? Listening is uncomfortable: it invites us into a place of vulnerability; it opens us up to all the hurt that has been caused by churches, and this could be overwhelming. But if we profess to be an embodiment of Holy Anarchy and we seek to grow into it, to 'become' it more fully, we must allow meaningful conversation around the gap between our own identity and the Holy Anarchy that we pursue. It cannot be a conversation that we control, because control has no part in Holy Anarchy; and it may be messy, discomfiting, shaking, especially for those of us who sometimes take the reputation and status of the church for granted. But as I shall develop further, at the heart of communities that seek to embody Holy Anarchy, there must be a willingness to engage in deep listening, not only examining ourselves but being open to others' examination of us. A multi-directional conversation in which questions and answers flow from all quarters, as we engage humbly in the desire to be honest, real, im/pure *in the midst* of the mess and ambiguity of life.

Revealed to infants: going nowhere fast

Returning to the image of the child, I am struck too by Jesus' gratitude for God's revelation coming not to those who are 'wise and intelligent' but to 'infants' (Matt. 11.25). It is a striking assertion. One that presumably, as adults, confounds us. How can *infants* testify to a revelation given to them? If it's true that this is the case, is it a *waste* to give it to people who can't proclaim it? I am sure that is the wrong question. It suggests that we imagine revelation must always be communicated; but there are glimpses in scripture of the faltering, even blocked, nature of God's revelation (e.g. Isa. 6.10); a revelation that closes our mouths and does indeed confound us. The sheer prospect of God's revelation coming to those who cannot communicate it is revelatory in itself – *because* it confounds us, those of us who always look for what is to be communicated. It also tells us again about the power of God, not coming through the common-sense of adult presumption ('we are the ones who know how to handle this'), but to those both relatively powerless to act intentionally on what they receive[7] and witnessing to it in ways we do not notice.

I love this, especially as someone grateful to be viewed occasionally as wise and intelligent! I am sidestepped by the revelatory power of God's weakness. It does not come to me in ways I might presume, expect, even demand. Instead, it humbles me. It diverts my attention, not upwards to the heights of power, but downwards, to a fragile infant. One who cannot speak, who cannot walk, who cannot feed themselves.[8] But one who teaches me about life and love. So, too, whenever churches presume *they* are the ones with the role, the capacity, the authority to receive God's truths and testify to them; they are humbled by the confounding nature of the butterfly, the seed, the yeast, the child. It is tempting, of course, to treat 'infants' as purely symbolic – of any people who show a childlike quality in their faith – but I am learning to beware such temptations. After all, when adults assume things about childlikeness, we often focus on those elements of childlikeness that confirm what we want to see: an innocence, a naïve trust, a sense of wonder. Things that adults sometimes yearn to recover in a messy world. Things that reconnect us with seemingly simpler times. And none of those things need be false – they may indeed be found to some degree in many children – but they are certainly not the whole story. And to focus on trust is to imply that faithfulness requires us to accept what certain people tell us; it can reinforce the status quo.

Children may be innocent in some respects, but are also profoundly alert to the brokenness and pain of things – more often than adults appreciate, or want to appreciate. They may be trusting, though it is not a passive trust that simply accepts reality, but an adventurous trust that fuels their risk-taking as they take a leap – while, on the other hand, children can also be understandably suspicious, conditioned by circumstances to be wary of situations or of adults, since adults have been the ones to harm them. Children may well express wonder at the seemingly incomprehensible, but they can also be strong-willed interrogators, demanding 'why?' or 'why not?' in the face of grown-up insecurities and intransigence.

The point is, to affirm childlikeness may not be as gentle on us as we might hope; it confronts us with real challenges too. So we should beware any 'idealized' version of the infant or the child, since childlikeness presents us with vulnerability, sensitivity to the pain of the world, suffering in the midst of adult negligence and cruelty, and the power of the persistent 'why?' question. In these senses, the 'symbolic' child is pertinent to our concern for Holy Anarchy, throwing open the possibility of renewed alertness to the nature of the world in all its awkwardness. As John Hull argues, 'an adult sees a danger where a child sees an exciting fact to arouse curiosity',[9] and surely the church is called to be curious! Adventurous. Risk-taking. Inquisitive and questioning. But at the same time, the turn to the symbolic child should not completely distract us from the actual infant. God reveals these things to infants, not only as symbolic bearers of various sensitivities, showing us how we can be childlike too, but as infants in themselves. The thought that God reveals things to people who cannot articulate them, or go around spreading them, is worth taking seriously. It takes us back to the question of listening, too, because it suggests to us, as the body of 'God the Child', that we should sometimes do less articulation, and less moving around, and more 'receiving' and more 'being'. Not that I am calling us to passivity, sitting back and letting the world happen around us, nor to perpetual navel-gazing. Rather, we should affirm that life in all its fullness is not only something that we may help to share with others, but something that others may certainly help to share with us. The church, as witness to Holy Anarchy and its upside-downing of the world, is called to embody this readiness to receive, not claiming to have all the answers, but recognizing and celebrating what others may give us. This, again, is 'mutual humanization'; 'becoming' more fully who we are called to be, in and through relationship with others.

But I recognize there is a particular element to this that people can find difficult. It has emerged in conversations about Christ as 'God the Child': an uneasiness that, if we view God in such childlike terms, this effectively makes God 'incomplete' – which is, after all, what 'becoming' also implies. If God is still 'becoming' who God is yet to be, this is far more problematic than a church that is in a state of becoming. It can be a problem even for some people's understanding of the church, if they are used to conceiving of church as self-contained, bearer of all the truth that is needed. For others, it is not difficult to affirm that the church is always learning, but this is aided by the reassurance that God is stable, the one from whom we are learning. But if God is also in process, currently 'incomplete', doesn't that make our own condition more precarious?

This relies on an assumption about God the Adult. It implies that if *God the Child* is incomplete, all of our metaphors for God *as an adult* are 'complete'. But where do we get that assumption from? At what age does a person become 'complete'? Why is it that we assume a child is 'incomplete' but an adult is 'complete'? I would argue, actually, that human beings are simultaneously both incomplete and complete, at whatever age. That is to say, we are not 'flawed' simply by being one age or another, with a bit of us 'missing' – so we are not 'incomplete' in those senses – but neither are we static or stable; we change; we grow; we learn; we have a sense of movement towards greater self-awareness – so we are not exactly 'complete' either. An adult is no more complete than a child, but they are different. A child is no more incomplete than an adult, but they are different. A child 'becomes' an adult, but this involves both gain and loss – which is why adults have a sense of wanting to recover certain features of childlikeness.

So when we use these metaphors of 'adult' and 'child' in relation to God, what is happening? As I indicated in Chapter 2, any metaphor involves an interplay of 'is' and 'is not', and so it is with 'adult' and 'child' in relation to the nature of God. One response to this could be to say that the 'incomplete' dimension of human children and adults is the untruth when it comes to God; that God is always 'complete'; that God does not need to learn, grow or change. Yet such convictions are shaped more by Greek philosophies of perfection – the idea that anything perfect must be unchanging, and that since God is perfect, God must be unchanging – whereas scripture, for example, gives us glimpses (however metaphorical) of a God whose mind changes, a God who enters into experiences and adapts through them, a God who cries, feels the pain of others' torment, and does new things. This growing nature of God, a perfect truth-in-process, ever-attentive to the awkwardly diverse, unpredictably dynamic and deeply pained universe, is what gives us, as the church, a foundation in our own provisionality: for we witness to a God in motion, impressing on us (but not imposing on us) the appropriateness of walking humbly with our God. The God who is unfinished.

So it is wholly appropriate, even if confounding, that God should reveal things to infants, those who cannot articulate them but who bear witness to them in their very being, in their cries and laughter, in their evoking in us a greater sense of mutual connectedness. In this spirit, the church should not only embody the Holy Anarchy of the God who grows, but should celebrate such good news through awareness of its beautiful infancy. Struggling to speak. Crying in hunger. Going nowhere fast.

Why have you forsaken me? A space of lament

From the beginning of life to the end of life, we turn to the crucifixion to highlight one particular aspect of the church's calling. It is the task of lament. When Jesus cries out to God, quoting Psalm 22, he gives expression to a profound agony – the sense of abandonment. Of course, this is not at all to avert our gaze from the actual pain of crucifixion itself, which many Christian theologies seem to do: to turn the torture into an abstract transaction, a balancing of the scales of divine justice, or a victorious vanquishing of sin and death. That is not my point, because the torment is real and should be reckoned with, as all torment, terror and torture should be reckoned with. It is our calling not to ignore, spiritualize or distort such realities. In fact, such realities are the basis for lament. It is because of the actuality of suffering that we sense God has abandoned us, an experience which catalyses the cry of lament.

It is part of the church's very nature and calling to help give voice to the discomfiting truth of the widespread experience of abandonment, forsakenness, alienation. The world is broken. To witness to the truth of Holy Anarchy breaking into this broken world is to face up fully to the depths of its despair. While we would prefer to soften the blow to ourselves of attending to the harshness of this reality; while we would rather not face it so squarely; while it seems to be profoundly 'bad news' – to name the many ways in which the world feels abandoned by God – it is an inherent part of what it means to witness to the alternative horizon on the edge of our world. It is not at all that the pain is *necessary* in order for the good news to be genuinely good, but that the seriousness of the bad news must be contended with if the good news is to mean anything.

Attempts to explain suffering are not the crucial thing here. In fact, they all fall short, simply by virtue of purporting to explain the inexplicable. Of course, the approach of Holy Anarchy does include a particular angle on the sheer existence of suffering, but its focus is not to persuade people of God's power, God's love, God's justice, since all such effort risks missing the heart of it: in the face of it all, why does it seem that a God of love abandons us? I could signal that in a dynamic cosmos – in which entropy pulls things towards decay and disintegration – our experiences of pain are part of reality, but that the oppression and injustice that channel these experiences in particular directions are a result of powers of domination, out of God's 'control' (since God does not exercise control), but that God's awesome weakness nevertheless catalyses multiple responses of empathetic neighbourliness. I could argue that God is therefore never absent, but it may *feel* like it because *solidarity in the midst* may not 'make itself known' as such. I could insist that God's power is not the sort of power to ensure certain outcomes,[10] but acts in childlikeness, evoking, inviting, luring, hoping that in small ways the disintegration of life in its fullness may be called out, and an overcoming may emerge. Holy Anarchy is at hand! But while such explanations may offer some help to some people, they can never 'answer' the question – and instead we must find ways of demonstrating solidarity with one another in the midst of 'abandonment', which includes helping to give voice to the cries of lament. This is the cry from the cross, which offers us a model not as an abstraction to signal the virtue of our oneness with others' suffering, but as a cry from the heart. We grieve and we cry.

Identifying ourselves with the crucified, however, runs a certain sort of risk. There is a danger that we, as the church, take on the clothes of victimhood, believing not that we speak in some fragile way for those whose cries have little traction in this world, but that the church in itself is the primary victim, as Christ's body. Of course, there are situations where Christians are persecuted, and this should evoke neighbourliness in us; but our neighbourliness should be evoked, across boundaries, not only where Christians are persecuted, but where any are persecuted, tortured, uprooted from homes through violence or disaster. It is the church's calling to give voice to the cry, in solidarity with others, but also to listen for the cry, from wherever it comes. After all, to identify ourselves with the crucified Christ is not to identify with someone who is part of our tradition; he was a Jew, one of the occupied, so we identify with all who suffer under the occupation of Empire in all its manifestations, all who suffer under powers of domination, patriarchy, racism, economies of exploitation, marginalizations of the 'indecent' and 'impure'; we identify ourselves with those who suffer under Christian imperialism, the sins of the church, including anti-Semitism, Islamophobia and the othering of many religious traditions; we head in a direction towards solidarity with all the cries of those whom we have silenced.

In other words, to lament is to identify not only with the crucified, but also with the crucifiers; to acknowledge where 'our side' has been the persecutor, tormentor, exploiter, abuser. In any case, there are difficulties with viewing the world simply through this binary, either as crucifier or crucified. As I have been trying to show, Holy Anarchy exposes the intersections between different structures of oppression, in which race, gender, sexuality, class, dis/ability can make many of us a mix of dominator and victim – but, at the same time, how those dynamics are understood is rightly in flux. There continue to be genuine differences in power between different sides, but the language of victim has been rightly problematized, as it undermines the agency of the survivors. So, too, the notion of identifying with 'the crucified' is too simplistic, because people may suffer under systems but still actively resist them, raging in solidarity with one another. But some forms of language may help some people, while other language gives resources to others, and different movements work at different paces, sometimes upholding one another, sometimes uncomfortably cutting across one another. The point I am making for our current purposes is that the church plays its part in holding the space in which many people's laments can be heard. Lament against the sins and suffering of the world at large. Lament against the church's own sins. Lament that uses one kind of language, and lament that uses another. So it is a space that does not try to tidy up the multiple conversations, or convert them into one vocabulary or an efficient programme for reform, but which allows for the uncomfortable starting-point: the sheer naming of the cries of abandonment.

It is not an easy task at all. Churches do not find it straightforward to handle emotion. And, as Karen Bray illuminates so powerfully, the *good news* of Christian faith makes us inherently drawn to positive feelings.[11] We do not know what to do with moodiness, mental ill-health, and the many uncomfortable feelings brought to the surface when we start to address, for instance, systematic racism – the shame, the fragility, the denial of our own power. This is not just a Christian problem; the nature of the globalized economy conditions us to be upbeat, expecting solutions, being drawn to efficient use of time and energy to make an impact; the dehumanizing 'functional rationality of the market' that measures our usefulness as productivity machines. But what of the many people who cannot be 'productive'? Or not in those terms. The very structures of our world work against us lamenting, even when it is so necessary. For example, churches emerging out of the pandemic have often grasped at ways forward, reviving solutions to our new normal, without necessarily lamenting all that has been lost. But there is so much to process, so much hurt to digest. And there can be this tendency to reach for the practical steps, to move on from the grief, to 'get over' a loss, without really attending to the feelings of abandonment, the cry of lament.[12]

But it is a vital task: not only to be the childlike community, recognizing its dependency on others, daring to be adventurous, being curious, inquisitive and questioning, because at one level much of that is about a certain sort of positive energy. The church witnesses to Holy Anarchy, and embodies it however partially, by also lamenting; reckoning more fully with the painful ambiguities of loss and potential, abandonment and integration, grief and hope. It is good news not simply to lean one way, towards the positive, but to be a community that enables healthy holding of the negative, allowing it to be voiced, acknowledged, taken seriously. It is good news, it is Holy Anarchy, to pause with the sense of abandonment rather than trying to fix it hastily, thoughtlessly. We are not only 'Easter people in a Good Friday world', opening up the possibility of renewed neighbourliness in the midst of structures that close it down violently; we are also 'Good Friday people in an Easter world', in solidarity with people's pain in the midst of inclinations to reach impatiently for happy endings, where agony is wilfully disowned. In fact, it is good news, in a world of so much indifference, to be a community that attends properly to despair.

What is written in the law? Interpreting scripture 'openly'

So far in this chapter, I have been offering a range of pointers towards the life of the church as an embodiment of Holy Anarchy. I have focused on ways of being, the sorts of habits we might cultivate with one another: alertness to pain, lamenting in solidarity, recognition of our dependency on others, our incompleteness, our need to be humble, our curiosity, inquisitiveness, questioning, our sense of adventure while acknowledging that we go nowhere fast. These are dispositions or features of a collective life that witness to the anarchic nature of God's alternative horizon, which does not tidy up the ambiguities of the world, but confronts the systems of domination and oppression.

But, I wonder, how might we think together about these habits? How might we resource one another to grow in them? It is one thing to identify them as significant signs of Holy Anarchy at hand, but how do we know that, and how do we keep unearthing what they might mean for us? In this section, I offer an approach to scripture to help resource the understanding and development of the habits of Holy Anarchy. I have written a little about this approach elsewhere,[13] but here I seek to direct the argument towards the cultivation of such habits.

The basic argument is this. Christians are often book-ish people, in the specific sense that we regard the Bible, a library of books, as the supreme authority for identifying how God is speaking with us. We mean very different things by this, with some adopting a 'literal' understanding of the words on the page, as the only way in which the words are true. But that relatively recent approach (a modernist invention) bears little in common with the approaches of the early interpreters or the many ways in which the Bible is read contextually now – that is, recognizing we bring lenses to it when we interpret it, lenses shaped in particular contexts that mean that we see certain things but not others. So to engage best with scripture is to recognize that no single interpretation is the whole truth; we as the body of Christ need the whole community of witnesses to help us listen for God's word through the conversation. However, it is not just that different interpreters give rise to different insights, each with truth to reveal to us, but that scripture itself is viewed as a multiplicity of voices – not so much a choir singing in harmony, but a cacophony cutting across itself. The community of interpreters helps us to navigate through that cacophony, to discern the strands of truth that are to be given more weight.

This is the issue. We are all selective with scripture, even those who say they regard it all as literally true. (After all, they give more weight to certain verses that lend themselves to such an approach, and less weight to other verses that challenge their ideology, their politics, their adherence to systems of domination. Literalism, for example, tends not to take so literally the instruction to 'sell all your possessions and give the money to the poor'.) But what is the basis for any of our selections? To answer this, from the perspective of Holy Anarchy, I must first establish that to be selective does not mean other parts of the Bible are edited out, overlooked, or rejected. Rather, it means that, looking through a consciously selective lens, with its own assumptions about scripture, we seek to *understand* what is going on in the 'other' voices and interpretations, since they are part of the awkwardness of the whole of reality, but we do not at all silence them. So the approach inspired by Holy Anarchy is to accentuate those voices within scripture that affirm the priority of truth-in-process, the empathetic neighbourliness that opens us up to others' experiences, pain and potential: the many voices in scripture that advocate love, for neighbour and for enemy; love and justice, for those oppressed and marginalized; love and mercy, for those struggling to fit in or who miss the mark. The voices of generosity, hospitality, compassion. The voices confronting systems of closure and cruelty. The voices in solidarity with the silent. On the other hand, there are contrasting voices, attached to a version of faith prioritizing certain forms of truth-in-hand, that would close us down to otherness – whether religious otherness or the experiences of those located somewhere else in the systems of domination. These contrasting voices are not ignored, but rather we seek to understand what experiences have given rise to them. What forces at work in the world cause religious communities to advocate wall-building, practices of separation, a purifying of devotion, and an emphasis on specific forms of belief?

Through this single question, asking whether a particular story or episode generates openness in us – openness towards our neighbours, including the neighbour of the Earth – we seek to discern the revealed voice of God in scripture. It is not that God is silent where scripture calls for closed-ness; rather, God is calling us into critical dialogue, to help us examine where our systems continue to evoke the call for unneighbourliness. But who says this single question can guide our reading of all scripture? Surely such a narrowing of the options is presumptuous and supplants the possibility of God's surprise. First, this approach is itself derived from scripture, the emphasis on 'the kingdom of God' (Holy Anarchy) breaking into a world of disintegration, injustice, suffering and despair. Where scripture breaks out as good news in defiance of powers and principalities, it is because of this emphasis on love, justice, mercy. Of course this is selective; of course this is a tidying-up of so many interweaving strands; of course this is imperfect but, first, it comes out of scripture itself, since scripture interrogates itself and encourages us to give more weight to some threads than others.

Second, this approach witnesses to a truth about scripture as embedded in the real world: the Bible (like all sacred texts) belongs to the human world in which we experience this 'civil war'[14] within ourselves, between the impulse towards truth-in-process and the inclination towards truth-in-hand, between empathetic openness and wary closed-ness. This tension does not only live in us psychologically, or in the political systems of our world, but in our texts, including sacred texts; they are true because they witness to this reality. Even where good religious people seek to respond faithfully to the same God, and the same events through which God seems to speak, they reach starkly different conclusions, not only in those communities out of which scripture emerged, but in the communities that continue to interpret scripture. We are torn people, not just now, but back then, and our text reflects this faithfully. Ambiguously. Awkwardly. Asymmetrically, even, because the voices advocating openness are not necessarily in the ascendency; sometimes they come from the edges of scripture, in the hidden transcripts of occupied people. That is to say, sometimes this approach to scripture is not the most obvious, because the authors themselves had to disguise it, since authorities were wary of seditious messages – messages beckoning people to live differently from the ways of the world. Now of course, as we have explored before, different religious groups each claim to dissent from the ways of the world, but focus on very different aspects of culture. And different groups align themselves with a different 'persecuted minority'. But what I am talking about here is the anti-imperial impulse, exposing and denouncing systems of oppression, but often in subtle ways – this comes through the insights of postcolonial interpreters who know what it means to live under oppression, or from women who know the struggle of life under patriarchy, or queer people who resist the binaries and 'purities' of the prevailing order, or from the Earth, denouncing its exploitation. Scripture itself encourages us to attend to the voices in its margins, between its lines; the unheard.

But third, even if this approach *claims* to stand with the multiple experiences and voices that have so often been silenced by religious and political power, is it not really just another version of White liberal bias? The answer to this is critical: it is an approach that is focused on *receptivity* to voices that do not fit with any prevailing system. Where White conservative voices prevail, it will certainly allow for more liberal voices, those alert to ambiguity, those with questions to ask, those who push against systems of control. But where it is White people in themselves who prevail, and their interpretations, this approach gives priority to experiences that challenge such privilege; it is open to the voices within scripture that enable this, however uncomfortably, and to the global community of interpreters who throw new light on the seemingly immovable dynamics of the world. It is a model that is meant to create the space in which 'interpretive hosts' are subject to critiques from those who feel like 'interpretive guests', those who feel like they are entering into someone else's space. But, more importantly, it is a model that seeks to disrupt assumptions about who is the host; the dynamics of power are interrupted; the 'normal' or taken-for-granted interpretations are humbled; the agency of those hungry for liberation and justice is taken seriously. And in any case, this spirit of multiple voices is not some European invention, though it is legitimate to acknowledge where Europeans have fostered it; but it is also very much a spirit springing out of many traditions, with allies and resources from many corners of the world. First Nation traditions, indigenous traditions, Asian, African, Dalit and Minjung – communities of interpretation in many locations give rise to the insight that power distorts how we see and how we relate, illuminating alternative paths before us.

I will come to the interreligious dimension of Holy Anarchy in Chapter 7, but here, in relation to the Christian scriptures, it is worth noting that an an-archic approach to scripture acknowledges that the Bible does not exhaust scripture. It would, after all, be a system of domination to superimpose the Bible on other traditions; but, equally, it is possible and appropriate to say that each scripture opens up reality differently – with distinct gifts, distinct insights, but also distinct areas of weakness with lessons to be learned from others. At the heart of biblical weakness is its alignment with a history of oppression, used by the oppressors to justify and deepen such suffering. It may well have a potent capacity to expose and subvert such alignments, but its legacy must nevertheless be reckoned with. This is also part of what it means to engage with scripture in terms of openness/closed-ness: are we open to see how it has been used to inculcate a spirit of closed-ness in those who honour it, at the expense of those who honour other texts?

The purpose in this discussion has been to uncover how the Bible may generate in us certain habits. First, such an approach helps us to appreciate the multiplicity of voices within scripture itself and in human community, a multiplicity that cannot be tidied up but must be engaged with constructively. This includes attending to the reality of voices that we find uncomfortable. So to be church, embodying Holy Anarchy, is to live healthily with diversity, without trying to deny the nature of the differences, demonize dissenting voices, or impose any uniformity. It is a community of deep conversation. (We return to this in Chapter 6.) Second, it draws our attention to the civil war within us – the tensions we live with when trying to make sense of the world and its interweaving truths. None of us is one-sided; none of us is simply good or bad, neighbourly or unneighbourly. So we should not idealize or demonize one another, but allow scripture to read us as we read scripture – and to do this in community is to learn to create safe space for one another and for those who feel less safe. A hard task, engaging our emotions and vulnerabilities, our need for good news and to lament. So, third, this approach encourages us to face up to the anti-imperial impulse of Holy Anarchy, which may sometimes be our ally and sometimes our judge, sometimes comforting 'our side' (however that may be understood) but often opening us up across borders to deeper solidarity with 'others', those voices from the edges of scripture or silenced by our tradition that have powerful insights for us to receive, which confront our complicity with injustice, and beckon us to new futures.

This is what scripture makes possible.

A hymn: Christ speak to me

Christ, speak to me, that I may speak
in living echoes of your word:
to speak the truth to powers-that-be,
until the song of freedom's heard.

Christ, stir in us the will to hear
deafening silence hushed at last,
to listen more attentively
to cries of pain that have not passed.

Christ, silence us if we shut down
others with stories they must tell;
so help us be communities
which learn to wait and listen well.

Christ, whisper words to reassure
we can bring questions, rage and pain
to you, receiving all with grace,
so teaching us to do the same.

Christ, speak through how we live and act,
through how we listen openly;
and where this voice is drowned by noise,
give signs that truth shall set us free.

Graham Adams (2021)
Suggested tune: *Fulda* – or create one
Inspired by Mark 1.21–28, and Lauryn Hill's song 'Black Rage' (2014) which
names the prevailing 'deafening silence' as one cause of black rage.

The shaken way, truth and life: *Ephphatha!*

What might this approach to scripture look like in a particular example?
In what follows, I bring two texts into dialogue, one that celebrates openness and one that at least tends to be used as though it defends a certain
sort of closure.

In Mark 7.32–37, in his encounter with a man who is unable to hear
or speak, Jesus proclaims, '*Ephphatha!*', meaning 'Be opened!' Since
individuals are not only individuals, but embedded in networks of relationships, so it is appropriate to assume Jesus' words are directed not
only at this one man. They are words of healing directed at a community, but specifically in a context in which people are conditioned not to
'hear' alternative voices and not to 'speak' alternative truths. It is a community of closure, an environment in which the powers of domination
inhibit such free and creative engagement and solidarity with divergent
experiences. In other words, it is not simply the man's condition that is
in question; it is the collective condition of the community – a condition that keeps this man in silence. To both, Jesus declares, 'Be opened!'
Deeper listening is called forth, but so too is honest speech, coming out of
situations of oppression, whether as cries of lament or longings for new
possibilities, evoking the transformative dynamics of mutual humanization. This is healing. Salvation.

To 'be opened' is to embrace the seed of an alternative horizon, emerging at the edges of the community, and confronting the forces that would
close us down to our neighbours. It is a shaking experience, especially for
those who enjoy the benefits of closure, whereas for those who are shut

down it is an open palm making all sorts of connections possible, in the cause of Holy Anarchy, a new world.

How does this relate to John 14.6? This is a verse widely connected with interreligious questions, to which we return in Chapter 7, but its relevance here is as an example of a statement apparently emphasizing the distinctiveness of Christian identity. In it, Jesus declares, 'I am the way, the truth and the life. No one comes to the Father except through me.' It seems very straightforward, presenting Jesus as the sole route to God as Father or the unique entry-point. The implication is that those who believe in other people or things cannot reach God. A clear distinction. A basis for the exceptional identity of Christian faith. A mark of legitimacy for the church's boundaries. The foundation for closure. After all, it's not as though people are unable to reach God – but they need to change their minds, turning away from false idols and discovering the one Way, Truth and Life.

But is it so clear and unambiguous, especially if we put it side by side with *ephphatha*? It may not be obvious that these texts should speak to each other, because *ephphatha* does not seem to address the question of the borders of Christian identity or questions of salvation as such. Even if they can speak to each other, why should it be that *ephphatha* impacts on how we read John 14.6? It could be the reverse. But I am working with the particular presumption that the gospel opens us up. This is not at all to say that the presumption is closed to being reconfigured – because the dialogue between any two texts can always open up surprising questions, unexpected wisdom, new possibilities. That is the point, but I am especially interested to see whether *ephphatha* can shed new light on John 14.6. After all, we need saving from the very powers that would close us down to deeper neighbourliness.[15]

Some people may be surprised that these perspectives can coexist in the same tradition or community – one apparently calling for faithfulness to the uniqueness of Jesus, one potentially for deeper openness, so that unheard voices may emerge. This raises interesting questions about Christian identity. If there is a gospel-shaped presumption that we are being opened up to deeper neighbourliness, what are we to make of John 14.6? It is possible, though, that through following Jesus as the way, truth and life, we will exhibit the greatest possible neighbourliness, including to those who do not belong. It may cause us to feel that the best way to inspire people to follow Jesus the Way is to reflect the awesome love that we know in Jesus, while maintaining that he alone is the way to the Father. This is possible.

But if Jesus is one who beckons us to 'be opened', is it possible that this means *not only* 'be opened to me' *but also* 'be opened to otherness'?

That he invites us to be attentive to whatever is outside of us, whatever is strange to us? That he reveals to us a horizon at which the whole of life is glimpsed differently, because it illuminates experiences, stories and potential which are otherwise silenced and shut down? Is it possible, in fact, that to understand him as the way, the truth and the life is to see in him what it means for God to shake us open to the greatest possible graciousness – which cannot be confined by belief-systems? And then we may notice, in the details of John 14.6, that 'coming to the Father' is not conditional on the basis of particular truths concerned with Jesus' life and death; there is nothing there about believing particular truths-in-hand, like the incarnation, or the atonement, or the resurrection, but simply that he *is* the one through whom people encounter the Father.

The truth could be this: that this way, this truth, this life, which may be embodied falteringly, imperfectly, in the life of the church, Christ's body, is the very spirit of shakenness, the anarchic power of God in the world. It is alertness to the unfinished God – the God who keeps doing new things, quietly, under the radar of powers of domination; who keeps risking truth as on an open palm, but through such a way that the connections between us are illuminated. The God who even enters into death at the hands of the powers, in solidarity with all who suffer at such hands, but opens up life that overcomes, life that is unfinished, life that shatters the boundaries between the false order of this world and the Holy Anarchy that is at hand. For Jesus to be the way, the truth and the life is for him to open up for us the way of openness, wherever systems would close us down, including in Christian faith.

Yet even as I make these claims, I recognize the tension remains, because of the apparently definitive boundary asserted in 14.6: 'no one comes … except through me'. But the tension in the biblical witness; the tension in Christian faith; the tension in the life of the church – they are not surprising, because they reflect our need for the boundaries of truth-in-hand together with the yearning for greater openness, the spirit of shakenness.[16] Perhaps the community of 'John', author of the fourth Gospel, especially needed such reassuring clarity. Perhaps their anxiety, in face of religious and political uncertainties, meant they longed to be affirmed in the distinctiveness of their commitment to Christ. This is wholly understandable, and the spirit of *ephphatha* opens us to be empathetic towards such longings, to hold together the authority of God in Christ with the generosity-of-spirit of God in Christ.

The intersection of these texts represents an example to us of the vision of divine love, its expansive truth-in-process, being hosted by the truth-in-hand of a community under pressure. This can comfort us, too, that even in the contexts of our own limitations and anxieties, even when we are in need of the reassurance of authority and clarity in a world of overwhelming uncertainty, whenever we expect others to fit in with our truth-in-hand, there is nevertheless the possibility of our witnessing to and sustaining the grander vision. We may be inclined to focus on 'no one' as though its meaning clearly closes things down, even as another impulse is at work, the way, truth and life of *ephphatha* – the expansive way of Christlike hospitality, the unfinished truth of divine receptivity, the abundant life in which all may participate.

The tension may not be neatly resolved. Just as we are a community of lament and of hope, daring to be in the midst of im/purities while affirming the agency of others, so too it can be possible to be faithful to Jesus, demonstrating that this involves 'being opened': to other parts of the church, other forms of Christian identity, and beyond, as a sign of our unfinished embodiment of Holy Anarchy. In fact, the edges may become the new centre,[17] as our opening-up launches us into an ever new future, becoming an ever new people.[18] Such is the movement of the unfinished God.

A hymn: Great Wisdom

Great Wisdom, calling us to notice
how you're at work throughout this Earth,
help us to gather round your table
all for the feast you brought to birth:

Great Wisdom, leading into all truth
including echoes we avoid,
help us embrace what still may stretch us:
those silenced voices from the void.

Great Wisdom, tearing down our high walls –
in love for all, so crucified –
help us to see you in all neighbours,
including those we can't abide.

Great Wisdom, healing all division,
inviting us to join with you,
help us expand our partial vision
until your reign makes all things new.

Graham Adams (2019)
Suggested tune: *Spiritus Vitae* – or create another one

Questions to ponder

1 In what ways may churches be called to deeper engagement and solidarity in the midst of situations of 'impurity'? And through such encounters with those who are 'othered', how may we become more fully human and more fully who we are called to be?

2 With regards to any of the following features of infancy/childlikeness and what they may mean for our embodying Holy Anarchy, can you identify ways in which churches could demonstrate them?
   - walking humbly through recognition of our incomplete grasp of truth
   - receiving God's revelation but being unable to articulate it clearly
   - going nowhere fast
   - being adventurous and risk-taking
   - being curious, inquisitive and questioning
   - appreciating our dependency on the gifts of others
   - being alert to the brokenness of the world

3 How might the church give voice to lament and create space in which abandonment, rage and despair can be acknowledged?

4 I suggested that scripture is a struggle between different voices – notably, those that open us up empathetically to greater neighbourliness and those that close us down. Can you think of examples of this struggle – and what difference might it make for 'ephphatha' (being opened) to have the upper hand?

Further reading

Graham Adams, *Christ and the Other: In Dialogue with Hick and Newbigin* (Farnham: Ashgate, 2010).

Graham Adams, '*Ephphatha!* – DARE to Be Opened: Scripture, Its Civil War and Shakenness', in Jione Havea (ed.), *Scripture and Resistance* (Washington DC: Rowman & Littlefield, 2019).

Karen Bray, *Grave Attending: A Political Theology for the Unredeemed* (New York: Fordham University Press, 2020).

John M. Hull, *What Prevents Christian Adults from Learning?* (London: SCM Press, 2012).

Janet Lees, *Word of Mouth: Using the Remembered Bible for Building Community* (Glasgow: Wild Goose, 2007).

Ched Myers, *Binding the Strong Man: A Political Reading of Mark's Story of Jesus* (Maryknoll, NY: Orbis, 1988).

Ann Richards and Peter Privett, *Through the Eyes of a Child: New Insights in Theology from a Child's Perspective* (London: Church House Publishing, 2018).

Notes

1 See Andrew Shanks, *Hegel and Religious Faith: Divided Brain, Atoning Spirit*, London and New York: Bloomsbury T&T Clark, 2011, p. 12, regarding engagement with ambiguities.

2 Marcella Althaus-Reid, *Indecent Theology: Theological Perversions in Sex, Gender and Politics*, London: Routledge, 2000, p. 92.

3 Althaus-Reid, *Indecent Theology*, p. 92.

4 Graham Adams, *Christ and the Other: In Dialogue with Hick and Newbigin*, Farnham: Ashgate, 2010, p. 3.

5 Al Barrett and Ruth Harley, *Being Interrupted: Reimagining the Church's Mission from the Outside, In*, London: SCM Press, 2020, pp. 128–31.

6 See e.g. https://www.nonreligionproject.ca/wp-content/uploads/2020/03/UK-Scoping-Report-Final.pdf – or https://www.abc.net.au/news/2021-10-24/religion-humans-are-hardwired-for-religious-spiritual-belief/100556060 (accessed 4 January 2022).

7 In Barrett and Harley, *Being Interrupted*, p. 114. Al and Ruth explain that children are often not 'productive'; the kin-dom may therefore not be about our own 'agency', but instead 'receiving' it in a world that thinks it's all about what we *do*.

8 Brian Edgar, *The God Who Plays: A Playful Approach to Theology and Spirituality*, Eugene, OR: Cascade Books, 2017, pp. 20ff.: Edgar emphasizes that to be like children is to be 'reliant', affirming the significance of grace rather than our own agency. But there is also a risk of reducing childlikeness to certain features, including reliance, as where Edgar notes several adult tendencies ('to examine life, to reflect on it and compare, assess and judge it') and asserts that children 'exhibit none of these' (p. 22). This is why 'play', for instance, to which we turn in Chapter 6, is significant, which Edgar celebrates.

9 John M. Hull, *What Prevents Christian Adults from Learning?*, London: SCM Press, 2012, p. 9.

10 See Jacques Ellul, trans. Geoffrey W. Bromiley, *Anarchy and Christianity*, Eugene, OR: Wipf and Stock, 1991, p. 37; he disputes notions of God's providence.

11 Karen Bray, *Grave Attending: A Political Theology for the Unredeemed*, New York: Fordham University Press, 2020, pp. 3–4.

12 See, for example, John Holdsworth, *Honest Sadness: Lament in a Pandemic Age*, Durham, NC: Sacristy Press, 2021.

13 Graham Adams, 'Ephphatha! DARE to Be Opened: Scripture, Its Civil War and Shakenness', in Jione Havea (ed.), *Scripture and Resistance*, Washington DC: Rowman & Littlefield, 2019.

14 Andrew Shanks, *A Neo-Hegelian Theology: The God of Greatest Hospitality*, Farnham: Ashgate, 2014, p. 112.

15 Shanks, *A Neo-Hegelian Theology*, p. 38.

16 In *Fragile Identities: Towards a Theology of Interreligious Hospitality*, Amsterdam and New York: Rodopi, 2011, Marianne Moyaert speaks of an appropriate 'restlessness and unease' in the tension between openness and closedness (p. 279).

17 Barrett and Harley, *Being Interrupted*, p. 165.

18 Richard Bauckham, *Bible and Mission: Christian Witness in a Postmodern World*, Grand Rapids, MI: Baker Academic, 2003, pp. 13–15.

6

Awkward Community and the Unfitting God

... so marred was his appearance, beyond human semblance,
and his form beyond that of mortals ...
(Isaiah 52.14)

Christ's awkward body

You may have noticed that some Christians tend to read the 'Old Testament' as though it is about Jesus. They identify in its pages a whole manner of ways in which he is present there, as the subject of what is being said. This frustrates me and I try not to do it. It is the wrong way round. Instead of the Old Testament being about Jesus, it is the text that shapes Jesus. Rather than his being present within its pages, its pages are present within him. After all, *before* it was ever the Old Testament, part of Christian scripture, it was the Hebrew Bible – and, crucially, it still is. Christians should therefore engage with it with some caution, as respectfully as possible, as the scripture of Jewish tradition, which 'we' have adopted and often misused. It is scripture that informs and inspires the life of Jesus the Jew, but that should not be read as a predictor of his ministry or straightforward bearer of Christian assumptions. In fact, to the extent that there is a single body of ideas called 'Christian assumptions', Hebrew scripture prompts at least as many questions in the face of them as confirmations. (I return to this in the next chapter, in the context of engagement with 'strangeness'.)

This difficulty comes into focus with regard to the song of the Suffering Servant in Isaiah (chapters 52 and 53). It is often read as though it is quite simply *about* Jesus, whereas its original landscape is often viewed as Israel's own servanthood. This caution is important, because it reminds us as Christians that where a text seems to be about an individual, it may actually be about a community. This is an approach I adopted in relation to the *Ephphatha* episode, in the previous chapter, and in relation to 'My name is Legion' in Chapter 3, because the healing of a person is the healing of community, and the healing of community is the healing of personhood. So when I read Isaiah 52.14, I confess that I partly do 'the Christian thing', seeing how Jesus' own suffering is interpreted through this vision of Israel – 'so marred was his appearance, beyond human semblance, and his form beyond that of mortals' – but at the same time I bring the Jewish insight into the sociality of the person and wonder how these words might illuminate our notion of the body of Christ, the church, a communal identity.

Christ's body, Christ's corporate body, is glimpsed as marred or disfigured; so much so that it is not recognizably human. (Indeed, too often the church does not seem exactly 'human', or not human in recognizable terms. Rather, it seems to talk an alien language. But what if it were better known for asking itself, 'What does it mean to be human?) Yet, Isaiah goes on, this body 'shall startle many nations' and 'kings shall shut their mouths' because of this body (Isa. 52.15). How shall this happen, this silencing of kings? The verse ends: 'for that which had not been told them they shall see, and that which they had not heard they shall contemplate'. What an amazing, truly incredible, vision: impressing on us that, in the world as it is, there are truths that kings do not hear, truths that are not brought to their attention, no doubt because they make it clear, one way or another, that there are certain things they do not want to know. Our leaders hold reality at bay, because it is inconvenient. Our powers of domination keep themselves from being confronted with disruptive truth. That is the current way of the world, the prevailing system, the TANA ('There Are No Alternatives') of our times, but in the face of it comes a disfigured face bearing witness to the unheard realities. This is the calling of those who are 'a light to the nations' (Isa. 42.6): to make known what they had not been told.

The song carries on, further impressing on us that this figure is not much to look at: 'no form or majesty that we should look at [it], nothing in [its] appearance that we should desire [it]' (Isa. 53.2). In fact, it is 'one from whom others hide their faces' (Isa. 53.3) – though the Hebrew can mean 'one who hides [its] face from us', another ambiguity. I have changed the translation from 'he' to 'it', to reflect my desire to explore the *social* nature of this vision: a church community that is undesirable, not much to look at, one from whom others turn away. That is not to say that where people reject the church, the church should regard this as an achievement, as though its unattractiveness signifies 'faithfulness to the gospel'. For it can be its unfaithfulness to the gospel of love, its prejudice and abuses of power that turn people away. It is understandable that, by contrast, some churches strive to be attractive, in faithfulness to the gospel; to be as accessible, even as impressive, as possible – but this can sometimes be superficial, or they confuse attractiveness with slickness.

After all, my point is that a church that plays its part in bearing the infirmities of others (Isa. 53.4) cannot easily be attractive; rather, it will be a site of struggle, in the midst of life's ambiguities and asymmetries.

Christ's body, the body of Christ, is an awkward body: not neat and tidy, not symmetrical or smooth-skinned, not fitting the world's image of the perfect body or even of good health. Rather, it is disfigured, while witnessing to the transfiguring power of God's awesome weakness. It is marred, damaged, not much to look at – even as it desires to be shiny and well-groomed. As Isaiah envisages, '[it] did not open [its] mouth' (53.7), yet it seeks to deploy clever propaganda to get its message across, wanting to be loved. How it wants to be loved! But it is awkward, an uncomfortable body, not always at ease with itself; trying to dance in a cool way, but caught between different rhythms (the rhythm of domination and the rhythm of an-archy) and often displaying a natural clumsiness. Nancy Eiesland speaks of the communion of struggle, in the context of the church, noting that 'there is no "perfect" body' but that in the midst of our struggles we are discerning 'the disabled God'.[1] It is therefore not surprising that we find ourselves being awkward, disjointed, ill-at-ease, because the song of the new horizon is quite strange; it is 'beautiful but not as we know it'; it is not easy to tune in to it.

I advocate this vision of the church for a number of reasons: first, ironically, to help us be more at ease with our awkwardness. It can be demanding, trying to be the body of Christ; we can expend enormous amounts of energy failing to live up to the one to whom we witness. Our embodiment of Christ is so flawed, and it is appropriate to live well with this awkwardness. To own our clumsy encapsulation of Christ. After all, it is not just that we, in our particular contexts, fall short of perfection, but that the one to whom we witness is not necessarily as 'shiny' as we want to be. Christ is, as I have argued before, the Shaken One,[2] in the sense that he witnesses to the shaking power of truth-in-process, opening himself up empathetically to ever new situations, but this is an unfolding experience, an ongoing reality; for he does not capture an end-point but reflects the road that leads there. And he does so while being, in certain respects, unappealing – because this is no smooth road and no welcome prospect for a world conditioned to see things another way. He is inviting us into a realm that does not immediately feel homely to us, because of its strangeness, its immersion in im/purities, its disconcerting dynamics, its upside-downing of things-as-they-are. This makes him and Holy Anarchy feel quite unattractive. No wonder then if we too feel a little disfigured, discomfited and discomfiting. It is a lot of pressure striving to be the peculiar body of Christ – not only because we fall short of it, but because it represents a challenging vision for us all.

Second, while there is a real challenge in trying to be this body, it is important to appreciate its liberating quality too. People who feel disfigured or marred by life; people who feel rejected and wasted; people who feel they have nothing more to give – these people can be the heart of the body, not its extremities but its very core, so witnessing to the awesome and subversive weakness of God at work in the world. The church has been known, after all, in particular circumstances, as 'rebels and misfits', precisely because it has been the space in which those who do not 'fit' elsewhere have found a home. This certainly has not always been the case; far too often the church has been the opposite, a place of conformity to the judgements of the world, or a place far more judgmental than the world. But its calling is to be for the unfit and the unfitting, because God, as revealed in Christ, does not 'fit' our assumptions or models, so the body of Christ embodies a generosity-of-spirit that transgresses prevailing expectations. So to 'own' our disfiguredness is to remind ourselves of the calling to be a community for those bearing pain, struck down by rejection, or despised on account of one thing or another (Isa. 53). But also, more positively, a community that affirms the gifts and agency of those who are dis/abled, differently abled, 'unfitting' the pervasive norms and landscape of society. It is a community of beautiful inefficiency, defiant diversity, and liberated liminality. An infant embodiment of Holy Anarchy.

Third, we fulfil the calling to be an awkward body when we do not succumb to a certain way of being beautiful. We may try to be beautiful in a number of ways. We may promote the positives in our story and identity, editing out the negatives, the mess, the shortcomings, thus presenting ourselves as innocent. We may focus on what makes Christian faith attractive, not what makes it demanding. Or we may seek to be as slick, efficient, productive and transformational as possible, like a top-flight business delivering the goods. In each of these ways we distort and tame Holy Anarchy. When we accentuate the positive, denying the negative, we close ourselves to the wholeness of things, our longing for innocence cutting us off from the lessons we are invited to learn. When we focus on being attractive, we risk editing the challenge of truth-in-process, out of impatience or particular institutional interests (such as anxiety over decline). When we prioritize being business-like, efficient and productive, we subsume the good news of divine solidarity into a capitalist project. Not that I am romanticizing inefficiency as such, since it too is capable of real harm; but to prioritize efficiency and productivity in human community is to treat people as machines, as though things like grief, bewilderment and contradiction have no place in our relationships. The alternative vision is one in which the mess of life is more fully owned, the demands of empathy are honestly acknowledged, and the awkward-ness of genuine community is risked despite its inefficiencies. This is the way of deep solidarity.

For Hegel, 'beautiful souls' are driven by a fear of hypocrisy, keeping them from engagement in the mess of the world, in case such engage-ment compromises their principles.[3] But, as Shanks explains, to maintain distance is also to risk hypocrisy, for failing to act on our principles. It is more honest to the good news of Holy Anarchy to embrace our hypocrisy, because whether we engage or not *we will be hypocrites*: so better to be one who at least attempts to make a difference, even if there are unintended consequences. And through the connections in the social matrix, there will indeed be unintended consequences, shadow-sides to the good that we do; but we cannot control the outcomes – we can simply trust that the butterfly of our contribution will generate more empathetic whirlwinds than ones that close down. The awkward body of Christ, which must reckon honestly with the depths of disillusionment and despair, is nevertheless graced with trust in the power of God's awesome weakness – a power that helps us live well with our hypocrisy, our dis-figurement and our inefficiencies, while encouraging us to witness to the liberation and solidarity of 'misfits'.

Marks of the anarchic church

In the light of Holy Anarchy's presence in an awkward church, what does this mean for the traditional 'marks' of the church – those characteristics that make something authentically 'church'? One, Holy, Catholic and Apostolic – understood differently by different churches and theologians; so what of them in this context?

First, to be *one*, united, is to be rooted in the common vision of Holy Anarchy. A vision in which we, as the church, know ourselves not to be the thing in itself, but we signal it, we embody it however partially, and we strive to further it in the world. But we can be humbled by our aware-ness that we 'only' host it rather than purporting to be its perfection, yet at the same time we are liberated because we needn't pressurize ourselves to be the horizon at which we're aiming. Our oneness, our unity, our common Christian identity, is defined around this organizing principle: the church witnesses to Holy Anarchy, the alternative horizon at which all domination is undone and life in its fullness is enjoyed by all.

But what if we do not all gather around this common vision? On the one hand, this question is unfair, because the very same issue applies to *all* claims to oneness – it is a happy ideal, but rarely realized. The point, though, is that oneness is itself both a gift and a goal; it is here in part, like Holy Anarchy, but not yet here in its entirety. So, too, regarding the claim that all Christians gather around oneness in the vision of Holy Anarchy. For many do not. Many are drawn much more to models of domination. As a Congregationalist, committed to church structures that should be as flat as possible, it is tempting to criticize other traditions that invest much more authority in individuals or elites, sometimes excusing imposition on the multitudes. It is an anarchic vision. But every tradition has its codes of domination, some more subtle than others and, as noted previously, more hierarchical forms of church have sometimes generated the most radical movements in theology and practice. This does not mean that any tradition is off the hook, unexposed to critique; rather, a healthy conversation evaluating modes of domination in every pattern of church is a proper function of the ecumenical movement – and extending that conversation to modes of domination in society too.

So we can quickly identify ways in which Christians are not united by a common vision of Holy Anarchy; the examples from Christian national-ism and explicit White Supremacy within churches testify to this disunity. But even so, the thing about Holy Anarchy is that it prioritizes truth-in-process, openness to the interweaving and contradictory truths that are part of the complexity of Christian tradition. And it would not be Holy Anarchy if it insisted that only those with a pure understanding of it can enter it. Rather, this 'common' vision of Holy Anarchy is understood and pursued explicitly by some, only implicitly by others, but defied and rejected by others, yet still there may be elements of common ground, invisible to many of us, cutting across all sorts of loyalties, including the boundaries between religions. Oneness in 'the body of Christ' will there-fore be ambiguous, as Christ was and is present in many unlikely places – so we, as his body, must be too. Its parameters cannot be controlled because it is a site in which control is negated; rather, it is about being alert to the elusive gift of unity, a solidarity that we pursue, amid our many differences: the third mark (catholicity).

Second, to be *holy* is to be engaged in the mess of life; 'set apart' not physically, but by commitment to engagement in pursuit of solidarity. Such holiness risks itself, in the face of divisions between the pure and the impure, the insider and the outsider, for the sake of human/divine immer-sion in the struggle for abundant life. God is holy by virtue of God's innate entanglement in the very stuff of existence, God's presence in the midst of every instance of brokenness and longing for healing. Nothing can separate anything from the love of God which, not least in Christ, is woven into the fabric of the cosmos. This is God's holiness, and our holiness is rooted in such interwovenness: so we should not be separate, but in the midst. Even as we strive to disentangle ourselves from structures and habits of Empire, there is no place of perfect isolation and we remain always embedded in the web of life, with its pain, perplexity and potential. To be holy is to be present to all of this.

Again, though, the church does not consistently reflect such holiness. We are too easily disengaged, or only partly embedded in the struggles of people. Of course, some churches are deeply present, at the interface of multiple injustices, baptized into the harshness of life, its disease and despair, while also attentive to people's capacity for wit and ingenuity in the face of systematic indifference. And even where churches are not engaged with these realities, they often want to do more. But it is not as such about our achievement; so we should not judge one another's holiness. Rather, we are beckoned to connect with one another, including those regarded as impure, indecent, unholy – thus troubling such boundaries. Holiness, then, is a direction of travel but, once more, a gift – not something we grasp. But what matters most is that we affirm its embeddedness in the struggles and mess of life rather than view it as an other-worldly disposition.

Third, to be *catholic* is to be a community of all-comers, of all classes. Not a sect of a spiritual elite or the self-righteous. Not a solidarity even of the like-minded, but a solidarity of those who are genuinely different from one another, across cultural, racialized, gendered, sexual and dis/abled borders, across distinctions in age or status. A solidarity of people shaken out of half-truths in a whole range of ways, or being shaken, gradually, sometimes patiently, sometimes impatiently, and often diversely. A solidarity among those alert to their complicity with oppression and those being liberated from such oppression – but awake to the power differentials between people, the need to give preferential space to those who have been silenced and dehumanized. True catholicity embraces the multiplicity of life, in ways we have not even noticed yet. It holds the open palm of faith, to represent such a depth of empathy, a willingness to attend to ever new realities.

But of course churches are often not so catholic; we are far more limited in our sensitivity, editing out so many voices, preferring those who fit with certain norms, leaving structures untroubled. Nonetheless, even in our inadequate embodiments of catholicity, we host a partial grasp of this greater vision. We may tame the horizon until it becomes almost unrecognizable, but even if it is seed-sized and under-our-own-radar, its latent potency remains, waiting to be set free. So, to all who fear the demands of such catholicity, may we first imagine it again, then celebrate its possibility and practise it intentionally. By way of example, if we strive to be a genuine intercultural church, we cannot maintain the norms of people from one ethnic background; we should decolonize our assumptions, habits and dreams, creating space in which multiple stories and truths may be recovered and received. To be catholic is to be inter-cultural, creating deeper solidarity among people (in the UK) from the various White backgrounds and UK Minority Ethnic backgrounds and Global Majority Backgrounds, a power-sharing community. It is also to be a solidarity among children and adults. A solidarity among genders and sexualities, abilities and neuro-diversities. Its diversity is uncon-trolled, but maximum participation is fostered, even if it slows down conversation and requires more of us in terms of readiness to attend to one another's stories and complexity. It generates in us a patience towards one another, an acceptance that true community takes time as well as space for difference.

Fourth, to be *apostolic* is to be sent, to be purposive, aiming at particu-lar goals – namely, to discern and celebrate Holy Anarchy, wherever it may be found; to embody it in our corporate life, however imperfectly; and to further it, in partnership with others, and in solidarity with those who suffer under powers of domination. But such apostolicity, such sent-ness, such *mission*-focus, can leave us with the impression that it is all about our agency. Whereas to live knowing we are sent – evoked into action by the awesome weakness of God – is also to know that the priority we are to give to truth-in-process involves openness and receptivity to the insight and agency of others. That is, to be sent is also to be interrupted, disrupted, even interrogated, by other communities, other traditions. In the face of our inattentiveness, others will bring their norms to us, or give us new insights into holiness. It is not only that we overlook things, though we undoubtedly do; but also that Holy Anarchy is intrinsically about building relationships across boundaries in pursuit of ever greater empathetic awareness of all the ways in which reality is conditioned by domination. So we should not think that it is our mission to testify to it alone. In Chapter 7, I turn more directly to the question of other traditions contributing to this process, but here I note that, in terms of the apos-tolic mark of the church, it is not for the church to think of itself alone as 'sent', 'missional', or the one and only apostolic community; rather, our very apostolicity brings us into encounter with critical reflections on the part that we play. Theologians like Lesslie Newbigin suggested that other religions may help the church to be true to the gospel[4] – but his presumption was that the church's gospel is nevertheless the answer of which others help to remind us; whereas I am arguing that the church's gospel incorporates reflexive mission, opening us up to insights *not that we have forgotten, but that we never knew*.

Once more, this mark of the church is not evident consistently in the life of real churches. Sometimes 'mission' is confused simply with 'evangelism', as though the only thing we are called to do is proclaim the good news and nurture new believers. Sometimes churches recognize that mission is so much more than this: it is also to care for those in need, to transform structures of injustice and violence, and to treasure the integrity of creation, as per the five marks of mission – even if these are given variable degrees of weight. And sometimes churches recognize that when we proclaim good news, or when we care for those in need, or transform or treasure, we need not be the only ones contributing to something greater than us; that others may also be contributing. But it is a further step to realize how others outside of us, at large in the community and in specific traditions, may help us to see things we have not seen and do things we have not done, in faithfulness to anarchic unity, holy im/purity, or deep catholicity. Whether or not churches affirm this dimension, it still remains a mark of the church, even if it is present only as a shadow of something more, just glimpsed at the edges, or buried like a seed.

In each of these respects, the marks of the church remind us that the church is always in a state of becoming; it is in process – a work in progress. Not that it should be self-loathing with regard to its incompleteness, because self-loathing makes us susceptible to manipulation by bullying impulses.[5] Nor should it burden itself with pressure, because it is not all about our agency. But it should allow itself to be liberated from missional self-regard, as though we have all the answers and are called to do it all, delighting instead in the unexpected power of chaos-events, in our own life and in the life of other communities; the capacity for surprising impact to emerge out of the cracks in the structures of domination. And it should hold before itself the vision of anarchic oneness, impure holiness, decolonized catholicity, and apostolic interruptedness, to help us flesh out our own embodiment of the horizon that beckons us.

Religious or spiritual? A community of friction

More and more people identify as 'spiritual not religious'. This is for a number of reasons, and it is an entirely understandable direction of travel. In the light of it, 'religion' – in terms of institutionalized expressions of spirituality – ought to be attentive to this phenomenon, to try to understand why people choose not to be 'religious'. It has to do with the harm that religion has done – the oppression, prejudice and dehumanizing that has resulted from authoritarian and intransigent ways of being; the spiritual abuse, denying the dignity and worth of particular people. It also signifies people's desire for more fluid expressions of what spirituality involves, not defined by the 'box' of particular forms and repetitions of devotion and worship, nor by the institutional trappings, the buildings, the decision-making, the habits and norms. People want greater freedom to piece their spiritual practices together in ways that are authentic, concerned that 'religion' creates a culture in which certain things are not 'allowed'. There is also an alertness to the ways in which 'religion' lives too easily with a gap between 'the talk', what people say they are about, and 'the walk', how their lives actually demonstrate their values; in other words, too many religious people are viewed as not practising what is preached to or by them, which undermines the integrity and value of religion itself – and the presumption to 'preach' at all.

In all these ways, it is understandable that people should opt for something more fluid, more authentically contextual to their searching, their needs, their aspirations. Religion has been, and continues to be, corrupt in so many respects, and even encourages complicity with unjust and oppressive dynamics. By contrast, 'spiritual not religious' people seek the safety and relative innocence that is distinct from religion. This should tell us something: that integrity matters; that issues of power and its abuse matter; that spiritual freedom and creativity matter; that questing rather than constraining matters. And all of these point towards Holy Anarchy, rather than the more limiting, damaging and corrupt notions of religion.

However, Holy Anarchy expresses a degree of friction with the 'spiritual' dimension that yearns for innocence, because Holy Anarchy does not envisage space free from corruption. The structures of oppression are so pervasive that we cannot avoid them, and there is something in trying to *own* this moral complexity. Religion that is faithful to this vision will therefore not be – or purport to be – innocent, but will enable the deepest possible self-criticism; this is not criticism of individuals, in a judgmental way like religion has often exacted, but criticism of itself, its corporate life, to expose its oppressive legacies. Of course, in many ways this is not attractive; it is challenging to envisage being part of a community that prioritizes critique of itself, wherever it lapses into bullying, exclusion or self-regard. But it must not simply be seen to do this, as an exercise in repairing the damage done to so many spiritual people; it must do this as an expression of its calling, to witness to Holy Anarchy, which alerts us to the structures of domination within which we live and move and have our being.

This is different from a dismantling of religion as such, because religion itself still has the potential to be a faithful witness to Holy Anarchy; it can embody it, however fallibly. But it is certainly a work in progress. The theologian Aloysius Pieris, who developed a distinctly Asian theology of liberation, identified the way in which western thinkers tend to dismiss 'religion' – whether in Marx's terms, on the basis of its distraction of those hurt by the 'System', or in Barth's terms, on the basis that religion plays God.[6] In contrast, for Pieris, in an Asian context, religion may well be flawed but it still has a liberative role, a capacity to foster people's liberation – if it learns to be truly attentive to the voices of those silenced by poverty and oppression. I agree that when it comes to embodying Holy Anarchy, communities are needed, which always involve some degree of organization, decision-making, priorities and purpose, and the risk of going wrong (in fact, the inevitability of hypocrisy) – and even though this certainly need not equate to 'religious institutions' as they are currently formed, 'religion' does have a particular role in self-consciously hosting and fostering such a vision.

Should we be 'religious not spiritual', then? No, but this provocative sentiment points to something helpful: the idea of owning the awkwardness of religious community, rather than expecting Holy Anarchy to be embodied simply in the lives of innocent, authentic seekers – because collective thought and action are intrinsic to the social dimension of Holy Anarchy. It requires organization, but is the most demanding organization imaginable. Barth suggested that religion tends to behave, collectively, as though it is a way of people earning divine favour. Even where its adherents don't believe that, it nevertheless often functions in that way, encouraging obedient servicing of the institution: an addiction to the truth-in-hand of religious form or message. Instead, religion should be about the social craft of living at the intersection between 'the world as it is' and 'the world as it could be'. It is an intersection responding to the risk of truth-in-process and which is marked by a certain sort of friction, as the alternative horizon exposes and disrupts the prevailing order. Other disciplines may also play their part in witnessing to Holy Anarchy – such as political movements, campaigning organizations and so on – but religion is a particular corporate response to an impulse, or calling, evoked by Holy Anarchy, alert to the uncontainable horizon that beckons.

What is actually required, then, is a holding together of religion and spirituality: an understanding of the role of community (with all the complexity it brings), constantly subject to the open-endedness of spirituality, while the longing within spirituality for something uncontaminated by religious corruption is also disrupted. After all, the 'holy' of anarchy is not pure; it is engaged in solidarity in the midst of the mess; and the 'anarchy' that is holy is a form of social relations that keeps interrogating any tendency towards domination. It is why both 'solidarity' and 'shakenness' are important: solidarity reminds us of the demands of building community, not only with the like-minded but with the different, and shakenness keeps opening up the inclination in any solidarity to become too settled, too institutional, too self-satisfied. So to be a religious or political community witnessing to Holy Anarchy, and seeking to embody it collectively, is to host the solidarity of the shaken.

But of course I am acutely aware that religion does not often look like that. I pray, though, that this might be its direction of travel.

A hymn

Reforming Christ – God's living, loving Word –
the Scriptures cradle and attest to you;
speak to us now, shed tears and light again:
for you are making us and all things new!

Reforming Christ! Nail questions to our doors
to make us think again, to seek your ways;
for we neglect debate at truth's expense –
so shake us out of each complacent haze.

Reforming Christ! Your faith enthrals my soul
and forms the righteousness your life enfleshed.
Call me to work for justice in all realms,
till church and kingdoms make your will their guest.

Reforming Christ! Expose what we indulge –
the things that seem to count, which miss the mark;
so help us see where faith is funding wealth,
and shake us to address the gap so stark.

Reforming Christ! Always reform your church!
Transform us till our minds conform to you –
Christ of the nails and faith that's for the poor –
for you are making us and all things new!

Graham Adams (2017)
Suggested tune: *Woodlands*
This was written for the 500th anniversary of Luther's 95 theses, calling the church to be self-critical.

Sacraments of Holy Anarchy: to play is to pray, to pray is to play

Praying for religion to embody the solidarity of the shaken brings me to consider the question of prayer directly – and its connection with a distinctly religious concern: 'sacraments'. To understand how they may be reconceived, we once again approach the discussion through the entry-point of childlikeness.

First, sacraments: baptism and communion are where the gospel of grace is specifically embodied in the worshipping life of Christian community. They signify the events through which divine generosity engages in human history, baptized in the very stuff of life, and feasting at one with all who are hungry for justice, peace, healing, acceptance and wholeness. They celebrate the uncontainable love of God the Child, embodied in Jesus' relationships: in baptism, demonstrating solidarity with all who are, in a sense, crucified by structures of oppression and closure, yet rising to new possibility, opening up space for all; and in communion, celebrating the forgiving love that accepts us no matter how we struggle to witness to such generosity-of-spirit, such hospitality, such solidarity with all. In these experiences, people are welcomed and re-welcomed into the life and ministry of Christ, even before it is a matter of our own agency, and whether or not our grasp of it is correct, inspiring us in our relationships to embody Holy Anarchy, within the church and beyond it, however imperfectly.

There is clearly a physical dimension to the entirety of our faith and discipleship, as it is entangled with questions of our own bodies, who we are, how we are regarded, where we are located, our relationships with others, the space we occupy, our connections with the Earth – all physical concerns; but arguably the sacraments give particular expression to the physicality of our worship. Through water, bread and wine, our collective memory of the life and purpose of Jesus, and our envisioning of new community, Holy Anarchy, in our midst, is felt, tasted, digested. It is tempting to think that these physical things are the means by which all people can connect with the good news of grace, because the sacraments do not rely so much on hearing or understanding; they open up other sensory ways of receiving, engaging and participating. But of course this does not mean everyone is enabled to access, because any single entry-point remains inaccessible to some people – as a result of limitations in physical wellbeing, sight, feeling, taste, digestion, and challenges of the physical space and expectations – which is why churches should always reflect on how to 'be sacramental' in as wide a range of means as possible, adapting the form to reflect the unbounded message. However, churches tend to make things more restrictive, not regarding the sacraments as means by which people can engage with the truth-in-process of divine love for all, but moulding truth-in-hand conditions, whether in terms of who can participate, what degree or version of understanding they should have, or what form the sacraments must take. In each respect, the fact that these sacraments celebrate the life of God the Child should tell us that childlikeness confounds those restrictions. More than that, there is a sense in which childlikeness embodies the truth of the sacraments more than un-childlikeness.

In the face of restrictions on who can participate, the child-shaped entry-point into Holy Anarchy calls us to make the sacraments not only open to childlikeness, but determined by it. This is why I believe strongly in the baptism of infants: it demonstrates the awesome weakness of divine love, in solidarity with those who cannot express agency in adult terms, who cannot articulate faith, but are recipients of – and witnesses to – love, thereby reflecting its upside-downing power. And communion too must be a feast for everyone: freeing all who are enslaved by structures of oppression and exclusion, including those adult-centred ways of thinking and behaving that condition the life of churches. The presence and participation of children in communion teaches us so much. The physicality of it matters to them, the open table matters; the inter-generational dimension, the party-like potential – and the capacity of children to be active in serving others, not merely the recipients of adult gifts. Childlikeness calls communities to take the risk of im/purity in defiance of such restrictions, to be anarchic where control closes things down prematurely, while also making it familiar enough to be safe space. In the face of notions of how things supposedly should be *understood*, again 'receiving it like a child' requires us not to expect certain interpretations to be normalized; participation should come *before* understanding, and even without it, since it is to be a space for people with intellectual disabilities, as well as for infants; a feast for all. To make it a pre-understanding space *is* to understand it, as being about grace that cannot be limited to truth-in-hand articulations of it; for sacramental physicality affirms the sacredness of all people, all space, all creation. Anything less would diminish its purpose. And in the face of the *form* it 'should' take, childlike inquisitiveness asserts the persistent 'why?', evoking the generation of ever new forms in multiple contexts, in solidarity with all who hunger after healing and hope.

Through all of these dynamics, baptism and communion can be considered 'play': water play and party play. After all, as Zechariah prophesied (8.5), when the hope of the exiled is fulfilled, children will once again be 'playing in [the] streets', capturing a key dimension of childlikeness.[7] But not just childlikeness in children's spaces, but in the streets, the plaza, the places of adult business; in the midst of adult games. When hope is realized, when Holy Anarchy comes, children get to play in the very midst – even in spaces that adults *presume* to control. And this relates of course to sacraments, spaces that adults presume to control, but in the midst of which children get to play. Quite rightly. The sacraments celebrate the solidarity of God the Child in our very midst, destabilizing our prevailing assumptions, norms and habits; so the form of the sacraments should reflect the message that is latent within them, but too often buried. The form of them should give at least a glimpse of the seed-like parable that bursts forth, through the cracks in adult control. The form of sacraments should reflect the playful energy that is alive in the very physicality of sacramental practice.

Play and imagination, after all, are not merely frivolous, as adults sometimes perceive it, but go to the heart of how children engage in being childlike while deeply processing experiences.[8] Play is a way of handling the struggles of life, including pain and frustration; even where it becomes fantasy, it is rooted in and emerges out of childlike managing of real-life fears, hopes, questions and relationships.[9] It allows its participants to experience the 'flow' of connection between aspects of reality.[10] So sacraments are well suited for childlike play – enabling participation, engaging with fears and pain, and fostering dreams of a more just world, where everyone can 'rise above' the waters of cruelty, exclusion, false order, and share in the abundant feast of life.

And this is prayer too. Not the whole of prayer, but a form of it. Sacrament is play, play is prayer,[11] prayer is sacrament – because in these connections we glimpse, we feel, we digest, we receive and enter into, we are immersed or submerged into, and we arise in the midst of, Holy Anarchy! It is their connective capacities that foster these deep possibilities[12] – as faith is connected with physicality, physicality expresses prayer, and we play at the orientation of faith, directing us towards a new and alternative horizon. It is the childlikeness of God's awesome weakness that enables us to cherish this sacramental approach to spirituality and prayer, *embodied* in the rituals of religion, but not 'dead' rituals; rather, ones that allow for and encourage playfulness, imagination, creativity, in the cause of that which cannot be contained by any single form of devotion, worship, service. Sacrament, seeming to pin the mysteries of faith down into a physical sign and moment, actually does something much more ambiguous; risking the messiness of engagement with the physical stuff of life, in order to open us up to our connectedness with all things, our rootedness in the stuff of the Earth, and our longing for all things to be reconciled through neighbour-love and justice.

Missional skills: mediation and agitation

Through this chapter, engaging with the corporate life of communities that seek to embody Holy Anarchy, we have considered a number of dimensions to the challenge. The awkwardness of the body illuminates its differently beautiful nature; its solidarity with those regarded as awkward or disfigured; its owning of its own imperfections, embracing the mess and muddle, but witnessing to a reality that is close at hand, by virtue of such disfigurement. This led to exploration of the marks of the anarchic church – 'one' but anarchic, subverting powers of domination, not neat and tidy, not with clear boundaries; 'holy' but not pure, embedded in the complexities and impurities of life; 'catholic' but decolonizing any tendency to tame diversity for its own sake, instead learning to receive the challenges of deep diversity; and 'apostolic', sent but also interrupted, alert to the ways in which Holy Anarchy prevents any tribe from conceiving of itself as the end with all the answers.

Such a community will attend to why people opt to be 'spiritual not religious', while reconceiving religion as self-critical, hosting the solidarity of the shaken, in partnership with other traditions and disciplines that also host it. It will be sacramental space, where the physicality and embodiedness of faith connects us once again with childlikeness, notably in terms of playfulness – as we process the brokenness and pain of reality through water-play and party-play, reimagining the horizon that beckons.

Running through these explorations, we may identify two missional skills: mediation and agitation. These terms come from Giles Fraser's 'Foreword' in Shanks's book *Against Innocence*,[13] where Fraser identified how some people tend towards mediation, working at holding awkward conversations peaceably, while others tend towards agitation, activists in confrontation with power dynamics. Arguably, at one level, these can be related to the solidarity of the shaken, where solidarity demands ongoing mediation between the many different voices in community, the challenge to build church communities that allow for and value such multiplicity, the anticipation of a new horizon close at hand in which the diversity of life is cherished and reconciled; and shakenness reflects the disruptive energy that keeps unsettling the presumptions of those with power and privilege, the agitation that prevents solidarity from slipping into acquiescence. But at the same time, shakenness can be the prompt for newly mediated perspectives; the awesome weakness that evokes in us an awareness that we have not really been listening to one another because our respective truth-in-hand has consumed us, and solidarity can express the politics of commitment to subvert prevailing social relations, alert to the ways in which structures of oppression inhibit deep solidarity, so agitation is required.

In other words, these two dynamics are woven together; there cannot be mediation without agitation or agitation without mediation. True, certain moments may call for one more than another, but the alternative horizon of Holy Anarchy implies the need for both – and the church's calling both to mediate and agitate represents a pioneering direction of travel. Too often it has focused on mediation, presuming that peace must take priority over justice, even as it has failed to mediate very thoroughly – not least because its presumed mediation has been in the context of a solidarity-of-the-like-minded. But it is called to agitate too, not in the cause of vested interests, silencing the forgotten, but in terms of solidarity in the midst, among the im/pure, among those disfigured by the distortions of life, among experiences of dis/ability, among the queering of identities and boundaries.

The church is called to be an embodiment of Holy Anarchy, a social vision, agitating in the face of systems that hold people in their place, in pursuit of the feast where everyone may gather around the table of life, mediated in their glorious but awkward diversity. Holy Anarchy is not a stable-state where all of this is resolved, but the means and the end, woven together, of communities wrestling with their 'unfitness' for such purpose while witnessing to a vision that cannot 'fit' within any single body or organization. This is the 'unfitting God' at work, delighting in the capacity of disfigured religion to reflect critically on the damage it has tried to disown while nurturing solidarity of all who are shaken in so many ways; and evoking in us a spirit of playfulness, unconfined by the rules of adult games.

A hymn

To God, gently moulding
　　this cosmos of clay,
which groans as it yearns
　　for that long-promised day,
we bring all our visions
　　and half-truthful dreams,
expecting the future
　　to be as it seems …

　　Wake us up! Wake us up
　　from our knowledge presumed;
　　Wake us up! Wake us up
　　from illusions consumed;

and come, like a thief
under cover of night,
to humble our hubris,
to be the world's light.

To God, surely judging
the ways of the earth,
denouncing the lies
and proclaiming true worth,
we bring our assumptions
and in/out divides,
expecting your justice
to bless the right side ...

Wake us up! Wake us up,
so we do not forget;
Wake us up! Wake us up,
to remember we met:
you came, like a judge
but whose bench was a cross,
exposing the sin
of condemning the lost.

To God, breaking open
fake versions of peace
which edit the cost
that is seared in this feast,
we bring all our wounding
and healing unborn:
may war be unlearned
and dis/order transformed:

Wake us up! Wake us up,
when denying the pain;
Wake us up! Wake us up,
for we have to be changed:
so come, like a clown
to disarm our deceit,
to join us together:
the last, lost and least.

Graham Adams (2013)
Suggested tune: *To God be the glory*

Questions to ponder

1 How might the 'awkward body of Christ' demonstrate that it is a community of honest hypocrites? How might we refrain from boasting, focusing instead on our capacity to build solidarity among all-comers (including those hurt by a boastful, complacent church)?

2 What do you make of the reconceiving of the marks of the church?

(a) To be 'one' involves being 'anarchic', united in our subversion of structures of oppression, and not anxious to tidy up our boundaries.

(b) To be 'holy' involves being engaged in solidarity with the so-called impurities of life, at one with those on the margins.

(c) To be 'catholic' involves being as diverse as possible, decolonizing our presumption to control the conversation on our terms, but receiving insights on many other terms.

(d) To be 'apostolic' involves being not only sent but interrupted, recognizing that others have things to teach us.

3 How might the church be 'religious', not as oppressive, authoritarian or exclusive, but as self-critical and alert to the limitations of its vision?

4 How might sacraments be as childlike and playful as possible?

5 What would it mean for the church to engage in mediation and in agitation?

Further reading

Graham Adams, 'Doubting Empire: Growing as Faithful Children', in Vuyani Vellem, Patricia Sheerattan-Bisnauth and Philip Vinod Peacock (eds), *Bible and Theology from the Underside of Empire* (SUN MeDIA MeTRO, 2016).

Al Barrett and Ruth Harley, *Being Interrupted: Reimagining the Church's Mission from the Outside, In* (London: SCM Press, 2020).

Brian Edgar, *The God Who Plays: A Playful Approach to Theology and Spirituality* (Eugene, OR: Cascade Books, 2017).

Samuel George, *Church and Disability* (Delhi and Singapore: ISPCK and CWM, 2020).

Lamar Hardwick, *Disability and the Church: A Vision for Diversity and Inclusion* (Downers Grove, IL: InterVarsity Press, 2021).

Molly C. Haslam, *A Constructive Theology of Intellectual Disability: Human Being as Mutuality and Response* (New York: Fordham University Press, 2012).

Nina Kurlberg and Madleina Daehnhardt (eds), *Theologies and Practices of Inclusion: Insights from a Faith-Based Relief, Development and Advocacy Organization* (London: SCM Press, 2021).

Stewart Rapley, *Autistic Thinking in the Church* (London: SCM Press, 2021).

Jarel Robinson-Brown, *Black, Gay, British, Christian, Queer* (London: SCM Press, 2021).

Mark Scanlan, *An Interweaving Ecclesiology: The Church, Mission and Young People* (London: SCM Press, 2021).

Notes

1 Nancy Eiesland, *The Disabled God: Toward a Liberatory Theology of Disability*, Nashville, TN: Abingdon, 1994, pp. 108–9.

2 Graham Adams, *Christ and the Other: In Dialogue with Hick and Newbigin*, Farnham: Ashgate, 2010, pp. 163, 165, 168–9, 176–7, 181.

3 Andrew Shanks, *Hegel and Religious Faith: Divided Brain, Atoning Spirit*, London and New York: Bloomsbury T&T Clark, 2011, pp. 14–16.

4 Lesslie Newbigin, *The Open Secret: Sketches for a Missionary Theology*, Grand Rapids, MI: Eerdmans, 1978, pp. 203–12.

5 Andrew Shanks, *Faith in Honesty: The Essential Nature of Theology*, Farnham: Ashgate, 2005, p. 144.

6 Aloysius Pieris, *An Asian Theology of Liberation*, Edinburgh: T&T Clark, 1988, pp. 91–3.

7 Brian Edgar, *The God Who Plays: A Playful Approach to Theology and Spirituality*, Eugene, OR: Cascade Books, 2017: he too picks up on Zechariah 8.5 (p. 114) and emphasizes how worship is play, of mind, body and imagination (pp. 29, 32–7). See also this review: https://www.christianscholars.com/the-god-who-plays-a-playful-approach-to-theology-and-spirituality/ (accessed 23 February 2022).

8 Rebecca Nye, 'Identifying the Core of Children's Spirituality', in David Hay with Rebecca Nye, *The Spirit of the Child*, London and Philadelphia: Jessica Kingsley Publishers, 2006, pp. 113, 120–1. In fact, for Edgar, in *The God Who Plays*, p. 1, 'play is of a *higher* order than seriousness', referring to Johan Huizinga, *Homo Ludens: A Study of the Play-Element in Culture*, Boston, MA: Beacon, 1955, pp. 211–12.

9 Hay with Nye, *The Spirit of the Child*, pp. 73–4.

10 Hay with Nye, *The Spirit of the Child*, pp. 68–70.

11 Edgar, *The God Who Plays*, p. 10.

12 Edgar, *The God Who Plays*, p. 45: play in particular enables relationships to develop.

13 Giles Fraser, 'Foreword', in Andrew Shanks, *Against Innocence: Gillian Rose's Reception and Gift of Faith*, London: SCM Press, 2008, pp. vii, xii.

PART 4

Love Kindness – Befriend Strangeness

In Parts 2, 3 and 4, I am naming and addressing the dimensions of False Order that obstruct Holy Anarchy. Part 2 was concerned especially with the structures of oppression, or imperial powers of domination, that colonize our internal and external worlds. They are the prevailing forces that condition us to accept and perpetuate systems of 'arche', rule-over, whether in religion, politics, economics, or in everyday social relations. These structures are addressed and dismantled through the alternative nature of Holy Anarchy's power dynamics – marked by awesome weakness, as demonstrated by God the Child.

In Part 3, we turned our attention to church communities, as those self-consciously aiming to embody Holy Anarchy, or at least to witness to its alternative paradigm. False Order, however, urges us to disown our mess, ambiguity and moral imperfections, in order to boast about our story, so cutting ourselves off from the fullness of reality. Holy Anarchy, by contrast, opens us up to the disfiguredness of the church, the shadow side that we bear within ourselves, both humbling us and liberating us from the distortions of self-delusion. Such a church, restrained from over-claiming while more at ease with itself, is in the process of embodying the Christ who is also in process.

Here, in Part 4, while dreaming of the dismantling of domination, and seeking to embody this alternative horizon within our own communities, we must address the challenge presented by the sheer fact of different communities with their own stories to tell. Where do they fit in? Are they different representations of the same big story, or are they doing distinct things in their own right? False Order urges us to tidy up the problem, either by viewing them as the same as us, or by demonizing them and holding them at bay. But Holy Anarchy prompts us to take seriously the sheer strangeness of the Other, which is the focus in Chapter 7.

Then, in Chapter 8, we return to the strangeness of Holy Anarchy itself, an alternative horizon beckoning us from the edge of reality – and it is this realization that shapes my understanding of worship. When we worship the God of awesome weakness, who makes the flourishing of life possible through the quiet bursting forth of Holy Anarchy, we are desiring, facing and pursuing something that does not quite fit in our world – it is a new landscape that unsettles us in fear and confounds us in bewilderment, so we find ourselves 'in two worlds', imagining what one of them might mean.

7

Structures of Closure and the Stranger God

*Do not trust in these deceptive words, 'This is the temple of the
Lord, the temple of the Lord, the temple of the Lord.'
(Jeremiah 7.4)*

Faith is Being Shaken

The prophet Jeremiah warns against deceptive words. He condemns the temple elite, which *professes* that the temple is indeed God's temple, even while the temple's behaviour actually hurts those it should defend (such as widows, orphans, refugees) and defies its vocation. To assert that the temple is true to its calling, the leaders use repetition to impress on their audience: 'We are the authority around here, so do as we say.' Do as we say, even if it's not exactly what we do.

Of course, the temple *could* recover its unique calling; the elite could remember what it means to safeguard the welfare of the relatively powerless in their midst. They could *be* the temple again, and it is logically possible for no other institution to be the temple in the way that *this* temple is called to be. Its vocation could be entirely unique. But actually, is that the intention here? Is the temple not called to witness to a way of being, that should extend beyond its own life? By failing to be the temple, it not only squanders its own purpose, but it neglects to affirm values that are lifegiving – wherever they may be demonstrated. Its deception represents a certain sort of slippage – not only falling short of its own 'terms of reference', but professing to be right, claiming to be good, while actually undermining other efforts in the world to be right and good.

The impact of such deception undermines not only people's trust in the particular institution, but the cause of righteousness and goodness at large. It is not just a 'trust' problem, but a profoundly moral problem. Jeremiah effectively says, in relation to all such failures, 'Do not trust in *these* deceptive words: "We are right, we are right, we are right", or "We are good, we are good, we are good"'; *wherever* institutions, organizations, religions or movements claim to represent the moral high ground, while denying it, negating it, mocking it. People may have faith in such institutions, but for a long time their faith has been shaken.

Now there's an idea: faith is being shaken. It's undoubtedly true that faith has been shaken – faith in all sorts of institutions, not least in religion, as we explored in the previous chapter. I suggested that religion, at its best, needs to aim to be a quality of community that demonstrates self-reflection – in fact, self-critique – to 'own' the fact that it has caused harm to many people, and that healthy communities reckon with this reality honestly rather than covering it up by boasting about their goodness. To own the reality is a mark of Holy Anarchy, destabilizing the False Order that suppresses messy history. Holy Anarchy opens us up to the fullness of who we are, as a flawed but potentially life-affirming community. This is hard work, precisely because faith has been shaken, and it is not easy to regain people's trust – but the possibility remains. Can faith be restored?

But there is an additional dimension to this: not only that faith in institutions has been shaken, but that *Faith, properly understood, is the very condition of 'being shaken'*. Arguably, this is what Jeremiah is impressing on his audience – that institutions may work hard to bolster their deceptive reputation, their supposed right to be what they claim to be, but that true Faith rises above such efforts to be an authoritative institution. For Shanks, to be more concerned with the wellbeing or moral authority or even the truthfulness of the institution or tradition in itself is, rather, 'church ideology' – which conditions 'faith' with a small 'f', as distinct from the higher truth of Faith.[1] Whereas Faith, which testifies to truth as truth-in-process, cannot be contained by the walls, boundaries or even the creeds of such things. Instead, true Faith builds neighbourliness that transcends the limits of any single identity. To believe Jeremiah is to be shaken out of the deceptions represented by 'this is the temple of the Lord' and to have faith, or Faith, in a greater possibility. The calling to 'be the temple' is not limited to this group of people at this time in this place, but extends beyond their flawed efforts. People anywhere can and do participate in safeguarding the wellbeing of widows, orphans, refugees, and any who are pushed to the edges by powers of domination, or by flawed institutions. Not building an institution with a good reputation for its own sake but a solidarity of the different, and in fact a solidarity of solidarities: communities and movements that cut across other, more limited, loyalties and commitments, in pursuit of something greater. The truth of such Faith is the very condition of being shaken out of more limited loyalties, opened up to deeper neighbourliness for the sake of the greatest possible solidarity.

It's a fine vision – but there's a problem. Faith, at least with a small 'f', often seems rather more focused on particular beliefs, particular loyalties, particular traditions. It does not always seem to be something that 'opens us up', but is often practised as though we are being closed down. It focuses our attention on specific events, as the means through which God reveals Truth and Salvation. And to have faith is to believe in these, to trust in these, and to commit to these, religiously. In Christian terms, it is about having faith in the details of 'the Christ Event' – the incarnation, the miracles, the atoning death on a cross, the resurrection from the dead, and the promise of eternal life for all who believe. The idea of being 'opened up' beyond these things seems to represent a dilution of truth, a denial of their supreme significance, and puts at risk the claim to salvation. After all, 'faith' shares a common root with 'fidelity', or loyalty – so to have faith is to be loyal to these truths and what they represent.

The Greek word for having 'faith in' something – *pistis* – can also mean the 'faithfulness of' something. So, in the ancient world, to have faith is to be faithful and to be faithful is to have faith. This builds up a picture of faith being very much to do with the particular *identity* to which one is committed: such as having faith in Christian truths; being faithful to Christian tradition; being loyal to Christian community. Since the early decades and centuries of the church were also forged in a context of insecurity, with tensions among Jewish/Christian communities and with various waves of localized persecution by Roman authorities, the church developed a particularly crystallized notion of Christian identity – which was ultimately reinforced by political power, when the church became entangled with the state. Christian identity became something capable of withstanding the arrows slung at it.[2] Something steadfast and trustworthy. Something demanding fervour, devotion, faithfulness, loyalty. To be faithful to Christian truth is to have faith in particular beliefs, defined in certain ways, and ruling out other forms. The sort of loyalty that institutions value: 'this is the temple of the Lord, the temple of the Lord, the temple of the Lord'.

This is not just an early church phenomenon, however. We see it expressed in arguments within Jewish tradition too. On the one hand, in the face of worship that seems merely designed to flatter 'God', to keep 'God' on 'our' side, the prophet Amos rages against such self-interest and speaks up for justice for its own sake (5.21–24). By contrast, as Shanks argues,[3] the prophet Hosea reflects something of a rather more limited vision, as desired by a jealous God, wanting followers to be loyal religiously (14.1: 'Return, O Israel, to the Lord your God'; 14.4: 'I will heal their disloyalty'). It is the same tension again: on the one hand, the tight connection between 'God' and the community's loyalty to such a 'God' and, on the other hand, the impulse that opens us up to the true demands of justice, towards ever greater neighbourliness in solidarity with those beyond us.

Of course, I appreciate that this can seem like a rather neat binary choice: either we are loyal to truth as revealed to us, or we are open to something more 'universal', perhaps vaguer, more diffuse. If that is the choice, it surely reflects a rather naïve version of the tension between truth-in-hand and truth-in-process. Either we grasp our truth and reject all others, or we express ourselves open to everything. But is this what I actually mean?

If we are drawn to truth as encapsulated by the claims of a particular tradition, somehow we are viewed as 'closed'. Surely that is not fair, if the truths at the heart of our tradition urge us to be loving and hospitable towards the stranger and outsider. And from such a perspective, the 'universal' alternative seems root-less, disconnected from any particular foundation. In fact, to opt for the perspective unconfined by the boundaries of any tradition is to be naïve about the roots of our commitments, the ways in which any supposedly 'universal' perspective is actually conditioned by unspoken contextual assumptions. And if that is what truth-in-process means, the criticism would be entirely fair. It would be absolutely right to judge such a claim to 'universal truth' as a delusion in itself, rooted in yet another temple that tells lies to itself and to others. After all, if I say 'my truth cannot be contained by the truth of a single religion, but transcends them all', I may not be alert to the ways in which these truths come out of particular histories, particular traditions and particular commitments – and I may overlook the colonial dimensions of this: how a wide range of ideas and practices may have been colonized and absorbed into my own religious empire, without the scrutiny or accountability that, at least in theory, can come from commitment to a particular religious community.

So the caricatures of 'truth-in-hand' and 'truth-in-process' are not good enough. This is why I have tried to affirm the necessary relationship between them: that even if we aim to prioritize truth-in-process, we should appreciate the role for truth-in-hand. To offer an open palm, ready to receive the awkwardness and complexity of truth, does not mean that we deny our own story, our own roots, our own loyalties. Instead, it means that, while learning to see where we stand, we also recognize that we do not have the whole of reality. In fact, our tradition itself – as reflected in scripture – consists of a civil war between different experiences and dispositions: some closing us down, others opening us up, some urging loyalty, others inspiring hospitality, with each challenging aspects of the other. In fact, our own story has voices within it that specifically open us up to other voices, other stories, other truths, other experiences. To be loyal to it can mean simultaneously being hospitable to others, ready to receive their strange wisdom.

This is the point: to be loyal and to be open need not be contradictions. But faith has often been conceived and presented as though they must be. Either we are loyal to a particular set of truths – and, with them, to certain institutional expectations and practices – or we cut ourselves adrift from sure foundations, putting our future at risk. Such a dichotomy is the work of religious Empire in itself, urging us to fear the consequences of openness, and to maintain a certain degree of closure. It is the temple telling itself, and telling those committed to it, that it *is* the temple of the Lord, the temple of the Lord, the temple of the Lord. Surely, if the truth is repeated, people will not stray. But it is a poor reflection of what the temple is for. A denial of the purpose of religious identity, not least Christian identity. Because at the very heart of Christian identity is the truth of divine truth-in-process, gracious attentiveness to reality in all its awkwardness, pain and potential, offering up the possibility of relationship, or solidarity, in the midst of all that keeps us dominated and divided. At the heart of it, we are invited to be loyal to a truth, and a practice, which defies anything that might contain it.

Ironically, it is the notion of *Faith* that particularly captures this uncontainability. It is Faith that best illustrates that Christian identity is about *being shaken open*, not violently or by brute force or by the demands of any dominion, but by the awesome weakness of God: making possible the alternative horizon that is at hand, at the edge of reality, or in the cracks, or buried, waiting to rise. After all, if we are saved – healed, reconnected, opened up to the truth of divine hospitality in the midst of all of the brokenness – not by what we do or what we believe, nor even by our 'faith' as such, but rather by *Christ's faithfulness*, then a whole host of possibilities emerge.

But why would I say 'not by our faith as such, but rather by Christ's faithfulness'? It is because Paul's phrase, in his letter to the Romans, represents such a crucial ambiguity (e.g. 3.22, 26: 'faith in' or 'the faith of' Jesus).[4] Of course, he *may* have meant 'faith *in* Christ' – that it is our own faith in, or loyalty to, Christ that is ultimately effective – but this has been so misused by the church to emphasize loyalty to particular beliefs and to the institution itself; and it also seems increasingly at odds with the emphasis on *what God has done for us*, which suggests our hope cannot be dependent on whether we happen or manage to 'have faith'. However, even if he did intend 'faith in Christ', this does not mean there is only one form of what that may look like, since the Gospel accounts give us many different examples of what having faith in Jesus consists of – though they tend to point to deeper solidarity among all-comers, rather than a solidarity of the like-minded.

So, alternatively, Paul may have meant *both things together* – that our own faith in Christ and Christ's faithfulness cooperate with each other; that we participate in Christ's faithfulness. This is a strong and attractive possibility, giving room for our own agency, our own contribution, while holding it in tension with our dependence on Christ's initiative.

But whether the two are intended together, or Paul really intended 'the faithfulness of Christ', there is a crucial shift here that we must acknowledge: first, that it is *not* about the adequacy of our faith in terms of assent to particular beliefs, the limitations of specific forms of truth-in-hand closing us down; but, rather, whatever role our own faith plays, it is relativized by the significance of Christ's own faithfulness – it is his faithfulness that makes the new reality possible. Second, the shift from simply 'faith in Christ' (which implies something relatively fixed) to a greater role for, or complete focus on, the 'faithfulness of Christ' (which implies movement) also draws our attention to the object of his faithfulness. It does not make sense simply as faithfulness to himself, but as faithfulness to – what? Where 'faith in Christ' views him as the object of our own agency, as though he is the identity to which we are loyal, the 'faithfulness of Christ', by contrast, views him as the subject oriented towards another object; he is showing us how to be loyal and opens up the possibility of our being loyal to it, *whether or not we are explicitly loyal to him*. There emerges a possibility of 'implicit faith', of being shaken open and oriented towards faithfulness to this something-other. I will return to this – but what is it that he was loyal to? To what does such faithfulness orientate us? I suggest it is Holy Anarchy.

Christ witnessed to Holy Anarchy. He embodied it, in relationships, however incompletely. He furthered it through his ministry, without doing it all himself; calling us to participate. He showed, through his connections with others, how Holy Anarchy 'shook' him to the reality in which he was embedded. He was shaken to the reality of the powers of domination, the System in which we are all conditioned, to which he was remarkably disloyal, against the odds, while also being shaken to the alternative horizon that is at hand, and to which he was peculiarly faithful. This shows us what faithfulness or loyalty means in the context of Christian faith and discipleship: learning to be disloyal to the demands of Dominion, the structures of oppression that condition and limit us, while growing in faithfulness to the alternative: an alternative that opens us up to ever greater solidarity among all-comers. It is the struggle – to disentangle ourselves from one form of matrix, while knowing ourselves to be embedded in the greatest possible solidarity. It is the conflict between one loyalty and another. That is why it is not simply truth-in-hand versus truth-in-process, but the demands of one truth-in-hand, which consists of the desired prioritizing of truth-in-process, leads us into conscious conflict between two kinds of faithfulness, two kinds of loyalty, two kinds of faith.

In fact, this is what Paul's distinction between 'faith' and 'works' may mean, even though it is not often heard in these terms. To believe we are saved or healed by 'works' is to put all of the emphasis on traditions and systems that accentuate the boundaries between us. Though we often think 'works' is about action, it is more specifically about particular kinds of action: the things that communities do to separate themselves from others, believing that those boundary-markers are the very means by which we fulfil our purpose.[5] They could be specific practices, like circumcision, or baptism, or participation in religious festivals, or they could indeed be subscribing to a creed or a particular interpretation of scripture, or a distinctive theology – as though such loyalty in itself is the answer. To emphasize such things is to work against the possibility of the greatest possible solidarity; it is to cut ourselves off from the awkwardness, pain and potential of others' truths, experiences, wisdom, gifts and struggles.

By contrast, Faith – as the condition of being shaken – is sparked in response to divine truth-in-process, the open palm that invites us to greater empathetic alertness. As such, it draws us away from loyalty to closed or self-contained systems and opens us up to a new kind of loyalty – faithfulness to the way of Christ, or Christ*likeness*,[6] or neighbour-love.

Faith in Christ therefore implies alertness to Christ's solidarity-building faithfulness, which reshapes our loyalties in the direction of Holy Anarchy. Therefore, such faith is not about being loyal to the boundaries of 'Christian faith' *as such*, except insofar as they open us up to otherness, strangeness and possibility. It would be deceptive words, were we to believe that a particular form of loyalty could encapsulate this faithfulness – 'this is the temple of faithfulness, the temple of faithfulness, the temple of faithfulness'. Rather, we are being shaken, the windows and doors of the temple opened, the thresholds lowered, the boundaries becoming more porous, the flow increasingly two-way if not multi-directional, as ever greater solidarity emerges through attentiveness to many stories, not least those so often silenced by dominant forces. Faith, then, *is* Being Shaken, even if it is so often expressed or presented as something more conditional, more limiting; even where such forces are at work, the implicit or explicit impulse towards empathetic openness remains present, like an open palm.

Being un/ique: the ambiguities of faith(fulness)

Of course, something in particular remains unclear: what is the exact relationship between truth-in-hand and truth-in-process? Or, to put it a little more straightforwardly, how can we know which aspects of Christian faith are to be trusted *in their own terms*, and which ones should be understood as inspiration for faith(fulness) that lifts us beyond the tradition in itself? After all, it is understandable that people would want to know, for example, whether something like 'the incarnation' is to be understood as truth-in-hand, a genuinely unique and fundamental foundation-stone of our faith, or is it rather something more elusive, pointing us to the power of shakenness at work within Christian tradition, orienting us to an ever-greater solidarity of solidarities?[7] Is it true, *in itself*, or is it true to the extent that it opens us up to deeper neighbourliness in the spirit of Christ's faithfulness?

For those seeking absolute clarity on this, my answer will be frustrating. The exact relationship between truth-in-hand and truth-in-process is necessarily ambiguous. If we give priority to truth-in-process, as demonstrated by the open palm of divine graciousness, there is always a degree of 'unknowing' when it comes to the precise relationship between words and reality, experience and reality, tradition and reality, faith and reality. Can our form of words, our expressions of faith, our grasp of core truths, ever fully reflect what cannot be contained in a grasp? This may be more evident further away from the question of core truths.

For instance, many of us will have had the experience of feeling that 'non-Christians' are often more 'Christian' than 'committed Christians' are. We often find ourselves puzzling over this, or where this intuition leads us. At one level, it simply shows us that correct articulation of traditional forms of words does not always flow into lifestyle – in fact, it often doesn't. So Christians may indeed 'talk the talk', but we repeatedly fail to 'walk the walk'. This is deeply problematic if we claim that the words matter hugely – because if we think the correct words, capturing the correct truths, are absolutely fundamental, then they ought to mean something; but it turns out that we use the words, but so often they seem to mean so little. The issue is often focused on the disconnect between 'talking of love' while 'walking the way of prejudice'. But it also applies to seemingly core beliefs, like the incarnation: because, if we say 'Jesus is the Son of God', this ought to *mean* something, in terms of our faithfulness to his incarnating of the divine life – life that is gracious in its dealings with the im/pure, the stranger, the outsider. Instead, though, we sometimes make it more about the words than the love. Meanwhile, people who do not use the words, and in fact who sometimes explicitly reject the belief-systems of Christians, nevertheless can demonstrate deeper and broader love. This picks up on the discussion in Chapter 2 of belief, grace and justice in the context of the two kinds of truth and the gospel.

Here, the problem can be expressed in these terms. Making it all about the correct words, through absolute devotion to a certain kind of truth-in-hand, even with regards to 'core' ideas like the incarnation, is more an expression of 'works' than 'faith'. We find ourselves focusing so much on the things that seem to make us unique that we fail to see how such focus cuts us off from more genuine demonstrations of our purpose, especially where those demonstrations are outside of our tradition. This nudges us towards two insights: first, it is an appropriate and lifegiving feature of Christian *faith* to be alert to all the ways in which faithfulness is demonstrated in the world. Not only faithfulness by Christians, but faithfulness by people in other traditions – and faithfulness as well among those who are consciously agnostic or atheist.[8] Faithfulness among social and political movements in the cause of Holy Anarchy. Of course, this goes against the grain of how faith has generally been understood – that 'people of faith' are explicitly responsive to the divine or a 'higher power' – so how can agnostics or atheists be 'faithful'? And surely they do not want to be seen as such in any case, so isn't it somewhat patronizing and colonialist to include them in a project that they do not own for themselves?

The point, though, is not to say 'they are really people of faith, but they just don't know it'. It is to recognize the ambiguity around faith and faithfulness, and to affirm what religious people often notice: that all sorts of people seem to live life more *faithfully* than many who are consciously religious. That is to say, many people demonstrate faithfulness, in terms of their loyalty to the solidarity of the shaken, or Holy Anarchy. Of course, it is not their language, as it is not the language of many within Christianity either – but I am trying to use this form of language as a way of cutting across other loyalties, to identify ways in which, though we may be different in so many ways, we nevertheless can contribute to certain dynamics, in the cause of anti-domination, embodying community, and engagement with those who are different.

This idea of cutting across other loyalties surely resonates with many people's experiences of spirituality, the ways in which spiritual identity does not fit neatly into religious boxes, the proliferation of religious and spiritual movements that defy such truth-in-hand containment. There are many who are implicitly and ambiguously, or indeed consciously and potently, pursuing the upside-downing of structures of oppression and seeking to build a greater solidarity, and the church should find common cause – however awkwardly and imperfectly – with such movements. However, it is worth noting a caution. After all, this affirmation of 'faithfulness' among all sorts of people also implies the converse: that those of us who *think* of ourselves as 'people of faith', and indeed faithful to our religious identity, may actually be more concerned with our religious 'works' (boundary-markers) than Faith; our Faith may be more apparent than real. This is partly what we were wrestling with in Part 3, in terms of the awkwardness and incompleteness of the body of Christ, seeking to be an honest and real community which owns the fragility in its 'faithfulness'. But at the same time, unlike 'works' which do indeed imply 'measuring up', Faith is not about judging the adequacy or otherwise of other people's faith(fulness). To be faithful – that is, responsive to the graciousness of the divine open palm, ever alert to what we do not know and the further demands of neighbourliness – is not to test one another by the extent to which we measure up. Although it evokes a spirit of self-critique within us, as we learn to confront powers of domination that insidiously prevent us from being as neighbourly as we hope to be, it does not require legalism of us, testing the quantity of our faith/fulness.

For sure, let us affirm faithfulness to Holy Anarchy, wherever it is found – whether consciously or anonymously, spiritually or religiously, politically or economically; wherever people are being shaken out of closed-ways-of-being and opened up to greater solidarity-building empathy, so fostering the alternative horizon that is quietly at hand. Equally, let us identify the ways in which even those who profess to be faithful can indeed negate such conviction; we can fail to walk how we talk. So we should build communities that are honest enough, and safe enough, to enable such self-reflection, learning and movement, without being paralysed by our inadequacy. And this is possible if we prevent such willingness to self-examine from becoming a crystallized truth-in-hand, measuring itself and others by how much 'proper' faith is shown. Instead, may the awesome weakness of divine/human grace work among us, even as we also continue to expose and confront structures of oppression.

The second insight, arising when we reckon with our inclination to focus on uniqueness, is that uniqueness is complicated. To put it simply, being unique is not unique! The uniqueness of Christian faith is not in itself, therefore, the answer to everything because other traditions are also unique. Placing a lot of emphasis on our uniqueness doesn't negate the uniqueness of others. In fact, the alternative to uniqueness is much rarer. There's no such opposite – being 'ique', a non-word, as opposed to un-ique – but in a funny way that is telling.

Every identity within the cosmos has elements of uniqueness about it, and even though every identity also shares some common ground with some other identities, commonality is actually quite hard to pinpoint. Two people may be men, but very different; children, but very different;

British, but very different; Black, but very different; gay, but very different; Christian, but very different; conservative, but very different; or have had enough of this sentence, but still be very different. So, when we focus on certain features of religious identity as the basis of our uniqueness, we soon find ourselves in muddy waters – with different voices arguing in opposing directions. For some, the emphasis is on 'these things can be found nowhere else except here', while others say 'but that's only true to a certain extent', finding equivalents of the Trinity, incarnation, grace and salvation in various places outside of Christian tradition, while in each case the first group of Christians respond that those equivalents are not quite the same. And both can be right! To an extent.

I am only making the points fairly superficially here, before giving an illustration in the following section, but the essence is that when we say 'this feature is particular to Christian faith' it often turns out to be not quite as particular as we think (such as the graciousness of God). Conversely, when we say 'this is universal across all traditions', it turns out to be not quite as universal as we imagine (for example, belief in 'God' is much messier than often assumed). So debates go on, with regards to the nature of the uniqueness in relation to the Trinity, incarnation, grace and salvation; but in the case of each debate, it is the attachment to a certain form of truth-in-hand that drives the problem. That is, when we hold to 'this notion of incarnation', it is inevitable that people set out their respective cases for and against the notion – each believing it is possible and necessary to win. Whereas truth-in-process asks something else of us: a readiness to attend to the mess, the ambiguity, the power dynamics, the unresolvable conundrum, and yet the possibility of ever deeper solidarity even among the different. Not an uncritical solidarity that leaves everything just as it is, but a robust conversation of mutual enrichment and challenge in which people do not seek to 'win', but to undo domination and build healthy, diverse community. This process may be understood in terms of John Cobb's 'creative transformation'.[9]

While conversations of conflict betray the predominance of truth-in-hand, battling with each other, a yearning for commonality, on the other hand, can also betray the allure of truth-in-hand, even if a different kind. So when people say 'all religions are equal', they have in mind a preconceived truth-in-hand about how to measure religion, not only imagining it is possible to identify and quantify the respective advantages and disadvantages of each religious tradition, and weigh them up, but presuming to have done so and reached a conclusion. But the equation is not possible. We cannot determine the precise validity or worth of different traditions and compare them in that way. Traditions are messy, understood in diverse ways even within themselves, let alone by others outside them, so their actual identity cannot be encapsulated – let alone quantified – in theological or moral terms. They are also dynamic, not self-consistent, making it even more impossible to compare like for like, or unlike for unlike. The conclusion of equality is unreachable. But it is possible to say something more modest: each religion excels in particular ways, but may be weaker in others, and these distinct contributions deserve to be heard in their own terms, rather than such diversity being dominated or filtered through a particular perspective. However, even this is not straightforward, because there is no 'neutral' way of valuing either the content or the 'right to speak' of religious traditions; every social context has its own history, matrix of competing values and power dynamics, making it difficult for religions to be given 'equal space'.

Take, for example, Paul's statement in his letter to the Galatian church: 'There is no longer Jew or Greek, there is no longer slave or free, there is no longer male and female; for all of you are one in Christ Jesus' (Gal. 3.28). At one level, it is an incredible affirmation of the all-inclusive solidarity of Christian faith, enriched by his further insistence, 'For in Christ Jesus neither circumcision nor uncircumcision counts for anything; the only thing that counts is faith working through love' (Gal. 5.6). In other words, it is not about any truth-in-hand loyalty, any specific marker of our faithfulness, except faith itself *working through love* – that is, through neighbourliness with all. An inclusive vision. Yet on whose terms? I was part of an interreligious conversation exploring passages from different scriptures, and it was a shaking moment to hear 'there is no longer Jew or Greek' through the ears of my Jewish friend. In this passage, Jewish identity is negated. It no longer is. While we could argue, as Christians, that this needs to be placed alongside more positive affirmations of Jewish identity found in other parts of Paul's writings, the discomfort remains: is the 'other' identity overcome by Christian identity, and who gets to say so anyway? No such statements, or practices, exist in a vacuum, and they are never simply a matter of theological convictions *as though theology itself is 'only' theology*. So if we ever proclaim with regards to the status or validity of other traditions, we should recognize that so many layers are interacting all at once: theological, ideological, political, as well as interpersonal and deeply personal.

To be un/ique, by contrast, is to own the fact that our religious identity is not simple and monolithic, but includes within it various voices that disagree starkly with one another. There are those who would wish me to be exiled from the tradition, while there are others whose company I may not want to keep. But even among those on more friendly terms, there is no agreement about the status of other religions – or even how to have the conversation. For some, other traditions are simply wrong; for some, they are partly right, but only on terms that it is our prerogative to determine; and for others, each tradition contributes something different to our grasp of reality in all its awkwardness. To know the un/iqueness of Christian identity is to recognize that there are things that, at its best, our tradition excels at, while others excel in other areas, from which we may learn. It is right that we should bring our own norms to bear on others, as Cobb argues,[10] because it is honest to do so, knowing where we are coming from, even as we recognize that we rarely bring them consistently, but are inclined to notice the speck in others' eyes rather than the log in our own (Matt. 7.3). So we bring our norms, for all their distinctiveness, but it is simultaneously faithful to the demands of Holy Anarchy to anticipate that others will bring their norms to bear in their encounters with us, destabilizing any power dynamics that presume to give 'us' an advantage, while also recognizing where any particular religious identities struggle to be heard.

A hymn: The gospel's scandal

This hymn was written during a conference. It tries to incorporate a number of different strands and I am not sure that it manages to bind them together as coherently as it might. However, it is an attempt to wrestle with this tension – between the gospel as having energy of its own, desires and goals of inclusion, justice and transformation, and yet seeking to be responsive and receptive, recognizing it continues to be rightly troubled and enlarged by experiences and stories outside of itself.

The gospel's scandal we proclaim
is love that can't be self-contained,
that overflows to all of space,
encountering every story's face,
receiving, too, what others share:
all prophets calling us to care.

For God in Christ declares and shows
such love that hears the cries, and grows
through making room for ever more –
the Earth who groans, the least and poor:
for love accepts what we exclude,
and shakes foundations which delude.

The gospel's scandal we confess
is love that does not judge the mess:
the things we tend to edit out,
the stuff that stirs up honest doubt;
for love is changed by those 'outside'
who shake our tribal prayers and pride.

For God in Christ reveals and sings
that even death, which surely stings,
shall not confine or kill off love,
once raised up on that cross above –
for life prevails and love expands,
defying nails with open hands.

The gospel's scandal we proclaim
is love that's not yet fully named:
unfolding love with truths unknown
as many stories find their home;
and nothing in creation's bounds
can stop it shaking barriers down!

Graham Adams (2017)
Suggested tune: *Sussex Carol* – or create another one

Practising xenophilia

At the heart of faith, which is the condition of being shaken, expressed
in our corporate commitment as a un/ique tradition witnessing to Holy
Anarchy, one particular practice is crucial: xenophilia.[11] Loving that
which is other, that which is strange or foreign. It obviously stands in
contrast to xenophobia, fearing the other and the strange; holding them
at bay; distancing ourselves, cutting ourselves off, on the basis that 'they'
do not belong with 'us'. Xenophilia instead says: you are different and we
love you for it. After all, we are different too – to them, but also among
ourselves. Our un/iqueness is not absolute. Differences run through our
own community and similarities cut across other loyalties. It makes little
sense to choose one single feature as the basis for cutting ourselves off
from one another. In fact, faith in Christ, as a response to the faithfulness of Christ, is all about loyalty to this very quest: the movement
towards ever deeper neighbourliness, in solidarity with those silenced and
oppressed by powers of domination, as a solidarity among the im/pure,

building awkward community, and befriending those who, in various respects, may be 'strange' to us. So we should work hard not to cut ourselves off.

As Marianne Moyaert argues, strangeness goes to the heart of Christian tradition. Because of Israel's experience of being strangers in foreign lands, and because of God's self-revelation to 'us' in the face of the stranger, there is a moral responsibility to welcome the stranger.[12] She suggests that this memory of oneself as stranger means that our identity is always partly strange to ourselves; that our identity is therefore 'fragile'. This is to say, we are in a state of becoming, as argued also by Claude Geffré.[13] Or, as I put it elsewhere, 'Strangeness, then, is not simply what one encounters "in the Other" but is that future version of itself into which a tradition may yet grow',[14] spurred in part by memories of past destabilization and reconfiguration in our unfolding story. For our story is one of dynamism – and understanding ourselves as partly strange, or dislocated, and loved, helps us to love others who are also dislocated or strange.

But we need to notice something: that when Christians speak of 'we' in relation to Israel, Hebrew scriptures, or the 'Old' Testament, as though Israel's story is 'our' story, and as though Christian assumptions about Jewish tradition allow us to treat it as our own, we collapse an important sense of strangeness. Of course, Hebrew scriptures were Jesus' scriptures and we see them in him (as noted in Chapter 6), but we need to be attentive to the tension: for just as Christian identity is both familiar and strange, even among itself, so our relationship with Jewish tradition is one of both closeness and strangeness. The point about its strangeness is not to hold it at bay, but to affirm how our indebtedness to its ethic of welcome calls us to welcome it. Yet we have used its stories as weapons against it, treading heavily in its space with our historic power, as the church, while also making ourselves the subjects of its narrative. We have occupied texts without due regard for their strangeness, their self-critical force, and have done so for colonizing interests.[15] Instead, we must affirm that it is their strangeness to which we are indebted,[16] telling the truth with reference to YHWH's different measure of reality; their traditions of profound self-examination;[17] their call to repent of the structures of domination with which we are complicit, not least in our denigration or denial of strangeness itself. Such resources help Jews and Christians to participate in repairing the world.[18] Such 'chosenness' is not at all about favouritism, but the discomfiting call for some to testify to that which is greater than their or our tradition, as it evokes us again and again to witness to divine hospitality to strangeness. The ever-open palm.

So yes, we are strangers in a foreign land, both in the sense that we should tread carefully when presuming to occupy other religious territory as though it is really our own, relearning how to examine ourselves in the light of such decolonial awakening, and in the sense that such a vision of transformed community is indeed rather alien – it is a strange vision – so we should maintain a constructive vigilance towards any who feel alien or strange in a broken world. Receive them. Love them. Learn from them. Do not make them fit our own story, but hear theirs on its own terms. And see what happens. After all, as Jewish tradition also teaches us: God comes to us in the stranger, so we should seek to be alert to such persistent possibility, appreciating how what is foreign and unexpected may bear the very face of God.[19] It is an insight that Kosuke Koyama had identified many years before: that too often churches manage only to love that which is familiar, whereas our tradition beckons us to love that which is unfamiliar, even if that shakes our preconceptions or muddies our notions of purity.[20] God is on the move, unsettling our temples and urging us to build temporary shelters, putting the lure of truth-in-hand in its place, and trusting in the God of new things.

Interestingly, 'xenophilia' is just one way of binding together 'xeno' and 'philia'. The Greek word for hospitality is actually *philoxenia*, where the terms are reversed. This is instructive: that love of the other, or the strange, is the very same spirit that defines 'hospitality'. Not hospitality that merely makes space for the guest, so that the host may tell their own story, but hospitality that helps the guest to feel so at home that the guest shares their story. In fact, even more than that: hospitality where the other is so loved that the distinction between host and guest is destabilized. Not that the guest is expected to pick up the responsibility of hosting, but their agency is valued if they want to play a more active part; their contributions are welcomed; and the power of the host is restrained in the cause of Holy Anarchy. Of course, this is harder where the host owns and controls the space; whereas if people meet in space owned neither by the one nor the other, this spirit of mutuality is more workable. But such space may be rare.

More often, we operate in space that belongs to someone, trying to welcome others into it, which is never easy to do well. And not just in terms of physical space, but intellectual or theological space too: for example, when 'theology' tries to 'make room' for new voices, who decides what theology normally consists of and who decides whose voices to include? The process never exists in a vacuum but always has a history. White voices 'include' Black voices. Men 'include' women. Straight and cis voices 'include' sexual and gender diversities. Able-bodied voices 'include' dis/abled, differently abled and neuro-diverse perspectives. And Christian voices 'include' other religions. To do this well, so much self-awareness is required, power needs to be reworked, and space and time need to be expanded. Anarchically.

By way of a brief illustration, capturing something of the earlier discussion around un/iqueness too, what of the 'hospitality' in the story of Jesus and Zacchaeus, or Zacchaeus and Jesus (Luke 19.1–10), and what sort of 'salvation' is declared to have come?

I begin with some strategic proposals: first, when it comes to religious diversity and the task of practising xenophilia, it is important not only to engage with texts and resources that are clearly relevant, but also to be attentive to other voices elsewhere. This story does not immediately seem to be concerned with religious diversity, but it has huge implications for it. Second, of course no single text can resolve such complex issues – despite John 14.6 often being used as though it can, as explored in Chapter 5. Rather, texts should be brought into dialogue with one another, to help name the different and contrasting impulses at work, and to see whether the knots that we struggle to disentangle can at least be illuminated more clearly, even if not quite 'overcome'. Third, when we engage in this way we will be left with loose threads, leading us to new questions.

So, Zacchaeus and Jesus: who is the host to whom? At face value, Zacchaeus hosts Jesus, but Jesus basically invited himself; so it is a complex dynamic. Both are men of some status, a tax collector and a wandering rabbi, though the tax collector's status is ambiguous – on the one hand, backed up by the possibility of armed force, as and when needed, and clearly exercising economic power over others by exploiting them, but on the other hand, still regarded socially and religiously as an outcast. In fact, Jesus' status is also complex: a religious teacher, but one who keeps touching and eating with the 'wrong' people, so not exactly pure, even if he is more popular (among the multitudes, but not the leadership). They represent complex constituencies and have different kinds of power, so the 'hospitality' is messy! But clearly Jesus expresses a sort of xeno-philia that others would not; his presence (at least) prompts Zacchaeus to promise that he will pay back those whom he has cheated. As such, Zacchaeus exercises power, at least willpower initially, which is yet to manifest itself in new action. As a consequence, Jesus declares, 'Today salvation has come to this house!' But what is going on there?

Jesus expresses hospitality to Zacchaeus, through using his moral status to express love for the outsider, as a result of which the outsider creates space to receive Jesus' generosity-of-spirit and responds through expressing his intention to do economic justice. This prompts Jesus' declaration of salvation. Zacchaeus has not declared faith in Jesus, as such. Arguably, he is responding to the open-palm truth of Jesus' generosity-of-spirit, but he does not name it or confess faith in the incarnation, the atoning sacrifice of Jesus' death on the cross, or the resurrection. The cross hasn't even come yet, but salvation has. In fact, Zacchaeus' statement of faith is inconveniently thin on the ground. Even so, Jesus declares salvation. It *may* be because of Zacchaeus' faith but, if it is, it is only implicit, not explicit – and Jesus' explanation is also inconveniently thin, not stating that salvation only comes because of him or because of Zacchaeus' faithful response.

Rather, the response – expressed here in terms of a commitment to do economic justice, though only in intention, because it hasn't happened yet – *could* be something that anyone *might* demonstrate, regardless of what or who prompts it. So another tax collector, in another town, who had never heard of Jesus, might also suddenly decide to pay back his victims. Assuming this is possible – and why wouldn't it be? – might this also be the basis for salvation? We cannot say from this text alone, but it makes no more sense to rule it out than it does to rule it in. So what matters here, potentially, may be the transformation that is underway rather than the uniqueness of the cause. And as for this salvation, which also means healing, in the Greek, Zacchaeus is experiencing the saving or healing of his broken self, damaged relationships, distorted dynamics. It is more than personal; it is many-layered.

In other words, this impure Jew, a collaborator with the Roman occupiers and an exploiter of poor people, is named a son of Abraham not because of a particular form of truth-in-hand, though a particular ethical intention certainly plays a part – rather than simply 'belief' or 'faith as trust'. His loyalty, his faithfulness, consists in a revised commit-ment. *Metanoia*. Repentance. Turning around. Changing his mind. It is an experience that many can recognize, in their own stories, whether or not it is prompted by a particular person, tradition or formalized reve-lation, and whether or not it takes a designated form, in a specific moment or over a period of time. What we see here, in this brief episode, is that hospitality, with all its messy and complex dynamics, can be the basis for great change – and this can transcend the distinctions between religious communities, between religion and politics, religion and economics, faith and ethics, pure and impure. But Christians often want to pin it all down, to determine the cause, the effect and the narrative, whereas the reality is messier, and salvation is beyond reduction; it has many sides, many faces, many dimensions, all of which – I suggest – reflect the impulse towards Holy Anarchy.

Loving strangers – or, indeed, loving strangeness, the sheer quality of that which is unfamiliar, in whatever guise – goes to the heart of this movement, because it is the hospitable basis of such transformation. And not only the transformation of others, but our own transformation, in and through such encounter. For God comes to us in the stranger, as stranger than whatever we currently hold, destabilizing our preconceptions and opening us up to the alternative horizon of new possibilities.

Engaging strangeness critically

So far it is arguable that I have given a potentially romantic view of strangeness, as though it is generally a beautiful thing to love and embrace. But are there some sorts of strangeness that we should rightly hold at bay? After all, some things are 'strange' precisely because their structures go against the dynamics of Holy Anarchy. For example, where a religious tradition perpetuates ecological destruction, patriarchy, racism, economic injustice, homophobia or transphobia, how can we 'love' its strangeness? This echoes certain issues we have encountered before: the tension between the love for justice (evoking solidarity among people in pursuit of certain kinds of transformation) and the love for enemies (evoking solidarity among those who work for quite different, even conflicting, goals). And, for sure, where a religious tradition (whether our own or another) is explicit in its defence of oppression or exclusion, does that not make it an 'enemy' of Holy Anarchy – yet somehow still to be loved?

In this regard, it is helpful to note two things: first, 'many theisms are headed in the wrong direction'.[21] In other words, it is wholly legitimate to call out theologies and behaviours that go against the spirit of Holy Anarchy. In Rieger and Kwok's terms, it is about the way in which 'God' and 'Empire' coalesce, such that religion becomes a clear defender of the status quo. It is often Christian traditions that play this role, but other traditions can certainly contribute to it too. The particular issue is not whether people do or do not believe in God, because belief in God is no guarantee of commitment to Holy Anarchy, as we have acknowledged. Rather, the issue is the question of our model of power: where it resists Holy Anarchy, in denial of God's awesome weakness, by upholding structures of domination, it needs to be named as such. Sometimes this will be movements within our own tradition, sometimes in other traditions, sometimes unnoticed and unexamined in ourselves, but Holy Anarchy evokes alertness in us to all these forms and processes. It is right to challenge such things, but what might it mean to 'love' such movements as 'enemies'?

Walter Wink's proposal that powers of domination should be 'engaged' rather than 'demonized' may help. He recognizes that any such powers consist of people, people who do not always know what they are doing, but admittedly they sometimes do; people who are embedded in these structures without the possibility of escaping into innocent space; people who are not simply 'baddies' as opposed to 'goodies', because loyalty to the System is messy, such that we can simultaneously collude with it and resist it. This is what intersectionality illuminates, identifying the different strands of identity and oppression interacting with each other. So if it is possible, it can be fruitful to humanize these systems, to see how we are variously embedded in them, while 'engaging' to see what alternative directions may be catalysed and furthered. But intersectionality also illuminates that some people are repeatedly at the bottom of the pile and that the systems dehumanize so many – so what does it mean to 'engage' such forces, rather than denouncing them straightforwardly?

This leads to a second insight: that the question of prioritizing 'love for enemies' looks very different depending on where you are in the dynamics of power. If you are relatively privileged, in certain respects benefiting from the prevailing structures, you might be inclined to favour 'love for enemies', to the extent that your privileges place you at odds with Holy Anarchy. In a number of respects, this is where I am, so I must be alert to the ambiguities in my own desire for 'love for enemies' to be prioritized, because I may need such grace extended to me. Meanwhile, if you are located rather differently, bearing the weight of several intersecting identities that are disadvantaged by the powers of domination, 'love for justice' may well be more urgent than 'love for enemies'. But not only more urgent. The prospect of being in a shared space with one's enemies, if they are one's oppressors, is actually a harmful prospect. This is where 'love for enemies' can be oppressive, depending who controls its meaning and structure.

In light of such dynamics, postcolonial experiences and perspectives can be particularly insightful. As Kwok Pui-lan notes, 'the issue before us is not religious diversity, but religious difference as it is constituted and produced in concrete situations, often with significant power differentials'.[22] She is highlighting that the sheer fact of diversity is never the whole story; it is always framed by histories of asymmetrical power, not least as a result of colonialism. So even where those of us of 'colonizer heritage'[23] seek to work positively with the voices of other traditions, it can be a way of bolstering our own cosmopolitanism.[24] Those of us who can take certain advantages for granted may desire to embrace the strangeness of other perspectives as a way of asserting our credentials as global citizens, without noticing how our historical privileges shape our assumptions and actions – in particular, the insidious grip of 'white mythology'.[25]

For Wonhee Anne Joh, in her work on the cross that uses Korean concepts to call for political love that is stronger than powers of oppression, there is a special role for people whose identities are hybrid:[26] that is, those whose identities have been reshaped in light of colonialism, such that they testify to the unequal interplay between the narratives of the colonizers and of the colonized. It is for them to be the 'watchdogs' alert to the ways in which EuroAmerican theories and practices are superimposed, as though they represent everyone. In fact, as Kwok argues, hybridity goes to the heart of Christian identity 'from the beginning',[27] since our categories for making sense of Jesus/Christ are conditioned by various levels of identity-complexity (Roman occupation of Palestine; Christian co-option of Jewish resources; Greek philosophical lenses through which to read biblical material; and so on).

These contributions show us that, even where we seek to engage positively with strangeness, the practice is informed by questions of power – so those of us with relative privilege should not automatically assume that 'the other' can always be loved, received and embraced. After all, as other religious traditions have also emphasized, the colonized did find themselves 'receiving' the strangeness of the colonizer, and it cost them their own identity and freedom. So when it comes to engaging with strangeness, and who decides whether to encourage it, there must be discernment, as I shall reiterate below.

At the same time, however, it can be those of us with relative power who are more anxious about the scope of strangeness which may be loved. Too much strangeness can threaten the integrity of the existing structures, pushing us too quickly away from a solidarity of the like-minded towards a deeper neighbourliness, the anarchic solidarity of the shaken. By contrast, those with less to lose can find allies among 'strangers', a whole host of experiences that have been neglected, suppressed and sacrificed by prevailing systems. So it is important, when faced with the task of how to engage with strangeness, to recognize the messy ways in which power dynamics shape things: dynamics that, on the one hand, encourage the powerful to say, 'you should love your enemies (because they may be us)', while, on the other hand, unnerving the powerful with too much awkward diversity, such that they proclaim, 'you should still conform within recognizable parameters'.

It is wisdom such as that from postcolonial perspectives, the watchdogs examining those of colonizer heritage, and with consciously decolonial visions, unpicking the grip of imperial possession, which challenges both voices in the heads of the powerful: so when 'love for enemies' is promoted at the expense of the interests of those who have been excluded, the insurgents declare that justice must take priority, holding to account those of us who would detract from its demands; and when 'too much strangeness' unsettles the powerful, the insurgents encourage such diversity *because* it unsettles the interests of the powerful.

What we see here is that our engagement with strangeness – whether in terms of religious diversity or any sort of variety of life – obviously throws up many questions. This is Holy Anarchy at work, because it cannot be witnessed by one single community or tradition; it cannot be contained or managed by a sole religion; it destabilizes such conformity and overcomes any instincts to close down the sheer awkwardness of the multiplicity of reality/ies. But this does not mean strangeness *per se* is to be romanticized, as though it is always a beautiful thing; because while it can be wonderful it can also be dangerous, notably when imposed. So we will sometimes have to choose, to take sides, not holding difference at bay for ever, but recognizing when the demands of justice, and the solidarity they evoke, must come first.

Missional skills: discernment, embodiment, friendship

Although I have not discussed 'strangeness' so far in the light of the usual framework of 'theologies of religious diversity' (TRD), it may help to explain where Holy Anarchy sits within such concerns. To do so is to begin to draw out certain 'missional skills' that may be pertinent when it comes to the question of witnessing to Holy Anarchy in a context of religious diversity, or indeed other kinds of diversity. As in relation to powers of oppression (Part 2), the discussion of which clearly overlaps with this dimension, we can identify three particular skills – discernment, embodiment and friendship – which, to an extent, are also the broader categories guiding us through Parts 2 to 4.

To discern is to see where Holy Anarchy is present: the alternative horizon at the edge of reality, or in the cracks, which reflects the divine truth-in-process of awesome weakness, exposing and subverting the prevailing structures that dominate and divide. This tells us, in relation to TRD, that exclusivist theologies and practices cannot wholly reflect Holy Anarchy: after all, the theo-politics of Jesus, by which I mean the way his theological and political commitments interact and embody one another in his ministry and vision, constantly challenge exclusiveness. He stood with those judged as im/pure; he affirmed the faith of those who did not belong; he pointed to an alternative reality that emerges beyond boundaries or in unexpected locations, so it is hard to see how such a propensity for generosity-of-spirit could justify a Christian attitude that denies the possibility of saving potential in other traditions.[28]

However, to discern Holy Anarchy at work also means we should recognize that it can indeed be hosted in apparently unlikely places – including within commitments to such exclusive theologies. After all, the vision and practice of Holy Anarchy consists of several things at once – so people and churches who are committed to the Christian faith as the only entry-point to salvation can also witness to the way Holy Anarchy subverts powers of domination, and they can seek to build messy communities of faith, holding together an awkward diversity of people shaken open or indeed who are closed in many different ways. They may also struggle to do these things – but we all do.

What of the skill of 'embodying' Holy Anarchy? In Part 3 we considered this in relation to the church in itself, and the call to be anarchically one, impurely holy, deeply catholic, and interruptedly apostolic. But how does this relate across religious borders, to our engagement with those committed to other communities? Here, we can consider how 'inclusivism' speaks partially to our embodiment of Holy Anarchy. According to inclusivist theologies, other religious traditions may potentially be included within our own framework, on the basis that the benefits of God's gracious acts cannot be limited to those consciously believing in them; but what this means is that Christian norms are the basis for any affirmation of other traditions – often experienced as a patronizing rather than dignifying approach.

With Holy Anarchy as my organizing principle, which is not only found in explicit Christian witness, but that can be *implicitly* discerned, pursued and embodied elsewhere, it certainly seems as though this approach could be characterized as yet another patronizing inclusivism. And I must 'own' the degree to which I am prepared to 'see' Holy Anarchy even where it is not others' language or concept, not only in religious traditions, but among those who are agnostic or atheist, wherever signs of anti-domination are at work and the flourishing of life in its fullness is encouraged. Of course, there is a degree of inevitability to this; we each 'see' from within a particular story (or cross-fertilizing of multiple stories) and we cannot help but frame what we encounter in terms that are familiar to us. This is the usefulness and prevalence of truth-in-hand; seeking out ways in which something different reflects aspects of what we already know; affirming it, even 'blessing' it, on 'our' terms.

Were that the whole of the story, that would certainly be a problem. If Holy Anarchy claimed to be anti-oppressive, decolonial and subversive of prevailing power dynamics, while colluding with business-as-usual – by accepting otherness only to the extent that it reflects what we already know – this would be a denial of the fullness of what Holy Anarchy means to be. However, as with exclusivism, it is important to acknowledge that

Holy Anarchy certainly can be witnessed to, and embodied, within inclusivist theologies, however imperfectly, because Holy Anarchy is always hosted by communities of more limited openness. But the reason why inclusivism *per se* cannot fully reflect the alternative horizon is because it does not have room for its own vision receiving from, and being troubled by, the strangeness of the Other.[29]

By contrast, Holy Anarchy involves a creative tension, because of the interplay between truth-in-hand (which asserts, 'Holy Anarchy is indeed our organizing principle') and truth-in-process (which acknowledges that Holy Anarchy is a risk, subject to revision through perpetual interchange with strangeness). It is an ambiguous dynamic between 'identity' and 'solidarity with what is unknown'. It is a *process* – which includes receptivity to the reconfiguring of itself. After all, the organizing principle may bear the marks of undiagnosed White mythology or western modes of thinking because of its roots. Even where it seeks to be as conscious as possible of these risks, it can never be alert to the whole of reality, because 'it' is always embodied in people, relationships and communities. So inclusivism is not enough, because the vision itself needs to be subject to critical voices outside of its current self-knowledge.

So it must surely find its home especially among 'pluralism': the approach to religious diversity that sees the value in traditions on their own terms, not because 'we' bless them on 'our' terms. But actually, pluralism often functions as an agenda in which people have already determined the validity of the Other;[30] there is not always scope for surprise, or even necessarily for criticism (except for criticism of exclusivist and inclusivist theologies). As such, pluralism does not fully embody Holy Anarchy either, because it is not always fully attentive to the strangeness of what is encountered; it tries to iron out the creases within traditions and between them to find a smooth sense of common ground and common cause. Where that happens, seeking out commonality at the expense of what is disruptively divergent, pluralism can nevertheless testify partially to Holy Anarchy, as we all can, but not fully.

Pluralism always needs some degree of correction from the approach known as 'particularism', in which traditions are said to be so particular, so distinctive, that any meaningful understandings between them are not really possible; difference in itself prevails. This is a helpful caution, correcting the positive presumptuousness of pluralism, but it cannot reflect the ambiguities that Holy Anarchy is alert to. So what is needed is a more deeply *pluralistic* theology which does not collapse into plural*ism*; an approach that is deeply receptive to strangeness, but without romanticizing it or converting it into something we already know. If there is anything that is predetermined by Holy Anarchy, it is that the priority of truth-in-process invites us to be open, even strangely open, while simultaneously bearing unusual witness to those experiences and stories that expose systems of domination.

If you like, once again openness and criticality are the two sides of the open palm: openness to reality in all its awkwardness, unfitting-ness, im/purity and multifacetedness, while giving greater weight to those voices alerting us to asymmetrical power-structures, so we can never be neutral. The solidarity we seek to build is indeed a solidarity of all-comers, mediated as (potential) friends, but the art of agitation continually confronts the systems that silence, suppress and sacrifice.

There are examples from other traditions to which I keep returning, because they offer up the potential for the dynamic between openness and criticality, the love for enemies and for justice, in line with Holy Anarchy's mediating and agitating energies. So, as Shanks suggests, a particular gift arising from Rabbinic Judaism is its robust introversion, a disclination to boast about attractiveness to others, because such restraint inhibits the will to dominate;[31] rather, it is more focused on working out how, within its communities, it can be true to the holiness of its calling in the midst of a broken world.

For the Muslim liberation theologian Farid Esack, the quranic tradition is inclusive of other traditions, on the basis that God creates diversity and sees the potential for interreligious solidarity against oppression. Such inclusiveness, then, is focused on certain goals: freeing humanity from injustice and servitude so they may be free to worship God.[32] He sees the connection between idolatry and injustice – that is, it is our worship of false gods that underpins structures of injustice, but Esack notes too that religion itself is not free from such dangers; rather, it is a battlefield between defence of the status quo and the determination to transform it.[33] So in these Abrahamic traditions we see marks of Holy Anarchy: the restraint of the will to dominate, the denunciation of idolatry-infused injustice, the need for corporate self-examination, and the possibility of a broader solidarity against oppression.

Traditions of the Indian subcontinent also bear the marks of Holy Anarchy in particular respects. Kristin Johnson Largen's comparative study, *Baby Krishna, Infant Christ*, underscores the potential for the ambiguity and dynamism of divinity as understood in Hindu traditions to enrich and disrupt the western philosophical models which have rather dominated Christian thought.[34] For example, divine *eros* (mutual love) and *lila* (playfulness) witness to the energetic, embodied connectedness between the divine and the human, which expresses divine delight in us at least as much as any divine judgement on us. Nevertheless, many Hindus affirm Christian faith for its implicit pursuit of the Hindu goal of union with the divine. But, among some, there is the view that any hierarchy of religious traditions places Christianity below, on the basis that its common attachment to exclusive claims impedes its capacity to embrace diversity – though at least there is the possibility that Christians may reincarnate as Hindus.[35] It is instructive to be humbled in this way.

For John Makransky, a Mahayana Buddhist, it is Buddhism that is best placed to recognize that no single tradition can contain absolute truth (an argument interestingly made by Shah-Kazemi vis-à-vis Islam, and by Vivekananda vis-à-vis Hinduism[36]), while affirming that non-Buddhists will be alert to certain aspects of reality by virtue of their commitments, which Buddhists may not see. He also argues that our historical conditionedness, rooted in particular norms and assumptions, means none of us can meaningfully rank the traditions, so even though he acknowledges that he regards Buddhism as best placed to affirm diversity, others will be better at other things, so an overall hierarchy is impossible.[37] Here we see the instability of Holy Anarchy, the refusal to succumb to the power of truth-in-hand, recognizing how we are conditioned yet still offering the distinctive good news that comes from particular locations in the matrix.

Overall, duly evoked by the invitation to Holy Anarchy, our engagement with strangeness, notably religious strangeness but all kinds of diversity (racialized, sexual, gender, dis/ability, neuro-diversity, and so on), is seen to be messy. Connections are made. Friendships are possible. Solidarity grows. We are enriched and challenged, while also potentially enriching and challenging others. But we must also be attentive to histories of colonialism, the harm done by one tradition to others, the risk of romanticizing the Other, turning them into an 'exotic' which excites our sense of global citizenship without due regard for the deep pain, the dehumanizing categorizations, and the refusals to hear stories on their own terms.

To engage strangeness, without idealizing or demonizing, is to risk being opened up in uncomfortable ways, not only to the ambiguities of reality that cut across our presumed boundaries and loyalties, but to the asymmetries of power that entrench patterns of domination and division. All of this needs to be handled with care – not as abstract food for thought, but as reality impinging on our attempts to worship the God of Holy Anarchy and witness to and embody such a vision. Such vocations cause us to turn to the question of worship as the space in which we engage not only with the strangeness of the world as it is, but with the strangeness of the alternative horizon to which we are being oriented.

A hymn: Let's go across

Christ calls us as disciples
to tread unknown terrain,
embark on new adventures
and change ourselves again.
'Let's go across the water,
on to the other side,'
and if a storm should greet us,
may peace and faith abide.

By faith we're called to follow
though like a mustard seed
we know our hope is fragile
and yearns to be set free:
but we are called in weakness
as waves crash all around,
God knowing our potential:
may peace and faith abound!

By faith we must remember
we've not passed here before;
this way eludes our mapping;
we're safer on the shore:
but we are called to follow
God's promises ahead
which break the flowing torrents:
in hope we too shall tread!

Christ, call us as disciples
to what we do not know,
to where the Spirit prompts us:
that mustard seeds might grow!
Let's go across the waters,
beyond what we can see,
that as your promise shapes us,
new worlds shall dare to be!

Graham Adams (2012)
Suggested tune: *Thornbury* – or create another one
Based on Mark 4.30–41 and Joshua 3.1–17.

Questions to ponder

1 If faith may be understood in terms of Christ's faithfulness to Holy Anarchy, what does this mean for our faith? In what ways is 'faith' like 'being shaken' – opened up to an alternative horizon that beckons us? How does this approach differ from the sort of loyalties often expected when we think of or practise religious faith?

2 What are the unique features of Christian faith that matter especially to you? On the other hand, what experiences do you have of shared commitments cutting across other loyalties – that is, having more in common with some people in other traditions than with some in your own?

3 How might churches demonstrate 'xenophilia' (love for strangeness) more fully? And what do you make of the approach to the Zacchaeus story in this chapter?

4 What kinds of 'strangeness' do you struggle with the most? Or, in other words, who do you find yourself treating as 'enemies', whether gently or fervently? And how important is it for churches to learn how to hold 'love for justice' in tension with 'love for enemies'?

5 Whether from the examples in this chapter, or from your own experience, what insights from other religious traditions have enriched or challenged you? And how do you feel about the prospect of your deep commitments being reshaped through encounter with others?

Further reading

John B. Cobb Jr, *Transforming Christianity and the World: A Way Beyond Absolutism and Relativism* (Maryknoll, NY: Orbis, 1999).

Catherine Cornille, *The Im-possibility of Interreligious Dialogue* (New York: Crossroad, 2008).

Jenny Daggers, *Postcolonial Theology of Religions: Particularity and Pluralism in World Christianity* (Farnham: Routledge, 2013).

Kosuke Koyama, *Three Mile an Hour God* (London: SCM Press, 1979, 2021).

Kwok Pui-lan, *Postcolonial Imagination and Feminist Theology* (London: SCM Press, 2005).

Marianne Moyaert, *Fragile Identities: Towards a Theology of Interreligious Hospitality* (Amsterdam and New York: Rodopi, 2011).

Andrew Shanks, *Hegel Versus 'Inter-Faith Dialogue': A General Theory of True Xenophilia* (New York: Cambridge University Press, 2015).

John J. Thatamanil, *Circling the Elephant: A Comparative Theology of Religious Diversity* (New York: Fordham University Press, 2020).

Notes

1 Andrew Shanks, *Hegel Versus 'Inter-Faith Dialogue': A General Theory of True Xenophilia*, New York: Cambridge University Press, 2015, pp. 2–4.

2 Andrew Shanks, *A Neo-Hegelian Theology: The God of Greatest Hospitality*, Farnham: Ashgate, 2014, p. 21: 'a community under constant pressure ... developed an authoritative hierarchy to enforce [its unity]'.

3 Shanks, *A Neo-Hegelian Theology*, pp. 71–4.

4 Here I am informed by, but not limited to, the so-called 'New Perspective on Paul', from E. P. Sanders, N. T. Wright, James Dunn and many other biblical scholars – for example, https://www.ntwrightpage.com/2016/07/12/new-perspectives-on-paul/ (accessed 7 January 2022).

5 See Shanks, *Xenophilia*, pp. 15–16.

6 Shanks, *Xenophilia*, pp. 1, 15.

7 Shanks, *A Neo-Hegelian Theology*, p. 114.

8 Andrew Shanks, *Theodicy Beyond the Death of 'God': The Persisting Problem of Evil*, London and New York: Routledge, 2018, p. 4: he speaks of God working 'undercover'.

9 John B. Cobb Jr, *Christ in a Pluralistic Age*, Philadelphia, PA: Westminster Press, 1975, pp. 21, 60–1, 80, 132, 181, 188, 203, 245; and John B. Cobb Jr, *Transforming Christianity and the World: A Way Beyond Absolutism and Relativism*, Maryknoll, NY: Orbis, 1999, p. 186.

10 Cobb Jr, *Transforming Christianity and the World*, p. 182.

11 Shanks, *Xenophilia*, pp. 1, 11, 26.

12 Marianne Moyaert, *Fragile Identities: Towards a Theology of Interreligious Hospitality*, Amsterdam and New York: Rodopi, 2011, pp. 261–7.

13 Claude Geffré, 'Double Belonging and the Originality of Christianity as a Religion', in Catherine Cornille (ed.), *Many Mansions? Multiple Religious Belonging and Christian Identity*, Eugene, OR: Wipf and Stock, 2002, p. 104.

14 Graham Adams, *Theology of Religions: Through the Lens of 'Truth-as-Openness'*, Leiden: E. J. Brill, 2019, p. 73.

15 See, for example, Mark G. Brett, *Decolonizing God: The Bible in the Tides of Empire*, Sheffield: Sheffield Phoenix, 2008, p. 41: Regarding Noah's curse, 'it is not just that the colonizers of modern history misconstrued these chapters in Genesis to serve their own interests. Rather, they *inverted* what the editors were setting out to do, and failed to see that the biblical texts potentially deprived them of legitimacy.'

16 Walter Brueggemann, *Redescribing Reality: What We Do when We Read the Bible*, London: SCM Press, 2009, pp. 4–5.

17 Shanks, *Xenophilia*, pp. 200–1.

18 Reuven Firestone, 'A Jewish Response to the Christian Theology of Religions', in Elizabeth Harris, Paul Hedges and Shanthikumar Hettiarachchi (eds), *Twenty-First Century Theologies of Religions: Retrospection and New Frontiers*, Leiden: E. J. Brill, 2016, pp. 323–4.

19 Moyaert, *Fragile Identities*, pp. 268–72.

20 Kosuke Koyama, *Three Mile an Hour God*, London: SCM Press, 1979, pp. 51, 65f., 74–5. He also wrote: 'Theology to be authentic must be constantly challenged, disturbed and stirred up by the presence of strangers', in Kosuke Koyama, '"Extend Hospitality to Strangers" – A Missiology of Theologia Crucis', *International Review of Mission*, vol. 82, no. 327 (1993): 283.

21 Joerg Rieger and Kwok Pui-lan, *Occupy Religion: Theology of the Multitude*, Washington DC: Rowman & Littlefield, 2010, p. 89.

22 Kwok Pui-lan, *Postcolonial Imagination and Feminist Theology*, London: SCM Press, 2005, p. 205.

23 Jenny Daggers, *Postcolonial Theology of Religions: Particularity and Pluralism in World Christianity*, Farnham: Routledge, 2013, p. 142.

24 Kwok, *Postcolonial Imagination*, p. 145.

25 Daggers, *Postcolonial Theology*, p. 19, citing Jacques Derrida, 'White Mythology' (1971), in Jacques Derrida, *Margins – in Philosophy*, trans. Alan Bass, Chicago, IL: University of Chicago Press, 1982, p. 213.

26 Wonhee Anne Joh, *Heart of the Cross: A Postcolonial Christology*, London: Westminster John Knox, 2006, p. 9.

27 Kwok, *Postcolonial Imagination*, pp. 125–49, 171–82.

28 See Andrew Shanks, *God and Modernity: A New and Better Way to Do Theology*, London and New York: Routledge, 2000, p. 42, and *Xenophilia*, p. 4, on the limitations of such 'exclusivism'.

29 Shanks, *God and Modernity*, p. 43, and *Xenophilia*, p. 4, on the limitations of inclusivism.

30 Shanks, *God and Modernity*, p. 44, and *Xenophilia*, p. 4, on the limitations of some pluralisms.

31 Shanks, *Xenophilia*, p. 201.

32 Farid Esack, *The Qur'an, Liberation and Pluralism: An Islamic Perspective of Interreligious Solidarity against Oppression*, Oxford: Oneworld, 1997, pp. 124, 146, 159.

33 Esack, *The Qur'an*, p. 176.

34 Kristin Johnson Largen, *Baby Krishna, Infant Christ: A Comparative Theology of Salvation*, Maryknoll, NY: Orbis, 2011, pp. 52–61.

35 Perry Schmidt-Leukel, 'Pluralist Approaches in Some Major Non-Christian Religions', in Harris, Hedges and Hettiarachchi (eds), *Twenty-First Century Theologies of Religions*, pp. 170–2.

36 Reza Shah-Kazemi, *The Other in the Light of the One: The Universality of the Qur'ān and Interfaith Dialogue*, Cambridge: The Islamic Text Society, 2006, p. 169; and Swami Vivekananda, *The Complete Works of Swami Vivekananda*, 8 vols, Mayavati Memorial Edition, Calcutta: Advaita Ashrama, 1989, vol. 3, p. 424.

37 John Makransky, 'Thoughts on Why, How, and What Buddhists Can Learn from Christian Theologians', *Buddhist–Christian Studies* 31 (2011): 130–1 (119–33).

8

Awe in the Garden and the Horizonal God

She turned around and saw Jesus standing there,
but she did not know that it was Jesus.
(John 20.14)

Between the old landscape and the new horizon: rewriting the script

Mary was the first to witness the emptiness of the tomb. The possibility that the old and familiar world was not quite the entirety of reality. The possibility of an alternative horizon, closer to hand than had been imagined. The possibility of Holy Anarchy. In John's Gospel, chapter 20, she tells Peter and another disciple what she has seen; they come, look, cannot understand, and return to their homes. But as for Mary, she 'stood weeping outside the tomb'. She stays there, facing it. The tomb, the empty space, the discarded cloth. An open palm, waiting. This is a basis for worship.

The gap, the crack in reality as we know it, which suggests the inbreaking of something different, or the outbreak of something un-remembered. And the emotion, the weeping, the grief – grief over what has been, and the yearning for what could be. The sense that she does not want to run; she wants to be there. Worship is the space in which we hold such spaces open – the silence, the weeping, the grieving, the yearning, the staying there, the waiting, the anticipation. Worship represents the opportunity for a different kind of encounter. Between the old landscape and the new horizon. Between what was, what is, and what might be. Between the tomb and its emptiness.

And then angelic figures asked her, 'Woman, why are you weeping?' It is an opportunity to ask the obvious – and the not so obvious. To give voice to grief and yearning. 'They have taken away my Lord, and I do not know where they have laid him.' It is an opportunity to wrestle with the ways in which we make sense of things, according to what we know: the truth-in-hand of reality, as it is currently understood. Jesus is missing, so must simply be laid somewhere else. It is the only explanation. TANA.

There are no alternatives. But something is nagging. Another possibility. Un-remembered but re-emerging. So she turned around – as though she knew that the direction she was facing was not everything. She turned around. And saw Jesus. There he was. The manifestation of the alternative horizon tugging at her. Holy Anarchy lives! But she did not know that it was Jesus. We do not know what stands before us. It is so hard to recognize what cannot be. What defies our truth-in-hand. She did not know. We do not know. And yet here we are, in this 'in between place'. Half-knowing. Giving voice to what cannot be. Grieving over what's been lost. Yearning for ... what?

This is a basis of worship. The shattering of the glass between two worlds. The tearing of the veil. The gentle trespassing of Holy Anarchy into foreign territory. But it's not really foreign – it has been here all along, if we had the figurative eyes to see it, ears to hear it, hands to touch it, or pulse to beat to it. But it's not exactly our fault. We were conditioned not to see it, not to hear it, not to touch it, not to beat to its presence. Conditioned by forces within us and outside of us, by the will to dominate that framed so much of life. So it was kept from us. Cut off from us. The possibility of this something-different. But we knew it was there, and sometimes we dared to sense its breath; to dance to its tune, however falteringly; to imagine ourselves as fully alive to its dawn. And we were given hints of it, we were urged to practise its dance-moves; we shared in stories telling of it; we even imagined that our communities of faith embodied it – but not as well as we had hoped. And here it is, again. Standing before us. But we cannot recognize it.

Jesus repeated the angels' words: 'Woman, why are you weeping?' Attuned to her grief. But added, 'Whom are you looking for?' Conscious that something, *someone*, is at the heart of this. A broken relationship. Disconnection. Fracture. And Mary supposes he must be the gardener. Projecting her prevailing-world assumptions as she tries to make sense of things – and is not yet able to recognize what stands before her. She asks, 'If you have carried him away, tell me ...' Help me understand. Help me grieve. Help me be with the one who made other things seem possible. Worship is a space for all of this embodied desire: to know, to weep, to be with one another. All of this matters; it is not peripheral to worship, as though worship is only the encounter with the new horizon. No, worship incorporates lament, the tragedy of existence, the wounds of the world. It gathers all of this into a space that has room for it. Like an open palm.

But it is also, for sure, a space in which the un-remembered or ever-new speaks, calling us by name: 'Mary!' She turned, again, because that's what resurrection evokes in us, and worship too: a readiness to turn again, to face reality differently, and again. Even when we're not ready for it, it startles us, sometimes quietly, in our peripheral vision, but sometimes starkly. She turned and this time must have recognized Jesus immediately, as she said, 'Rabbouni!' (which means Teacher). Of all the terms she might have used, her instinctive response is that this is a teaching moment, a revelatory event, shaking her out of one form of knowledge and alerting her to another. The veil is torn! Holy Anarchy is not just close at hand, but right next to you. Even so, 'Do not hold on to me', he says. The open palm may be revealed, for all its awesome weakness, the possibility of truth beyond the fist of violence, outside the grip of domination, the clench of closure – but do not try to turn it into something to be held, grasped, clenched. Let it be. For this is resurrection, a basis for worship: what is being revealed to us remains uncontained; small but at large; present but absent; comforting but discomfiting.

So worship is the space in which the dominant scripts of life begin to be rewritten. As James Smith explains, our desires are reoriented[1] – away from the prevailing desires, towards desire for the kingdom (or Holy Anarchy). That is to say, the fact of desire is not negated or undermined at all; far from it, our nature as desiring creatures is crucial, but what is it that we desire? We are conditioned by Dominion, the colonization of our consciousness, to want certain norms, certain goods, certain structures to remain in place, securing the vested interests of those with privilege. But instead, when the alternative space of worship happens, our desires are reoriented towards the new horizon; we learn to want what God wants, we learn to act as God acts, we learn to connect as God connects. Witnessing to Holy Anarchy. Embodying Holy Anarchy. Furthering Holy Anarchy.

When leading worship, I have occasionally thought to advise the gathered congregation that they are being brave: not because they have come when I am leading, but because worship can be unsettling, destabilizing, upside-downing. It can illuminate the way things are, encourage us to name the many facets of reality, bringing our grief and lament and yearning, while offering a vision of something strange and encouraging us to believe in and act on its possibility in the here and now. Every aspect of that is disruptive: the illumination of things as they are, the encouragement to name the pain and grief, the encounter with a strange alternative, and the at least implicit demand on us to act as though it's here. Unsettling but liberating, shaking but hopeful, confounding but 'possibilizing'. Making possible what otherwise might not seem possible.

Resurrection is not the solution, fixing the cracks in the System, restoring order in a world of chaos. Rather, it is the crack in a world of order; it is the fracture in the glass, the tear in the veil, the earthquake-event, destabilizing life as we know it. But it is also not a universal experience, an everywhere-event, but is local, personal, small. It comes to us as a crack, not everywhere all at once, but somewhere particular, trusting that the cracks might spread, the tremors might reverberate, the tunes might echo – through us. So if it is the call to dance to a new tune, the tune of the alternative horizon which is closer at hand than we imagined, it is not a song and a dance that everyone everywhere can grasp immediately. Instead, it is an under-the-radar dance lesson, starting small, covert even, under the nose of Empire, in the early-morning dawn, in the shadows at a tomb, in the garden of remembrance, which we falteringly join in with, and find others are learning the steps too, some of them conscious of the horizon, some of them less so, but more and more picking up on the possibilities that it evokes.

This, too, is worship. Not a fix, but a crack; not a closing-down of solutions but an opening-up of reality's possibilities; not an experience of grandeur or finality, necessarily startling with glory, but an under-the-radar dance lesson,[2] combining the rhythms of lament and hope, in some respects dancing against our conditioned instincts and in other respects finding ourselves entering into a new flow; where our scripts are being rewritten, and the potential for rewriting the scripts of the powers-that-be is fostered; where old tunes are revived and re-worked and new harmonies and cacophonies are added; where the strangeness of an alternative horizon stops us in our tracks and inspires us to take new roads. In worship, the glimpse of Holy Anarchy is brought into focus; the invitation to Holy Anarchy is broadened; the need for Holy Anarchy cries out; and the possibility of Holy Anarchy knocks on the window and helps us to believe. It might be so.

A hymn: God, you do a brand new thing

God, you do a brand new thing,   *Alleluia!*
waking us with news to sing!   *Alleluia!*
You confound familiar ground,   *Alleluia!*
turning all things upside-down!   *Alleluia!*

Old horizons lose their grip;
Empire's fabric starts to rip.
Life renewed, un-held and free,
opens up how things may be.

Life we cannot recognize –
since the Christ was crucified –

names us, loves us into change,
so we see You in the strange.

New horizons glint and form;
age-old landscapes are transformed;
nothing now can stay the same:
see, the future lives again!

Graham Adams (2018)
Suggested tune: *Easter hymn*

Living in both worlds: failure and forgiveness

As should be clear by now, worship is an 'in between space', not a resolution, not a pacific state where all is well; but a space in which the
gravest tensions are held, between the depths of pain and injustice, on
the one hand, and the heights of liberation and fullness of life, on the
other. But also between the failures of our efforts, the shattered dreams,
the catastrophes of institutional hypocrisy, and the breadth of divine forgiveness, the generosity-of-spirit that always has room for us. In worship,
we encounter this double-reality, up close and personal. The two sides
of the open palm: openness and criticality, but openness has/is the upper
hand. The criticality comes from the mirror that worship holds up to us,
helping to illuminate what we may rather not see – but not so much the
personal weaknesses that churches often ask us to confess;[3] rather, the
structural dynamics and distortions that underpin and exacerbate injustice, fracture, suffering.

In worship, prophetic incisiveness also brings us up against the things
we're often deeply conscious of, but which we would prefer to gloss
over – the cries of the Earth, the struggles of poverty, racism, alienation
and isolation. And our failures to address them. Failure is obviously a
spectrum, where some instances are over-emphasized, deepening people's
sense of self-loathing and paralysing us with guilt, but other instances are
under-played, or belittled, because they are almost too great to handle.
The systemic failures that repeatedly disappoint and damage so many.
The things we name in passing, such as poverty or racism or ecological
catastrophe, but which are hard to reckon with in their entirety. Obviously naming failure is not good news, and yet it can be worse to bury
it; so to recognize it and hold it, in one another's company, offers up the
possibility of not being entirely defined by it: because the divine open
palm receives our failures, integrating the multiple stories wrapped up

with them, without causing them to eat us from inside. Rather, there is the potential for them to spark new insights and actions, however small, however inadequate. Worship expresses divine/human solidarity with the depths of our failures, while also creating the space for reflection, regeneration and renewal.

This is why 'failure' is not intrinsically a negative experience – which is not to belittle the effects of it on those who bear the burden of systemic injustice. But the point is, in a world fixated on success, failure can be the raw material for the emergence of new shoots of life. As Jim Perkinson argues, indigenous cultures traditionally prized compost as 'the goddess of failure', since so-called waste has the potential to nourish and nurture new beginnings.[4] In fact, I suggest Holy Anarchy is necessarily and generously attentive to 'waste': whether it is food-waste, the wastage of people and gifts, apparent time-wasting, as well as wastelands, all of these signalling how what is so often overlooked must be cherished for its unacknowledged worth. To waste food, land, people, gifts is to squander parts of the web of life, each with an integrity and worth in themselves. Meanwhile, to think in terms of time used less productively as 'time wasted' is to misunderstand the rhythms of human experience, our need for calm time, playful time, creative time, or 'being' time. We should not succumb to the expectation to be machines of productivity, but should allow for and encourage patience, retreat, wondering, day-dreaming and night-dreaming. All of this has a place in worship, which has room for everything.

Worship also recognizes that to pursue Holy Anarchy is to be in it for the long haul, not relentlessly moving 'forwards' as though to let go of the past, but instead returning again and again to stories of old, the things we assumed were done and dusted but that continue to bring forth new life, the resources that may have been wasted but which can be reaffirmed, the moments when it all went wrong but which nevertheless act like manure for future possibilities. Not that we should be held captive by such traditions either, since there must be room for surprise, but it can be ancient resources that generate the surprise. So by thinking differently about failure, too, and how we allow some experiences to 'go to waste', we rediscover the wholeness of life, of who we are, and of the truth-in-process of divine generosity-of-spirit, with room for every detail. A cycle, or spiral, of rediscovery, reaffirmation, repurposing, and resurgence – surging forth, like resurrection, in the midst of apparently dead space, dead time, with what Walter Brueggemann calls 'the threat of life'.[5]

But does worship always facilitate this integration, this solidarity, this 'possibilizing' through which we may grow and reorientate ourselves to

Holy Anarchy? Clearly not. Its form and message are rather more frequently focused on something other than Holy Anarchy. The insidious presence of powers of domination means that worship can often be a space in which vested interests are secured; high priests of propaganda proclaim messages of purity and righteousness at the expense of those who do not 'fit'; and the truth-potential of outsiders is given no airtime. Even though it's always true that quiet signs of Holy Anarchy can be latently present, under the noses of such worship-empires, like surreptitious yeast mixed in with the dough of prevailing liturgies, it's nevertheless apparent that worship often directs us to the projected 'God': a God of control and order, a certain kind of belief and loyalty, insiders and outsiders. But the words of scripture, hymns, prayers, conversations, sermons, and of our own personal hearts and minds, and the silence in between, can still offer resistance to this; pointing us to the alternative horizon beckoning from the edge of worship.

Like the woman doubled over, in Luke (13.10–17), it is a sign of the way in which 'the edge of worship' has the capacity to become the centre. Jesus was teaching in a synagogue on the sabbath. The woman appeared, bent over, unable to stand up straight. And as Luke notes, 'When Jesus saw her, he called her over.' In other words, Jesus who must have been in the centre of things *called her over*: so she was at the periphery, but he brought her into the centre. Defying people's expectations of worship, defying purity codes and hierarchies. Allowing her to interrupt what polite society and respectable religion expected to carry on regardless of life at the edges. So no wonder the leader of the synagogue was 'indignant' – whereas Jesus called them out: 'You hypocrites!' He called the woman 'a daughter of Abraham', so downgrading their status and upgrading hers. Consequently, according to Luke, it was not she or Jesus who were 'shamed', despite the prevailing honour/shame culture, but his opponents – and 'the entire crowd was rejoicing', because Jesus was allowing even this environment of worship, laden with expectations and norms, to be the site of Holy Anarchy!

And Luke immediately goes on to tell us that Jesus asked, 'What is [Holy Anarchy!] like?' A mustard seed! An infestation![6] A nuisance! A weed! An unwanted shrub that, when grown, gives home to outsiders – birds of the air, with all their unpredictability. This is the power of worship when 'the edge' is attended to; when interruption, disruption, unpredictability is given room. When those deemed expendable, or treated as invisible, the waste of society and religion, are given prominence. When wildness takes root, upsetting false order. Like disruptive children. Like people who exclaim at the 'wrong' moments. Like communities that are genuinely hard to hold together, let alone to grow, because they do not consist of the like-minded, or people who look alike, but are awkwardly diverse, brilliantly unconforming, weirdly wonderful.

Of course, not all churches are the same; not all acts of worship are the same. Some are shamelessly complicit with patterns of domination, led by a clique with the same experiences, uncritically deploying their power to urge obedience to Christian Empire. By contrast, some are much more attuned to divine truth-in-process and the call to solidarity among all-comers. Most are in between, a mix of different dynamics and values, sometimes alert to the risks of faith, but often not. So what helps to foster the necessary alertness and spirit of solidarity? Participative worship, to validate the agency of people and the co-production of worship. Conversational worship, to help tease gently to the surface what otherwise might rest in privatized minds and lives; helping one another to make new connections between faith and life. Space for creativity and play, to embody worship and solidarity, to practise childlikeness, to affirm that worship is something we 'do', inside, outside, upside-down. Symbolic actions to enable people to give expression to questions, pain and yearnings, whether in words or in silence. Liturgies that allow fresh air to breathe through them, but not constantly filtered through the same minds and experiences. Worship that keeps working at the relationship between spontaneity and safety, familiarity and surprise, space and pace.

This doesn't mean at all that formal worship intrinsically works against Holy Anarchy, because sometimes it is formality that gives thought and space for divergent voices to be heard, experiences at the edge to be named, and new forms to be given affirmation. Sometimes supposedly 'free' worship can be all too controlled according to unspoken rules. Dominant cultures find a way of maintaining order. Nonetheless, worship cannot be taken for granted, as though its forms or content will witness to and embody Holy Anarchy quite automatically; rather, it needs to be evaluated together, in light of the horizon to which it draws our attention. Not simply by those who lead it, but in meaningful dialogue with all-comers. In fact, to reflect on the practice of worship is itself a Spirit-inspired activity; not mere business, but about making connections with one another in the light of divine truth-in-process.

Such reflection is about being vigilant against self-justifying inclinations that what we do already demonstrates 'this is the temple of the Lord, the temple of the Lord, the temple of the Lord'. After all, worship ought not to be a space for boasting about how effective we are, or how all-conquering our version of 'God' is, but rather the holding space between the two worlds, in response to the awesome weakness of God: reckoning with the pain and injustice of life, while also delighting in the small victories of Holy Anarchy in our midst. It is a place of wrestling, weeping, wondering, asking the simultaneous 'why?' in the face of 'there are no alternatives' and 'why not?' when alternatives are hesitantly unearthed.

This wrestling and dreaming leads to co-creation of new forms, which may be personal and interpersonal, under-the-radar and public, anti-domination and ecological. The ecological dimension is significant, because it is increasingly clear that the missional calling to ecological care is a real catalyst for the renewal of worship – which makes perfect sense. In worship, we remember that we are part of an ecosystem, a web of life, a solidarity of the different, a solidarity of all creatures and of the Earth; we remember that we are not at the centre of the cosmos but orbit around one star among trillions, within an impossibly diverse and dynamic creation; the truth-in-process of which is an affirmation of our connectedness and a dream for shalom, wholeness, the reconciliation of all things.

So, in worship, we remember that we are part of creation and we co-create new ways of being, new ways of relating, reviving ancient ways and unearthing – or re-earthing, re-wilding – new possibilities. It must have room, then, for grief and despair in the face of ecological crises,[7] even while also affirming that every small action we take in care of creation, however insignificant it seems, plays its part in the web of action. And worship carries on, through the ebbs and flows of life, the weeping and the wondering, the routine and the revolutionary, the holiness of the mundane and the hoped-for anarchy that subverts every empire.

Of course, what this also requires is sensitivity to those who feel they are in no state to handle such demands. This is one of the most difficult but crucial aspects of worshipping space – holding those who are ready for the destabilizing that Holy Anarchy evokes, together with those who need most security. It is the solidarity among those who are being shaken open and those who need to remain closed for their own wellbeing, since they are already bruised and traumatized by distorted systems. As I have indicated before, those who find themselves being shaken open are never to impose such a dynamic on others, which would be an act of further domination; but what we can do is recognize empathetically the complexities within us all: for I may be prepared to be shaken open in some respects, and may be ready to understand the stories of those who have been closed down by powers of domination, but I should neither compel people to share their stories to satisfy my own desire for growth, nor should I imagine that I am 'a shaken person' as though there are not other ways in which I too am 'closed'. This is where the language of 'open' and 'closed' certainly has limits; it appears pejorative, purporting that we can identify whether someone is one or the other, whereas the reality is always messier.

This complexity is a helpful basis for worship, reminding us that we cannot construct hierarchies – between the 'strong' and the 'weak', the 'open' and the 'closed'. Rather, it is a space in which greater mutuality and solidarity can be encountered and furthered. So we would do well to suppose that a broad mix of awkwardness, pain and gifts are brought into public worship, entangled within and between each of us. Some of these will be expressed, though never fully, but many will remain latent or even unknown. Worship, after all, is concerned with the reorientation of desires, towards the alternative horizon, so we can never be entirely conscious of what is going on for us or for others. It is for those facilitating it to be sensitive to how our (un)consciousness may be decolonized from the forces of domination and division, slowly disentangling us while knowing ourselves to be embodied in alternative patterns defined by Holy Anarchy.

These challenges need not paralyse us, however. I am often struck by how people are grateful for an act of worship, because of how it touched their needs in a particular way, which was never something I would have imagined the particular act of worship addressed. This is the positive side of the 'risk' of things, or the potential chaos-event at play – because connections can be made beyond those intended, precisely because we are not 'in control' of this. Other subtle agencies are at work, in and through the relationships – which may be the Spirit of solidarity, who leads into all truth, notably all truth-in-process. While the reverse is also true, worship can indeed be 'successful' or effective even where it feels 'unsuccessful' or flawed.

So in worship there is room to acknowledge our worship failures and to appreciate that it is a forgiving space, a generous space – not slick and efficient, not stripped of the mess and muddle that is inherent to humanity, but at one with the multiple, interweaving stories that are brought to it, the awkwardness, pain and gifts that help to shape it, and the invitation that it represents, to live in two worlds more justly, more lovingly, more humbly.

A hymn: What kind of victory is this?

What kind of victory is this –
of Christ the crucified?
What kind of winners are we –
amazed but terrified?
What kind of gospel is this,
if marked by thorns and nails?

What kind of resurrection –
redeeming Love that 'fails'?

What kind of faith supposes
that victory is the end?
For, surely, resurrection
makes Hope our restless friend;
it doubts what seems so certain,
subverts the Empire's force:
Christ, rising in defiance,
cross-questions history's course.

The good news of this victory
is not success or height
or outcomes to be measured
or prowess in a fight,
but gambles on earth's 'losers'
and those cast out, unclean –
the beings barely human
in whom God's truth is seen.

For resurrection glory
shakes how we think and see;
it questions what is failure;
it calls out what may be:
its victory is sedition
in face of powers-above!
One like a human being
prevails by wounded love.

Graham Adams (2015)
Suggested tune: *King's Lynn*

Worship as gathering up the fragments

God bless us as we gather the fragments of who we are:
our lament and our joy, that nothing may be lost
God bless us as we gather the fragments of our ideals:
our stumbling and our rising, that nothing may be lost
God bless us as we gather the fragments of renewed vision:
our hope for the hungry to be fed, that no-one will be lost

In John 6.12, in the account of Jesus feeding a very large crowd, Jesus tells the disciples to 'gather up the fragments left over, so that nothing may be lost'. This again reflects the sense in which God sees nothing as waste: even the crumbs of life, of relationships, of stories, and of faith and discipleship, are worth gathering up, which is what we do in worship. For those fragments were gathered up and filled twelve baskets, symbolizing the renewal of Israel – a community of gathered-up fragments.

In an act of worship inspired by that instruction, we considered what it may mean in three ways. First, to set out gathering up the fragments of our pain and our joy, particularly in the light of the pandemic. Our sense of dislocation, isolation, disconnection, bewilderment, grief – these need to be named, not glossed over; because we were affected at many levels, not always consciously, though in some respects it certainly became a window giving us new glimpses into inequalities, structural racism, food poverty and hunger, and deepening our grasp of the climate emergency. While we may also have felt real gratitude for those working in emergency services, hospitals, care homes, shops, deliveries, and in so many unseen capacities, worship should gather up the mix of fragments that defined the asymmetric experience.

Second, whenever we gather for worship, or as church, or as any community, we should recognize that we come with all our diversities – 'we' are not monolithic, or neat and tidy, but gloriously different and fragmented, though potentially seeking solidarity. Worship must always be ready to be queered, to have dominant norms destabilized as we learn again and again what it means to become one another's guests, rather than including 'others' on 'our' terms. I am reminded of a pastor of a church that is constituted by people from a particular Global Majority Background, who expresses frustration whenever he feels some pressure to make his church 'more multicultural' – because for him a multicultural church is a myth, since diverse churches are always based around one culture being the norm and others are invited on such terms. This is a helpful caution against naïve claims to be 'for everyone', because to be genuinely for everyone is to be constantly attending to issues of power, control and agency: who runs this show? Nevertheless, there are examples where churches do have diverse leadership representing diverse constituencies and a genuine sense of an 'intercultural' life, embodied in mutual flows of giving, receiving, listening, learning, weeping and rejoicing in solidarity. Of course it is difficult, but a vision worth pursuing.

Third, the gathering up of the leftovers also represented a different model of economy. A flow not defined by the price of scarce bread but by the abundance of gifts. To gather up the fragments is therefore to be part of an alternative vision, a protest against prevailing norms, and a party that defies them. Not just doing charity, which only ever goes so far. But fostering new patterns, small subversions of the dominant system.

Worship therefore becomes space in which we gather up the fragments of our emotions, our life-experiences, our mixture of pain and joy, disillusionment and desire, together with the fragments of our diversity, the rich potential that dwells within the multifaceted nature of who we are, unsettling claims by any single group to be 'the norm', and fragments of an alternative vision, no matter how imperfectly formed or practised; fragments of social, political and economic commitments to the new horizon that is at hand. In worship, we gather these many dimensions, for they are enough to fill twelve baskets, representations of new community.

A hymn: In the bleak pandemic

In the bleak pandemic,
breaking what we knew,
much of life was housebound,
so Earth breathed anew.
Birds we had not noticed
showed us how to sing
in the bleak pandemic,
changing everything.

In the midst of trauma
'normal' is revised;
all the world seems stranger;
hugs are sacrificed.
In the bleak pandemic,
work and rest are strained;
many people hunger:
Come, O God, and reign.

In this time of waiting,
helpless as we are,
keeping social distance,
neighbours seem so far;
in our sense of numbness,
ill-at-ease and lost,
God, be born among us;
bear with us the cost.

In the place less stable,
in the cry for bread,
in the midst of trauma,
come, God, make your bed.
In our heart-felt longing,
glimpsing simply this:
in your fragile advent,
peace and justice kiss.

Graham Adams (December 2020)
Suggested tune: *Cranham*

This hymn obviously does not describe everyone's experience of the Covid-19 pandemic. Other 'pandemics' have continued to be more devastating in many parts of the world, as outlined in *Doing Theology in the New Normal*: pandemics of injustice.[8] So, for example, the assertion in the first verse that 'everything' changed is an overstatement – and regrettably far too little has changed as a result of the pandemic, despite its being a potential 'portal' to a new world (Arundhati Roy).[9] Nevertheless, this hymn attempts to articulate the sense of dislocation experienced by many during the disorientation caused by a virus.

In the Appendix, I offer some examples of worship materials which can be seen as attempts to gather up such fragments and point to the alternative horizon. In addition to resources that engage with texts and themes for use throughout the year, there are also materials relating to specific festivals – Advent and Christmas, Passion and Easter, and Trinity Sunday – in which Holy Anarchy may be understood as emerging under the very nose of Empire and getting under our skin, generating new possibilities.

A Palm Sunday hymn

Ride on, ride on, to nowhere fast,
except the future born at last –
the realm at hand which lifts the least
and welcomes outcasts to the feast.

Ride on, ride on, your judge awaits,
beyond the crowds and city gates;
he'll barely catch this palm parade
and wash his hands of Law's charade.

Ride on, ride on, to mock such rule –
to satirize on colt and mule,
with bands of dreamers, children, stones,
no legion drilled in deadly tones.

Ride on, ride on, though well aware
your circus troupe will stop and stare,
their bold, defiant hopes but lost,
to see you hanging on that cross.

Ride on, ride on, with foolish love
that dares confront the powers above
who hold the world within their lies:
ride on, that Life might yet arise!

Graham Adams (2020)
Suggested tune: *Winchester New*, or create one

Questions to ponder

1 In what ways do you see worship rewriting the script of our lives and of the world, reorienting us to an alternative horizon that beckons us? Or, in what ways could it do so?
2 How does worship, as you know it, reflect this tension – between the world as we know it and the world as it may become? And how well does it hold together pain and joy, disillusionment and hopefulness, failure and forgiveness?
3 How might worship be developed to gather up the fragments of life, in all its mess and ambiguity, so that nothing may be lost?
4 How might worship enable us to do something new, right under the nose of the System, as we celebrate Holy Anarchy under the very skin of life?

Further reading

Cláudio Carvalhaes – https://www.claudiocarvalhaes.com/, see blog, Liturgies (accessed 7 January 2022).

Cláudio Carvalhaes, *Liturgies from Below: Praying with People at the Ends of the World* (Nashville, TN: Abingdon, 2020).

Hannah Malcolm, *Words for a Dying World: Stories of Grief and Courage from the Global Church* (London: SCM Press, 2020).

Reimagining worship – https://www.reimaginingworship.com/ (accessed 7 January 2022).

James K. A. Smith, *You Are What You Love: The Spiritual Power of Habit* (Grand Rapids, MI: Brazos Press, 2016).

Ruth Valerio, *L is for Lifestyle: Christian Living that Doesn't Cost the Earth* (Downers Grove, IL: InterVarsity Press, 2019).

Notes

1 James K. A. Smith, *You Are What You Love: The Spiritual Power of Habit*, Grand Rapids, MI: Brazos Press, 2016, p. 25. See also James K. A. Smith, *Desiring the Kingdom: Worship, Worldview and Cultural Formation*, Grand Rapids, MI: Baker Academic, 2009.

2 Again, similar points are made by Brian Edgar, in *The God Who Plays: A Playful Approach to Theology and Spirituality*, Eugene, OR: Cascade Books, both in terms of 'dance' (p. 119) but also the way in which 'living in the kingdom' involves play, 'as if' we are 'living in a different world', valuing 'make-believe', which is to 'bring about new realities that previously only existed in [our] minds' (p. 23). The difference, though, is that Holy Anarchy is not only within us; it is also a living reality, not only on the horizon, but in the cracks around us, and at the tomb.

3 Andrew Shanks, *Faith in Honesty: The Essential Nature of Theology*, Farnham: Ashgate, 2005, p. 139.

4 James W. Perkinson, 'Coronavirus Cacophony: When the Dwarf Rebukes the Giant', in Jione Havea (ed.), *Doing Theology in the New Normal: Global Perspectives*, London: SCM Press, 2021, p. 236.

5 Walter Brueggemann, *The Threat of Life: Sermons on Pain, Power and Weakness*, Minneapolis, MN: Fortress Press, 1996.

6 Andrew Shanks, *Hegel Versus 'Inter-Faith Dialogue': A General Theory of True Xenophilia*, New York: Cambridge University Press, 2015, pp. 164–5.

7 See Hannah Malcolm, *Words for a Dying World: Stories of Grief and Courage from the Global Church*, London: SCM Press, 2020.

8 Havea (ed.), *Doing Theology in the New Normal*, p. 67 – racism, economic distress, and more.

9 Arundhati Roy, 'The Pandemic is a Portal', *Financial Times*, 3 April 2020, https://www.ft.com/content/10d8f5e8-74eb-11ea-95fe-fcd274e920ca (accessed 7 January 2022).

Conclusion

*Thus says the Lord: Do not let the wise boast in their wisdom,
do not let the mighty boast in their might, do not let the wealthy
boast in their wealth; but let those who boast boast in this, that
they understand and know me, that I am the Lord; I act with
steadfast love, justice, and righteousness in the earth, for in these
things I delight, says the Lord.*
(Jeremiah 9.23–24)

The gospel of awesome weakness

So what is the gospel? It is the good news of the awesome weakness
of God! Awesome weakness like an open palm, impossibly attentive to
reality in all its awkwardness, pain, diversity and gifts. Awesome weakness illuminating the power-play at work in our world, the structures
of domination that clench their fists, which leave little room for the
ambiguities and potentials that defy capture; the structures that close us
down and cut us off from one another. Awesome weakness that shows
up the forces of Empire, the assertion that 'There Are No Alternatives',
the practices of Dominion, exposing them, even subverting them through
foolish chaos-events of seeds, yeast, childlikeness. As Caputo puts it: 'first
the weak force of God, then the mad and scrambled character of the
kingdom where the power of powerlessness reigns'.[1] For this is how it
comes to us, the alternative horizon, the realm beckoning to us from the
margins, through the cracks in the fortresses of power, in the shadows,
fluttering fleetingly like the glimpse of a wild butterfly – Holy Anarchy!

Holy, but deeply in solidarity with the mess and impurities of life.
Anarchy, because this is a new form of power, where no-one lords it over
another; even God is marked by awesome weakness, not in control, but
evoking, risking, making possible ... It is close at hand, even within us,
but so easily obscured by the delusions and domineering systems that
detract us from its possibility. In particular, three patterns of False Order
obstruct the emergence of Holy Anarchy.

First, the pattern marked by the will to domination. It is embedded in
social structures and practices, but also in our psyches, conditioning us

to see it as normal, inevitable, even as just and divinely ordained. It instils a sense of order, but it is order that suits and serves the interests of those already with privilege, guiding us towards futures that perpetuate such hierarchies. There Are No Alternatives. TANA. It is just how things are. And its grip is tight. In economics. In politics. In religion. In our handling of the Earth. We are closed to more empathetic possibilities, cut off from one another's realities. Even where good intentions seek to temper its worst effects, it still prevails, having conditioned such hopeful enterprises, so we are always walking uphill in our efforts to transform it. But it can be exposed. It is indeed exposed by a broad coalition of movements and experiences. It can be subverted. Cracks within it can be opened up. It is the childlikeness of God's presence, embodied in community, which witnesses to entry-points to the alternative. A seed-like presence, buried but loaded with disruptive power. A sprinkling of yeast. A chaos-event. Making possible what seems unlikely. Even when the alternative seems dead. The emptiness of the System's efforts is revealed. Love lives again. A different future cracks the glass between us.

Second, we are inclined to imagine that our communities of faith can resemble and embody this alternative to such an extent that we may boast about it – disowning the messier reality that we are ourselves compromised. But we are indeed compromised, infected, distorted. Our efforts are far from perfect even where they produce some good. Whether it is patterns of power that have held us enthralled to such delusions, or simply a failure to recognize the unforeseen consequences of our best intentions, churches tend to edit their story. But to embrace the fullness of it is to make something different and better emerge: an awkward body at one with the awkwardness of life, in solidarity with the mess and im/purity, honest about hypocrisy, attuned to cries of lament and despair. It is to be different by way of being real, defiantly *not* cut off from the struggles of the world, but in their very midst.

Third, though, such efforts can make us inclined to focus on our own community, unconcerned with the truth-potential beyond us. Any community can do this, going with its own flow without asking more far-reaching questions about those outside of it. Indifferent, even, to those who are rather too strange to be engaged with. Holding them at bay. Allowing ourselves to presume things. But this can be addressed. We can learn to love what is strange, and resources within our tradition can enable it. The gospel itself evokes it. Loyalty to the tradition resources it. We can grow in deeper neighbourliness for those who may teach us things we had not imagined. And, as a result, Holy Anarchy is closer at hand.

This is the gospel of Holy Anarchy. Dare we believe it and be loyal to it?

Anonymous anarchy

In 2 Kings 5.1–27, the military commander Naaman only comes to the point of encounter with Elisha and the healing power of God because of his wife's slave-girl, unnamed. We may call her No-Name, a representative of the multiple people through the Bible and through our lives who affect our stories but whose names go unknown. Even though she did not need to do so, she gives the information to help Naaman. Then again, in Acts 16, another slave-girl, another No-Name, triggers a series of events that lead to Paul and Silas being imprisoned, then to their being set free – in fact, 'the foundations of the prison were shaken'. These No-Names act like chaos-events, prompting transformations beyond themselves.

They are like Anonymous Anarchy: the unnamed presence of God's alternative horizon evoking change in the world. It is different from what some Christians have referred to as 'Anonymous Christianity[2]', where people in other religions are regarded as *effectively* 'Christian' because they are potentially saved by Christ without knowing it. Anonymous Christianity is about presuming that, on the basis that aspects of other traditions reflect the desire for relationship with God, the God who first reaches out to them, they are assessed as being sufficiently the same as 'us'. It is well-intentioned, and challenges the church to think more expansively about its gospel of grace, to open its doors from the inside. But it still seeks to bless others on our terms – and, in response to it, other religions have been known to say that Christians are Anonymous Muslims or Anonymous Hindus: the irony that no-one has the monopoly on projecting their own expectations into other space. But Anonymous Anarchy aims to be different. It affirms a vision that is itself broader than Christian faith, not even defined by our parameters; in fact, others contribute to it in ways that Christians cannot know – they can shake our foundations, disrupt our assumptions, open our doors from the outside, as we learn to see the limitations of what we currently know to be true.

Yes, this entails the recognition that to belong to a particular tradition, Christian faith, involves practices of discernment that have implications beyond itself. So it is inevitable, and I believe legitimate, to *own* the ways in which we belong 'to this' while engaging constructively with what is different, even as we look through our own lenses while learning to see and hear and touch through the experiences of those who are different. This sensibility is encouraged and enabled by our own tradition, but enhanced and reconfigured through engagement with the resources in other traditions. After all, any religion is not simply concerned with its own identity. Or, rather, its own identity is intrinsically a dynamic relationship between particular features ('this is who we are') and more universal aspirations ('this is how the world could be'). In the case of Christian faith, our particular features are defined by the narratives of Israel and Jesus, the biblical witness, the traditions of the church. But at the same time those narratives and traditions are about 'more than' being Christian; they point towards God's broader purposes and desires: such as justice, peace and the reconciliation of all things. Other traditions, too, consist of such dynamics, between their particular features and their universal visions. In some respects, the particular features overlap with those of other traditions (such as some material in the Bible and the Qur'an between Christianity and Islam, or traditions of grace in Jesus and Krishna, or ethics of love in Jesus and the Buddha, and so on), but real differences run deep as well.

What is notable, however, is that the universal visions also have some overlap – not at all that they are identical, but they share some commitments to justice, peace, reconciliation. Obviously each tradition understands those goals from within its own particular commitments. So even where the goals appear similar, there remain distinctive (or un/ique) underpinnings – so 'justice' or 'peace' or 'reconciliation' do not mean the same to everyone, and each will have insights to contribute to the others.

An advantage of re-naming the kingdom of God as 'Holy Anarchy' is that, while it remains very much rooted in Christian faith and we should never deny this connection, it nevertheless reflects a more universal aspiration, a grand narrative beyond the borders of Christian 'truth-in-hand', in the sense that its truth-in-process is alert to the unfolding possibility of an ever greater solidarity. This universal aspiration means, first, that contributors to it can indeed be more anonymous than Christians or others may imagine, since they need not be attached to the language of 'God', let alone 'kingdom'. When Jeremiah says 'let those who boast, boast in this, that they understand and know me', it is arguable that what may be 'known' is that which acts in steadfast love, justice and righteousness (Jer. 9.23) – that is, the power of the open palm evoking empathetic openness in the cause of Holy Anarchy. That agency in the world that persistently opens us up to one another's otherness, that we may grow in neighbourliness and thereby dismantle structures of dominion. It is of course possible to believe that others can contribute to 'the kingdom *of God*' too, as I do believe; it is nevertheless clear that language can be a significant barrier. Changing the language is not, however, a mere act of propaganda, to deceive people into accepting something undesired but, again, is to affirm something crucial about the very nature of Holy Anarchy. After all, people in other religious traditions, or indeed in secular movements working for justice and peace, would rather that Christians explain what they mean. That said, as theologians like Stanley

Samartha and Aloysius Pieris affirm, other traditions – and people of no particular tradition – can contribute to this goal which transcends Christianity, in ways that can surprise us.[3]

This leads me to the second point: that the term 'Holy Anarchy' reflects the intentions of God's kingdom more clearly than the language of kingdom, in terms of power dynamics. In effect, it reflects who we aim to be, as Christians, subverting patterns of lordship and fostering the flourishing of life. It is true to who we are. However, this is not immediately apparent. Not only is it an ongoing argument within Christianity, since many would see it differently, but it is far from evident in our behaviour. For the church has repeatedly exacted domination and oppression, in its collusion with Empire and its persecution of various groups, closing down dissent and maintaining cultures of control. But despite this, and in many small ways witnessing to an alternative, its truth-in-process is inspired by the awesome weakness of God, which evokes a different model of power and relationships, community and solidarity, in which the dignity, worth and agency of the least, the little and the last are celebrated, and psychological and political structures honouring 'the first' are humbled and dismantled. As such, Holy Anarchy more fully reflects the intentions, trajectories and practices demonstrated in Jesus' ministry and relationships, embodying God the Child: a wild way of personal, social and ecological transformation. And there are certainly many strands in other traditions that resonate with comparable vibrations, even as there are norms and structures that resist them too.

Third, though, it is crucial that Holy Anarchy does indeed allow for the anarchic reconfiguring of Christian assumptions. While there is always the risk that, in seeing traditions through our own lenses, we may patronize and misunderstand others and superimpose our assumptions and practices on them, there is also the necessary corollary that we are seen through their lenses – and this leads to reappraisal of our preconceptions. Both our preconceptions about our own identity and our preconceptions of others. So even where others do not 'know' that their experiences, stories and wisdom are contributing to something that we may call Holy Anarchy, the capacity remains for us to learn from such encounters. The very nature of Holy Anarchy is that Christians cannot control it, for it is indeed anarchic. So what we assume to be the case, how we presume it unfolds in history, will be shown to be partial. And people such as No-Name in one situation or another play crucial roles in prompting us to see and appreciate what we otherwise fail to grasp, whether or not they follow all of the consequences of what they initiate in us.

Holy Anarchy is, after all, concerned with the emergence of a solidarity of solidarities, cutting across more limited loyalties, not to denigrate the particular commitments of each tradition but to affirm them and build on them, in a spirit of mutual enrichment and challenge, exposing and rooting out structures of oppression and nurturing the fullness of life. Obviously this involves a subtle but intentional recognition of the many ambiguities within traditions – the ways in which each tradition is an awkward solidarity of diverse strands and insights, often conflicting with one another – and between traditions, as we engage with the similarities and differences, the moments of choice between 'either' and 'or' and the invitations to embrace 'both/and', and indeed the multiple mysteries where we cannot make sense of one another's otherness.

To regard Holy Anarchy as present in Anonymous Anarchy, in those so-called No-Names beyond articulation, whether within particular traditions or not bound by any specifically, is to recognize both that this goal is interconnected with so many interests and movements – not only religious, but political, economic and ecological, any who in subtle or explicit ways seek to foster alternative patterns of power and the flourishing of life in all its fullness – and that it is profoundly messy! It is indeed chaotic. Because a small instance, the size and strength of a butterfly in the scheme of things, can somehow play a disproportionate part in the grander unfolding of reality. So for all its scale, identifiable in multiple religious traditions, campaigning movements, political struggles, processes of liberation and justice, it is vital to remember that Holy Anarchy is also evident in the briefest of encouraging encounters with those who would not imagine that their contribution is weighty.

The weight of small things

Though two copper coins are not much, they nevertheless have disproportionate power. The story of the widow who gives to the temple just these two coins (Mark 12.38–44) is often taken as a celebration of costly giving, therefore urging people to make other such offerings to God. Now there may be a place for such a message in particular situations – notably, where the grace and justice of God are cheapened by complacent or indifferent forces, which cause us (or certainly the privileged) to assume that God's purposes can unfold without much effort or without *metanoia* (profound mind-changing and turning-around). And in a sense, Jesus does seem to commend the widow – he sees her as more impressive than those who gave out of their wealth. But this is no celebration of giving in itself, nor of its costliness as such. Rather, her two copper coins have a different power: the power to illuminate dynamics and structures. So her gift is indeed weighty, and should be celebrated.

For without her, Jesus would not have drawn people's attention to the systems that demanded such costliness of her[4] – the temple treasury that he sat 'opposite', to position himself against its ideology and effects. He denounced the scribes who 'devoured widows' houses', requiring them to give what they could not afford, and immediately following this episode he sets himself apart from those who are impressed by the grandeur of the temple structure, so he shows no allegiance to it – a blasphemous positioning on his part. So his observation that she gives 'more', even in two copper coins, is both very much at one with his broader affirmation of the value and worth of what seems small (seeds, yeast, childlikeness) and in tune with his denunciation of apparent greatness: the structures of imperial or temple-state oppression, colonizing the minds, hearts and behaviour of widows, so they do what they cannot afford. And any such systems, religious, political or economic, that exact such self-denying obedience in the interests of those with privilege are also denounced.

A hymn

Just two copper coins from the humblest of widows –
the barest of gifts through the eyes of the proud;
but Jesus sees wealth in the smallest of offerings –
the size of a whisper that dwarfs what is loud.

Just two copper coins may seem nothing to temples
which pay no regard to the cost for the poor,
but Jesus, positioned opposing the system,
exposes what's wrong when the rich ask for more.

Just two copper coins are enough for revealing
how cheaply we stand by the world that we know,
but Jesus, while seated to judge all oppression,
invests in a future that's waiting to grow.

Just two copper coins – in our wallets or wisdom,
aware that we're short of so much, but your grace,
for Jesus gives worth to the smallest abundance,
which helps us believe every gift has its place.

Graham Adams (October 2021)
Suggested tune: *Bard of Armagh/Streets of Laredo*

Again and again, Holy Anarchy strikes us, emerging through the cracks, distracting us or drawing our attention, in unlikely people, unlikely moments, unlikely places. Beckoning us to see. And to get it. And to join in.

But whether it is anonymous or explicit, whether like an earthquake-event or something as subtle and everyday as two copper coins, it prompts attributes and sensibilities within us. First, skills of discernment, enabling us to identify both the structures that dominate and the alternative that calls to us. We have resources within our own tradition that help us – the biblical witness which 'opens us up' – but also draws our attention to the way in which other voices would have us closed down, in collusion with patterns of domination and division. There are voices, too, like No-Name in Acts 16, who 'divine the spirits', contributing to our grasp of what is happening. Some are in other specific traditions, some are spiritual seekers, some have no explicit 'home', but in their wandering they help to point us to truth-in-process which we often neglect.

Second, as we discern, we also seek to disentangle ourselves, to reckon with the forces that hold us and others in place. But as we do this, we recognize too that we cannot be separate from them. Purity is not an option, only im/purity. There is, in fact, holiness in our very immersion in such a struggle, to be in the very midst of life, in solidarity with the laments, the despair, the dreaming. Nevertheless, we seek to be a distinctive community, offering the possibility of something different from the overbearing structures, even as we know ourselves still to be conditioned by them. So we build church, the awkward body of Christ, infected by the disease we seek to address, but nonetheless witnessing falteringly to its overcoming. We represent a foretaste of a different world, even in our recognition that we have sometimes failed so dramatically and need forgiveness institutionally. We offer sacraments of Holy Anarchy in our weakness, praying patiently and playing at the art of childlikeness. We mediate between our conflicting voices, in our striving to be the most catholic of bodies, decolonizing the space in order to enable multiple experiences to be heard and cherished, so also agitating wherever some would seek to control others. We know that even as we aim to disentangle ourselves from the matrix of False Order, we are nevertheless embodied as agents of it, belonging in effect to two empires – but still, and still again, the hope does not die: we bear witness to a truth that cannot be extinguished. The alternative horizon is small enough to live under the nose of the System, even under the nose of the very church that sometimes denies it; and gets under our skin.

So third, while discerning it within ourselves and beyond, and disentangling ourselves imperfectly while embodying a partial witness to the alternative horizon, we also find ourselves learning the art or skill of reconfiguration. For we are not the whole, or the end. We are markers along the way, constantly learning. Our minds are changed. Our hearts too. We turn around. We evaluate where we have reached. We see the limitations. The damage. We hear the cries. We own the hypocrisy, the im/purity. We open ourselves again. We restrain our desires to boast, or to make others like us. We remember the possibility of a solidarity not of the like-minded but of the different, and of a solidarity of solidarities. And we remember, too, that faith orientates us to such a possibility. To be loyal to Jesus Christ and his vision may even require us to be neighbourly, hospitable, receptive, not only in relationship with those who are already much like us, but with the strangers, the different. To be xenophile. To be loving to that which is other. In whom God comes to us. To shake us open again. So we are reconfigured. We must therefore be receptive to such a possibility, and know it to be good news.

This is what the gospel gives to us, and requires of us, and makes possible among us, in solidarity with others. Discerning the systems that condition us with the spirit of False Order, and discerning the alternative horizon that comes from the edges, through the cracks, in two copper coins. Disentangling and embodying: realizing how we are embedded in distorted relationships and structures in subtle and interconnected ways, making purity an impossibility, but also facilitating the very resistance to such captivity, as the social practices that harm are also, ambiguously, the social practices through which we learn and foster new possibilities. For the awesome weakness of God is at work even where it is suppressed; and communities conditioned by its negation are nevertheless charged to grow it, point to it, celebrate it. And through such dynamics, we also reconfigure ourselves, recognizing the limitations of our efforts, drawing on the wisdom and gifts of others, being open to the possibility of an ever greater solidarity of solidarities. Holy Anarchy at large!

They said nothing to anyone, for they were afraid

It has been exciting to write this book, but also somewhat scary. Some of the insights that have emerged along the way, one or two of which have surprised me a little, have the potential to frighten some people: whether because Christian faith is being expressed as anarchic rather than orderly, or divine power is awesomely weak, or the truth of it is profoundly open to the experiences and gifts of others. I recognize such things can be unsettling; and when directed at those of us with relative power, they are meant to be. But they can also disturb people with relatively less power, who value the securities and boundaries of prevailing models of faith. This makes me hesitant. It is not a comfortable situation to disturb those who already feel precarious. Nevertheless, I do believe that risking the possibility of Holy Anarchy opens up alternative space, alternative dynamics, even alternative relationships in which different and liberating modes of being are released: the pain of disruption may be honestly reckoned with, previously suppressed experiences and wisdom may be taken seriously, and steps towards a new future may be developed collaboratively. That potential is there.

But still. Like the first witnesses to the resurrection, fear and amazement can overwhelm us. The sheer possibility that it does not have to be this way is in itself unnerving. We can feel amazed by the presence of an alternative horizon in our peripheral view, startling us with the prospect of overcoming the weight of the status quo: is anti-domination really possible? Can we honestly build communities that understand and appreciate their own awkwardness? Might we dare to love that which is strange and allow it to reconfigure what we think we know? The truthful answer, in a sense, is Yes and No. Holy Anarchy represents the invitation to Yes! It is possible to identify the structures that stand in the way, to practise alternative habits by which we dismantle such things and build something new, and to do so in partnership with others whose insights and gifts may be different, that we may keep learning. It is possible. But at the same time, it isn't. The fullness of Holy Anarchy may not 'fit' in any single programme, any identifiable community, any anti-domination movement, since the traces of Dominion will keep reappearing. After all, Holy Anarchy is not about the final vanquishing of all such ambiguities, but about living more constructively in such a world. It is an open palm in a world so often defined by closed fists, so it risks the reality that closure is not what it seeks. And there are things we do not currently see, which we will be alerted to in due course, and there are challenges in the future that we do not know yet, so Holy Anarchy helps to keep us open.

They told no-one, because fear consumed them. The new reality was too strange. What would others make of it? But actually two things are true simultaneously: on the one hand, there is a sense in which it is not quite possible to tell people about it, because any attempt will be flawed, as this is. The reality of Holy Anarchy defies efforts to tell people, and sometimes silence is a better witness, like the silence of an infant who cannot articulate it, the silence of a butterfly's chaos-event, or the silence that goes hand in hand with doing justice, the sheer practical commitment to deep solidarity. On the other hand, the text is not quite telling the truth, because they did tell people, even what could not quite be captured in words; they did tell of the empty tomb and ripples began to spread. At one and the same time, Holy Anarchy can't be confined to certain forms of expression – the words themselves will have a degree of emptiness to them if they are not reflected in practical solidarity – yet what we can witness and proclaim is the emptiness itself: the truth of the gospel is in the emptiness. The truth is, Holy Anarchy is not there, not held, not captured, not contained. It is at large. It has gone ahead of us. It waits.

An Advent hymn

Praise God the childlike dreamer
   who beckons valleys, 'rise!',
whose weakness brings down mountains –
   the wilderness surprise!
Give praise to God whose advent
   reveals how things could be,
that we may dare imagine
   new possibilities.

God speaks: 'Awake, my people,
   to face what's waiting here:
the world you sometimes hide from,
   the shadows that you fear;
it's there that I am sighing
   among the depths of pain
and asking awkward questions
   till deserts bloom again.'

Praise God the wildest dreamer
   who bears creation's groans,
and dares confront the powers –
   those resting on their thrones:
the greed consuming futures,
   indifference to Earth's cries,
which call for *metanoia*,*
   that all of life may rise.

God comes, the fiercest fire
   and yet a mother hen;
a hand stretched by a child
   above an adder's den;

God, wreak your holy havoc
  where systems hold in place;
come, help us reimagine
  till love fills every space!

Graham Adams (2021)
Suggested tune: *Ellacombe* – or create your own
Based on various texts, including Isaiah 11.8.
metanoia: changing minds, turning around, radical reorientation. (Or change
the word to 'transformation' instead.)

Questions to ponder

1 What do you make of the outline of the gospel offered in this chapter?

2 Think of examples of the smallest possible ways in which people can contribute to Holy Anarchy. They may be anonymous contributions, – that is, without people realizing that's what they're doing, or explicit and intentional. Like 'two copper coins', these small things may contribute by exposing the systems of domination, or by reflecting God's affirmation of littleness in itself. Think, too, of the small ways in which you have been touched by the gifts of others. Give thanks for all of this.

3 Take the first task: discerning features of the system of domination that frames our lives, and discerning the alternative horizon beckoning to us from the edges. In light of the latter, what might it mean to disentangle yourself from the former – even to dismantle it, stone by stone?

4 Take the second task: embodying a community that seeks to reflect that alternative horizon, however awkwardly, impurely and slowly. What might this mean in your context?

5 Take the third task: reconfiguring our assumptions and practices in the light of those whose experiences and insights are different. What are the obstacles to this? On the other hand, what encourages you?

6 What frightens you most about this enterprise of Holy Anarchy? Conversely, what intrigues you, excites you, or encourages you?

Notes

1 John D. Caputo, *The Weakness of God: A Theology of the Event*, Blooming-ton, IN: Indiana University Press, 2006, p. 17.

2 In particular, see Karl Rahner, *Theological Investigations*, Vol. V, London: Darton, Longman and Todd, 1966, pp. 131–2; and Karl Rahner, *Theological Investigations*, Vol. VI, New York: Seabury Press, 1974, pp. 390–5.

3 See also Andrew Shanks, *Faith in Honesty: The Essential Nature of Theology*, Farnham: Ashgate, 2005, p. 105.

4 See Ched Myers, *Binding the Strong Man: A Political Reading of Mark's Story of Jesus*, Maryknoll, NY: Orbis, 1988, pp. 320–2.

Appendix

Worship Materials

Gathering up the fragments

Here are some worship materials. Several are formal 'responses' (with different 'voices'), designed to gather people together or to send them out, in light of the call and solidarity of the gospel – though the materials may be adaptable for other purposes. Some are prayers, some are brief guidance notes for an activity, and some offer summary notes of a sermon or reflection. By no means are they definitive or exhaustive. After all, they were created for particular contexts, so cannot be expected to speak into all situations. On the one hand, since they were not the product of conversations with diverse participants, they cannot reflect everything that I have been saying. It would have been better had they emerged more organically – and in the everyday sense of the word they are not particularly 'anarchic'. On the other hand, they attempt to reflect some of the impulses of Holy Anarchy. Please feel free to use them, 'preserve and overcome' them, or treat them as prompts for your own innovations.

* * *

BEING CHRISTIAN COMMUNITY – A MATTER OF BELIEF, BEHAVIOUR OR BELONGING?

Opening Up in engagement with the Bible

In particular three sample verses: Acts 4.12 ('there is no other name ... by which we must be saved'), 1 John 3.18 ('let us love, not in word or speech, but in truth and action'), and John 10.16 ('I have other sheep that do not belong to this fold').

Introductory exercise

You could distribute some one-line statements to a number of people in the congregation – statements that reflect a bias towards belief, behaviour *or* belonging. (For example: 'I believe Jesus is unique, and I think other people should believe it'; 'Jesus said, "Go and do likewise", so the focus of my faith is on action'; and 'I don't always know what to believe or do, but I know I am part of Christ's body'). Ask the speakers to say their sentence three times, speaking over one another. Then ask everyone else if they could identify what was being said. After this, ask for the statements to be said in turn.

Discussion

You could explore how this 'mix of views' resembles people's experience of faith and church – both from inside and from the potential perspectives of those outside. You could explore the appropriateness of the mix, since it reflects different emphases within the tradition. By contrast, how different is it to hear them in turn? Does that feel better or worse? It might be better because it's clearer, but worse because it's possibly less 'honest' – and when each is said in isolation, does it become a little separated from the others, perhaps judged against one another? You could draw out the significance of our bias towards one or another – and the importance of building a community in which different biases are heard.

Reflection

You might focus on faith/faithfulness, as understood in Chapter 7. That is, faith as loyalty to the impulse of divine truth-in-process. This involves believing and behaving as though there is something greater than the limits of Christian community; something that opens us up to ever greater neighbourliness, a solidarity of all-comers – God's kingdom, or Holy Anarchy!

Blessing

God whose truth is steadfast love for all
bless us with faith beyond words and walls.
Christ who defies the limits of custom and the cross
bless us with hope that is open to ever new life.
The Spirit who leads into truth that sets us free,
bless us with love that cannot be contained: Amen!

* * *

BE SILENT (Mark 1.21–28)

The original context of this was over Zoom during the pandemic, which explains some of the wording of the prayers – and questions were discussed in break-out rooms. This can easily be adapted to other settings.

Theme: the tension between being silent and being vocal – when to be one or the other. And who decides? There are always issues of power involved, because if a dominant person tells others to 'be silent', it can be dangerous and damaging, but to silence bullies is potentially liberating, creating space for other voices to be heard.

Opening prayers

God of words and silence,
Sometimes, in a world so full of noise, it is good to be able simply to be, and to be silent;
in a world so often full of sad news, we find ourselves seeking hope, the breaking-in of your good news, so we come seeking your voice:

God who *speaks* to us … **we listen for your word of life and grace with deep gratitude.**

But we also know, with thanks, that we can bring all our confusion, bewilderment, and rage; we can bring all our emotion, our pain, our empathy and tears; we can bring our struggles, and so:

God who *listens* to us … **we bring our words and silence to you with deep longing.**

We come into this moment, this space, where we are face to face with the fact that we are separated, and yet we are finding ways to connect, imperfect ways, but sharing our need for mutual support:

God who *speaks* to us … **we listen for your word of life and grace with deep gratitude.**

And into this time, into this space, with unreliable connections, with occasional awkward silences, small signs of the strangeness of this world, we bring who we are, our connections, our brokenness:

God who *listens* to us ... **we bring our words and silence to you with deep longing,**

because we long for greater connection, but we also long for people to be safe; we long for healing, but we also hunger after time with family and friends; we do not have the words, but you receive us:

God who *speaks* to us ... **we listen for your word of life and grace with deep gratitude.**
God who *listens* to us ... **we bring our words and silence to you with deep longing.**

So we bring all our prayers to you, as we long for peace and healing, in the name of Christ, Amen.

Reflection

Jesus tells the unclean spirit to be silent. Dangerous words. But the spirit here represents the forces of domination which keep people in their place. The institutional bully. The powers of oppression. The clichés, assumptions and habits that stop us from questioning, and which keep us cut off from one another's realities. The experiences of male-dominated cultures, racism, class-ism, homophobia, transphobia, and so on – wherever 'this' is taken for granted and it is difficult to voice an alternative. Jesus silences this power. What might that feel like? What might happen? What is the risk? What is the good news?

Discussion in groups

Any experiences of being silenced, or seeing it done to others? What does it feel like? And how might churches ensure they create safe space for voices to be heard – not the dominant ones, but the unheard?

Blessing

God, who spoke your word of life into the silence,
be with us as we listen for your word in the world today.
Christ, who called for silence amidst the noise,
be with us as we give space for quiet voices to be heard.
Spirit, who leads us into all truth,
be with us, guide us in wisdom and bless us with peace.
Amen.

THE PARABLE OF THE GLOOP:
AN INTER-GENERATIONAL ACT OF WORSHIP

Bible readings

Ezekiel 17.22–24 and Mark 4.24–35.

Words of gathering and welcome

God of welcome,
help us to make this a place for all people –
with room for questions and dreams,
with space for peace and play,
with doors open wide for all that we bring
and all that you give us this day. Amen.

Reflection

Jesus was nurturing a vulnerable community. It may have been tempted to look for the quick-fix, to force change by compromising itself – but, to him, seeds grow and we don't always know how; it happens. As for the popular saying, 'to those who have, more will be given', he called it into question ('beware what you're told'), contrasting it with the gospel of small things, like seeds. This fits with his affirmation of children too – as also identifiable in Ezekiel 17.22 (celebrating the sprig) and 1 Samuel 16.7 (don't judge by stature!).

Illustration

Make some gloop (you may know it as 'oobleck' – it's basically cornflour and water). It behaves as a liquid but also as a solid. Invite people to play with it. (Be mindful that some people do not like getting messy.) It can be a way of 'being childlike', running it through hands, being captivated by its mystery. It also shows how things that seem a certain way can actually be different – like seeds, like yeast, like children, small but loaded with chaos-capacity: the potential to evoke big changes!

Blessing

God who inspires us to be curious about creation,
bless us with faith that lives well with questions.

Christ who inspires us to seek justice for the small,
bless us with hope that a fairer world is at hand.
Spirit of truth who inspires us to play joyfully,
bless us with love for all people and all creation.

* * *

BELONGING TO TWO EMPIRES (DISCUSSION-BASED WORSHIP, OR BIBLE STUDY MATERIAL)

Bible readings

Isaiah 9.1–4, Matthew 4.12–23, 1 Corinthians 1.10–18 (but focusing on Matthew).

Reflection 1

'*The missing city and the hidden empire*': It is so fascinating that Sepphoris, an imperial city not far from Nazareth, is never mentioned in the Gospels. It is as though the storytellers wanted to free themselves from its overbearing presence – to edit the empire. The fact that the city is missing represents the agency of those on the margins, determined to write history differently. Meanwhile, their alternative empire (*basileia* = kingdom/empire) has come near, calling us to 'turn around' (*metanoia*/repent). So today: might there be imperial frameworks that are prevalent and dominating, but that we would prefer to be separated from? And are we seeking to give our allegiance to an alternative empire, that beckons us?

Activity

How could you explore the missing city and the hidden empire ... on maps, in pictures, in the stories we tell ourselves? Do we notice Empire at large in our world today, and how do we hear the call of the alternative?

Reflection 2

'*Who do we belong to?*': Paul is addressing the temptation among the Corinthians to put themselves in different camps. He urges them to unite. But note: Empires ask people to unite too, in order to silence dissent. So how do we know what to unite around? Paul's vision of unity is rooted in Christ's way of foolishness – that is, it is unlike the norms of Empire. And yet we belong to both. We are not 'purely' in God's realm; we are shaped by the other Empire – but, even so, we can 'turn around' again and again. The tension between the empires will even affect how we read the Bible: for example, whether 'fishing for people' is simply about growing the church (and potentially sidestepping the challenge of Empire) or 'catching out' the rich and complacent, and building a fairer world instead, so practising the subversion of Empire. Even as our loyalties remain divided, the good news is that light has come – the challenge is being illuminated and what it means to give allegiance to the alternative empire is taking shape in our midst ...

Explore

How do we belong to different empires? Where are the pressure points in terms of our allegiance to one or the other? Where is it difficult to notice our allegiance or to change it? For example, in our interpretation of the Bible? And how can we encourage one another to 'turn around' again and again for the sake of Holy Anarchy?

* * *

BEING ATTENTIVE
(Jeremiah 23.1–2 and Luke 1.69–71, 78–79)

Reflecting on the way in which God 'attends' to things that the world does not attend to (Jeremiah 23.2: 'I will attend to you'), but speaks to us through distractions, drawing our attention to the margins (Luke 1.79: 'light to those who sit in darkness and in the shadow').

An Invitation to Communion

Come, come round this table –
    be distracted by God who pays us attention,
    be distracted, for a moment, by the story and life of Jesus of
    Nazareth,
    be distracted, from whatever it is that occupies you, by the
    movement of the Spirit.

Come, come round this table – and hear the great story –
  of the God who pays us attention, attending to creation in its scale,
  in its every atom, in its pain,
  of the God involved in the lives of the smallest and unlikeliest, those
  like Abraham and Sarah,
  of the God paying attention to the cries of those enslaved, and
  demanding, 'Let my people go!'
Hear the great story –
  of the God who pays attention to a wandering people, as they long
  for the security of Egypt, as they move into new space, as they pull
  down and as they build, as they are conquered and exiled,
  of the God who pays attention to exiles, and offers a vision of a new
  society, of ripe vineyards and long lives, of bad shepherds being
  humbled,
  of the God who speaks to shepherds of a new birth, having paid
  attention to a young girl, who becomes the mother of God the
  Child.
Hear the great story –
  of the God who pays attention to lepers and outcasts, tax collectors
  and sinners, women and children, so many little ones in a world of
  power,
  of the God who pays attention to those who have no right to show
  such faith,
  of the God who reveals to us a new realm, glimpsed in the smallest
  of things, seeds, yeast, buried treasure, children, small acts of
  defiance.
Hear the great story –
  of the God who is a distraction, who plays with people outside
  the rules and the boundaries, distracting us from good order and
  imperial peace,
  of the God who draws people's attention with a new vision, and
  who must be silenced,
  of the God crucified on a rubbish dump, making visible the very
  truth of what is invisible.
God who is in the midst of our troubles,
  in the midst of creation, exile and Empire,
  in the midst of our pain,
  in the midst of our tension,
  distracting us from 'there are no alternatives',
  with a vision of a very different future,
  which does not stay buried in a tomb:

for God pays attention even to the dead,
   even to what seems lost,
   broken dreams, a people in despair, the end,
   and distracts us from those persistent lies
   with the quiet boldness of resurrection:
   the ultimate distraction:
   thanks be to God!
So in this meal, let us pay attention – let us remember – God in Christ attends to us, in these fruits of the earth, graced by God, and in our brokenness, and in our renewal and transformation.
Let us pay attention to the one who sets us free from the things that distract us from reality: the reality of God's presence in the midst, and God's promise of new creation, which is close at hand.
Come, meet the one who pays you such attention.
The feast is ready: thanks be to God! Amen.

Blessing

God, present 'in the midst' of our trouble,
give us faith that we may be attentive to you.
Christ, making visible what is invisible,
give us hope that we may be attentive to pain.
Spirit, drawing attention to what consumes us,
distract us with love that binds all together.

Under the nose and under the skin

In this final section of resources, I offer some materials concerned with particular Christian festivals – Advent, Christmas, Palm Sunday, Easter and Trinity Sunday.

* * *

THE ADVENT OF CHAOS

Bible readings

Isaiah 64.1–9 and Mark 13.24–37.

Setting the scene

You could set out the chairs in random ('chaotic') groups or curved lines, but close enough for groups of people to discuss questions together.

Reflective discussion-prompts

The mountains will quake (Isaiah) and the powers in the heavens will shake (Mark) – the advent/coming is a disruption. The signs of it, in Mark, are allusions to Jesus' passion – that is, his death on the cross (evening, midnight, cockcrow, dawn), because it is in his death that his glory is revealed: a subversive advent. In other words, his coming in majesty is not the sort of event we might expect, but is a 'rupture' in the systems and norms of our world, in the midst of powers and powerlessness; and we are being 'woken up' to this hopeful impossibility: the good news of God's love is its weakness, like the butterfly, or chaos-event, as discussed in Chapter 4; the awesome weakness of the open palm, or the child in a manger, or a dissident nailed on a cross, evoking Holy Anarchy among us.

James Alison's insights, in *Living in the End Times*:

> the state of alert ['keeping awake'] in the face of his coming is a *training in perception* ... of the way that all the majesty of God is to be found in the almost imperceptible victim. (p. 149)

> hope appears ... as an unexpected rupture in the system ... exactly where we have a tendency not to look ... from a rupture in impossibility. (p. 174)

Questions to discuss

1 How does Christ's coming disrupt, or rupture, the world's order?
2 How is your perception being changed?

Blessing:

God who quakes the things that seem immovable,
bless us with faith that can move mountains!
Christ who comes to us in the victim of false order,
bless us with hope that ruptures the system!
Spirit of truth who leads us into freedom-giving truth,
bless us with love that casts out all fear,
now and until God's heavenly will is done on earth,
Amen!

* * *

CHRISTMAS

Bible readings

Psalm 96, Isaiah 9.1–7 and Luke 2.1–7.

Opening prayer

Sing to God a NEW song!
Sing praises to the God of NEW life!
Living God,
You do a NEW thing among us
and although we make it something to repeat every year,
you still speak through it –

you shake us and wake us up
   with a NEW beginning
which is for 'us', for every 'us',
   and for the whole world:
So our hearts praise you,
   for you are making
      all things NEW!

Sing to God a NEW song!
Sing praises to the God of NEW life!
Living God,
Under the nose of a vast Empire, and still in forgotten places,
you get under the skin of our world in a NEW way –
you surprise us with unlikely messengers,
and make known to us that something NEW is happening!
While wrapped just in cloth,
you show us
   how fragile we are;
so help us to do something NEW
by showing love to all people:
So we share our lives,
for you are making
   all things ... NEW!
      AMEN!*

Reflection

In Isaiah, a child has been born 'for us' – but who is 'us'? It is so easy to say 'everyone', but the effects of the child are not the same for everyone; the good news is more intense for those who are 'in darkness', so how might we be mindful of the targeted impact of Christ's coming, to bring healing where there is brokenness, justice where there is injustice, peace where there is violence, hope where there is despair? Meanwhile, Luke tells us there was no room 'for them' – drawing our attention to any 'them', those for whom there is 'no room'; prompting us to make room, not only at Christmas, but wherever people are not given space, of any kind.

---

* Graham Adams © 2019, 'Seasons of the Spirit' Prayer Handbook, The United Reformed Church.

Art

Using the many global examples of art depicting Mary and Jesus can help to explore the multiple possibilities of 'them' and 'us'.

Blessing

Through the Bethlehem baby,
a child born *for us* –
   one and all,
may God bless us in our hearts
   and bless others through our lives.
Through this child,
born where there was no place
   for them,
may God help us to make space
   to break the barriers between us.
Through this child,
   called Prince of Peace
   and Light of the World,
may God bless us with the peace
   that makes all things new.
Amen.

***

PALM SUNDAY

Reflection 1

'*Why are you doing this?*' (Mark 11.1–11) – prompting us to consider why it is that we celebrate this strange festival. It is a public act (in the streets), in situations of crisis, where the Roman military procession enters at the opposite gate, as a show of dominating power. It defies expectations (on a colt), contrasting with that military procession (and in Matthew's account – 21.7: 'he sat on them' – Jesus is on two animals, suggestive of ironic street theatre, mocking kingship). And it leads to Jesus 'looking around', being attentive to what is going on in the Temple-State, centre of the imperial presence, the debt economy and religio-political power; attentive to the very structures of domination ... so how may we practise faith publicly, in the midst of situations of crisis? How may we defy expectations? How may we be attentive to the very structures of domination in our world today?

Reflection 2

Judgement Day (Mark 11.12–19) – overturning the moneychangers' tables is a provocative act (the leaders plot to kill him), it confronts the structures of oppression (which he calls a 'den of robbers'), waking people up to the reality (the whole crowd were 'spellbound', captivated by this growing illumination), reminding them of the alternative possibility (the temple as a house 'for all nations'), extending beyond more limited solidarities ... so how, then, are we called to overturn structures provocatively, to wake ourselves and others up to the reality of things-as-they-are and the possibility of things-as-they-could-be?

A hymn: The road

The road towards the city gate,
once paved with palms to celebrate,
still marks the way that people tread
towards the things we crave and dread:
for up ahead, as Christ knew well,
our demons wait with lies to tell.

The road proceeds to seats of power –
the Empire, judge and temple tower,
from where the systems that oppress
co-opt us all, we must confess;
but Christ upsets the robbers' den:
it's time for justice – now as then!

The road, both past and still today,
excites our passions on the way;
for like disciples desperately
we want Christ throned in majesty!
But he knew more the path and cup:
no gold for him when lifted up.

For if we walk this Christlike road,
where expectations still implode,
we're drawn towards his judgement day
when raised the new-creation way:
no mighty lord or warrior-king –
but Love who changes everything!

Graham Adams
Suggested tune: *Sussex Carol*, or *Melita*, or create one

Blessing

God of palm-processions and public protest,
bless us with purpose to live out our faith.
Christ of table-turning anger at walls of injustice,
bless us with courage to live out our hope.
Spirit of wise judgement and boundless comfort,
bless us, so we may live by your steadfast love.

* * *

EASTER

Call to worship

God of life, you do a new thing among us:
Help us to trust in the new thing you do.
Help us to doubt that things will stay the same;
Help us to trust in the new thing you do.
Help us to doubt that violence is the last word;
Help us to trust in the new thing you do.
Help us to doubt that division will always prevail;
Help us to trust in the new thing you do.

Reflection – 'Mary!'

It was still dark when I first got there, and I was alone.
I needed to go alone, just to be close to him, to feel his presence one
more time, even though he was gone; I needed to be as near to him as
possible, because of all he had meant to me.
But when I got there, I couldn't believe it – it didn't make any sense –
the stone was rolled away.
I felt sick at first. I could barely breathe. Like I was winded. Dizzy.
Terrified. Lost.
Briefly I wondered if my eyes were mistaking the darkness of the
empty tomb for something else, because it was still so early and the
sun had not risen.
But I realized it was real – the hole – the empty space – the place where
he should have been; where we had laid him. Empty... Empty... How
could it be? How could it ...?
So I ran.

I ran to the others, I ran all the way back, and I told them.
The look on their faces.
I wasn't sure that they believed me.
I wasn't sure that *I* believed me.
But it was real. It was.
The emptiness.
So they ran to the tomb, and found it just as I'd said. Empty.
I went back there as well, but they ran off again.
So I was alone.
Empty.
Then this voice spoke. Or was it two voices? Like angels.
'Why are you weeping?'
Why am I weeping? What a stupid question! So much I could have
said in reply.
Jesus was gone. My Jesus. My teacher. My friend. My companion.
Dead. Buried. But gone. Jesus. That's why I wept.
Then I turned, and saw someone standing there.
I didn't recognize him. How could I? No-one would have recognized
him, not at first.
I don't know, it made more sense that he was the gardener or
something.
And I wondered if he'd taken the body. I accused him. You see, I
didn't recognize him.
But then.
He said my name.
Mary!
And nothing was the same. Ever again.

Communion liturgy

O give thanks to God, who is good;
whose steadfast love endures for ever!
Let us give thanks, for God has become our salvation.
We offer songs of victory and recall God's acts;
God opens the gates, so we may enter!
The stone rejected by the builders
has become the chief cornerstone –
this is God's doing, turning things all around:
so let us rejoice and be glad in it!

We come to this Easter garden, not quite knowing –
and with tears for all that has happened.

Yet as we come, we are called by name, and known,
but with eyes that struggle to make sense of it.
For as we come, Christ is here, but not yet known,
though with an invitation to glimpse a new world.

And as we reach out, perhaps we begin to see –
we remember his parables telling of a new world
revealed in faith the size of a seed, or hidden yeast;
we remember he told us to become like children
risking, venturing, questioning, vulnerable but bold;
we remember his care for the least and the last
calling us to be an upside-down community for all.

Slowly, perhaps the new world comes into focus:
we remember the healings, the new beginnings;
though it has a cost, a risk, a cross for us to bear;
we remember that night, the bread and wine:
broken and spilt, as signs of God's generosity;
we remember dashed hopes, the deepest loss –
it was the end of the world … or was it a new birth?

We come to this Easter garden, not quite knowing –
and with tears for all that has happened.
Yet as we come, we are called by name, and known,
but with eyes that struggle to make sense of it.
For as we come, Christ is here, ready to be known,
and inviting us to share in the new world,
where all creation enjoys abundant life: Amen!

Blessing

Though we do not always recognize it,
God, our gardener, you nurture beauty and truth.
Though we do not always recognize you,
Christ, our living future, you call us and love us.
Though we do not always grasp the truth of it,
Spirit, you help us to pursue this different future
where all creation enjoys abundant life. Amen.

TRINITY

Come, worship the wild God –
Worship the God who cannot be contained by the walls of a building,
or even by a tomb;
Worship the God who will not be limited to a far-away heaven, but is
present through all creation;
Worship the God who is not captured by human ideas or schemes, but
confounds and surprises us;
Worship the God whose love is ungraspable, beyond our own versions
of it, yet makes itself known;
Worship the God whose promise of a new heaven and a new earth is
revealed in a helpless child –
Worship the God of scandalous generosity and boundless grace who
makes us all welcome, as we are

Blessing

May God, our father–mother,
divine fire and refuge,
the source of life,
bless us with wisdom,
that we may notice wisdom
wherever she dwells.
May God the Child, Jesus of Nazareth,
prince of peace, water of life,
bless us with wisdom,
that we may love foolishly
   and defiantly.
May God the Spirit, comforter and judge,
gift-giver and guide into truth,
bless us with wisdom,
that we may be people of hospitality and hope,
now and until the kingdom comes
in all its fullness.
Amen.

Index of Scripture References

Index of Names and Subjects

212, 213, 215, 218, 221, 225,
228, 242–3, 244, 248, 250
alternative 13, 57, 74, 116–18,
242–3
British 23, 74
'Empire within' 73, 94
'Empire throughout' 84, 95
emptiness, emptying 14, 205,
222, 231, 252
empty tomb 2, 11, 205, 230,
251–2
ephphatha 147–51, 153
evangelise, evangelism 117, 161

failure 23, 47, 86, 110, 175,
209–10, 214–15, 219, 222
Faith (as distinct from lower-case
'faith') 176, 179, 181, 184
faithful, faithfulness 6, 19, 43,
45–6, 53, 57, 60, 79, 122, 136,
144, 148, 150, 154, 161, 162,
177, 179–84, 186–7, 188, 192,
202, 238
False Order, *see also* dominion,
empire 36, 67, 81, 90, 113,
130, 149, 167, 173, 176, 211,
221, 228–9, 247
friend, friendship, befriend 9, 27,
58, 71, 129–32, 134, 173, 186,
189, 196, 199–200, 215, 240,
252

gender, gendered, *see also*
LGBTQI 10, 12, 13, 19, 28, 38,
47, 49, 56, 57, 77, 81, 84–6,
89, 100, 115, 118, 120, 121,
140, 159, 160, 190, 200,
generosity, generosity-of-spirit,
generous 20, 40, 48, 54, 81,
82, 103–4, 108, 118, 143, 149,
156, 165, 191, 196, 209, 210,
214, 253, 254

God the Child 110–13, 115,
124n21, 137, 165–7, 173, 225,
244, 254
Good Friday, *see also* cross 142
grace, graced 41–9, 53, 78,
103–5, 116, 117, 121, 122,
134, 147, 152n8, 157, 165–6,
183, 184, 185, 194, 223–4,
226, 227, 239, 240, 245, 254

Harley, Ruth, *see* Barrett
Havea, Jione 32n27, 95, 97n43,
98n55, 99n62, 123, 124n23,
124n25, 124n28, 125n30,
125n34, 125n35, 151, 152n13,
220n4, 220n8,
Hegel, G. W. F. 55, 57–8, 65n32,
157
Hindu 51, 119, 199–200, 223
horizon (alternative) 1–2, 3–5, 7,
10–12, 17, 18, 28–9, 42, 50,
55, 57, 71, 81, 90, 91, 101–3,
108–9, 116, 118, 121, 122,
128, 139, 142, 147, 149, 155,
157, 159, 161, 163, 167, 168,
169, 173, 179, 180, 184, 193,
196, 198, 200, 202, 205–9,
211, 212, 214, 217, 218, 219,
220n2, 221, 223, 228–30, 232
hospitable, hospitality 41, 104,
116, 143, 150, 165, 178, 179,
189–92, 229, 254

imperial(ism), anti-imperial, *see*
empire 17, 19, 23, 27, 54, 56,
57, 58, 71–2, 74–6, 78, 80–2,
84, 88–90, 92, 95, 100, 102,
105, 112, 114, 117, 118–19,
121, 140, 144, 146, 173, 195,
227, 242, 244, 249
im/pure, im/purity 9, 21, 29,
35–6, 39, 41, 45, 53, 57, 70,

McDonald, Chine 63, 65n29
mediate, mediation 2, 168–9,
171, 199, 228
metaphor 12–17, 72, 104, 107,
109, 110, 137–8
Mignolo, Walter 77, 96n15–16,
99n75
mission, missional, missionary 2,
19, 22–3, 28, 52, 56, 60, 62,
67, 71, 73, 75, 87, 115–18,
119–22, 160–1, 168, 196, 213
missio Dei 115
mission Christianity 84, 119
Moe-Lobeda, Cynthia D. 30,
30n2, 63, 77, 80, 85, 95,
96n17, 97n29, 98n46–7
Moyaert, Marianne 152n16, 189,
202, 203n12, 204n19
Muslim 199, 223
Myers, Ched 72, 96n3, 133, 151,
233n4

narrative, *see also* story 24, 75,
81, 88–9, 113, 115, 124n27,
189, 192, 195, 224

oikos 91–2, 95, 116
openness 2, 37, 41, 43, 47,
55, 58, 64n12, 80, 103, 105,
106, 108, 110, 143, 144, 145,
147–9, 152n16, 158, 160, 179,
181, 198–9, 209, 224
divine openness 41, 43, 47, 55,
105, 106, 110
empathetic openness 41, 43, 80,
106, 110, 119, 144, 181, 224
open palm 38, 40, 41, 42, 48, 49,
50, 55, 67, 70, 103–6, 108–9,
111, 117, 119, 122, 148, 149,
159, 178, 181, 182, 184, 189,
191, 199, 205–7, 209, 221,
224, 230, 246

overcome, overcoming 13, 44,
50, 55, 57–60, 62, 71, 82, 127,
128, 140, 149, 186, 191, 196,
228, 230, 237

patriarchal, patriarchy 18, 49, 52,
59, 75, 85, 93, 140, 144, 193
Perkinson, James 63, 112–13,
124n23, 210, 220n4
Pieris, Aloysius 31n3, 48, 64n21,
162–3, 172n6, 225
play, playful, playfulness 1, 2,
26, 62, 76, 100, 104, 112, 116,
118, 123n3, 124n17, 129,
131, 132, 152n8, 165–9, 171,
172n7, 172n8, 172n12, 199,
210, 212, 220n2, 228, 241,
242, 244
postcolonial, *see also* decolonial
18, 54, 69, 88–9, 144, 194,
195
process theology 106–7
psyche, *see also* consciousness
71–2, 76, 78, 82, 85, 88, 221
psychological, psycho-social 20,
39, 53, 56, 67, 69, 71–3, 77,
80–1, 84, 144, 225
purity 21, 36, 39, 41, 53, 73, 92,
129–31, 134, 161, 166, 190,
199, 211, 222, 228–9

'race', racial, racialized 10, 27,
28, 38, 47, 57, 63, 75, 84, 85,
86, 89, 100, 115, 118, 120,
121, 140, 159, 200
racism, racist, anti-racism 1, 28,
33–7, 44, 49, 51, 55–8, 59–60,
62, 73, 74, 84, 113, 140, 141,
202, 216, 220n8, 240
reconfiguration, reconfigure,
reconfiguring 14, 17, 54, 77,
102, 113, 115, 120, 130, 134,